THE SEA TURTLE

BY THE SAME AUTHOR:

Handbook of Turtles: The Turtles of the United States, Canada and Baja California

The Windward Road: Adventures of a Naturalist on Remote Caribbean Shores

Ulendo: Travels of a Naturalist in and out of Africa

THE SEA TURTLE
So Excellent a Fishe

by Archie Carr

University of Texas Press, Austin

International Standard Book Number 0-292-77595-4
Library of Congress Catalog Card Number 86-50717

Second printing of University of Texas Press edition, 1992
Published by arrangement with Charles Scribner's Sons

∞ The paper used in this publication meets the minimum
requirements of American National Standard for Information
Sciences—Permanence of Paper for Printed Library Materials,
ANSI Z39.48-1984.

The line illustrations for this book were prepared
by the Graphic Arts Division
of The American Museum of Natural History.

Previously published as *So Excellent a Fishe:
A Natural History of Sea Turtles*.

597.92

CONTENTS

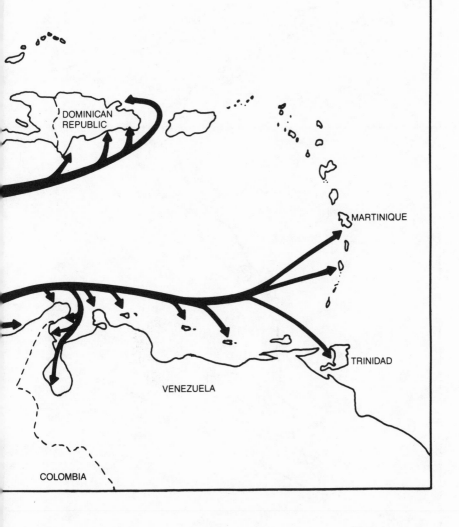

DISTRIBUTION OF 1005 INTERNATIONAL RECOVERIES OF GREEN TURTLES THAT HAD BEEN TAGGED ON THE BEACH AT TORTUGUERO, COSTA RICA, 1956–1982.

DOMINICAN REPUBLIC

MARTINIQUE

TRINIDAD

VENEZUELA

COLOMBIA

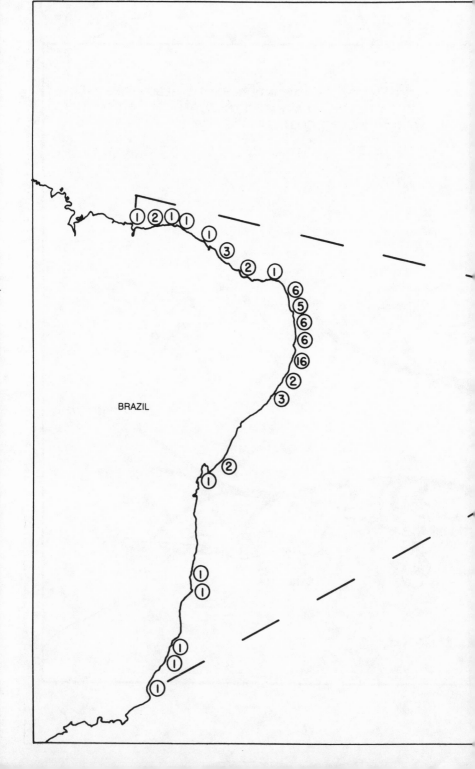

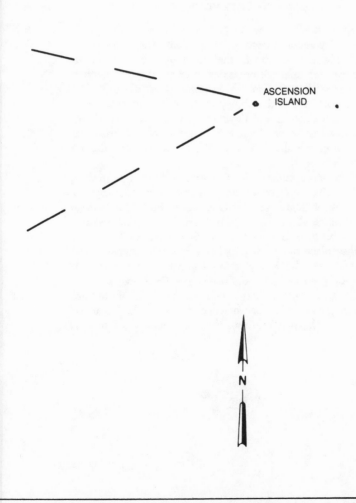

AFRICA

DISTRIBUTION OF THE 64 LONG-DISTANCE RECOVERIES OF FEMALE GREEN TURTLES THAT HAD BEEN TAGGED AT ASCENSION ISLAND, 1960–1978. ALL THE TURTLES WERE RETAKEN BY FISHERMEN ON THE BRAZILIAN FEEDING GROUND OF THE POPULATION. NO TURTLE TAGGED AT THE ASCENSION NESTING GROUND HAS EVER BEEN FOUND NESTING ANYWHERE ELSE IN THE WORLD.

ASCENSION
ISLAND

N

The Bermuda Assembly, 1620:

AN ACT AGAYNST
THE KILLINGE OF OUER YOUNG TORTOYSES

In regard that much waste and abuse hath been offered and yet is by sundrye lewd and impvident psons inhabitinge within these Islands who in their continuall goinges out to sea for fish doe upon all occasions, And at all tymes as they can meete with them, snatch & catch up indifferentlye all kinds of Tortoyses both yonge and old little and greate and soe kill carrye awaye and devoure them to the much decay of the breed of so excellent a fishe the daylye skarringe of them from of our shores and the danger of an utter distroyinge and losse of them.

It is therefore enacted by the Authoritie of this present Assembly That from hence forward noe manner of pson or psons of what degree or condition soeuer he be inhabitinge or remayninge at any time wthin these Islands shall pseume to kill or cause to be killed in any Bay Sound or Harbor or any other place out to Sea: being wthin five leagues round about of those Islands any young Tortoyses that are or shall not be Eighteen inches in the Breadth or Dyameter and that upon the penaltye for euerye such offence of the fforfeyture of fifteen pounds of Tobacco whereof the one half is to be bestowed in the publique uses the other upon the informer.

THE SEA TURTLE

I

THE TURTLE MOUNTAIN

The big pied slate-and-orange airplane roared down the tree-walled river. Water spouted from under the hull and blotted the view through the portholes. Just opposite the camp we hit planing speed and rose to the surface of the river, the ports cleared, and I could see Larry Ogren, a student from the University of Florida and my staunch assistant in the Tortuguero turtle work. He was waving from the dock, and Leo Martinez, our Creole *mayordomo* was with him. They were staying behind to gather little turtles for the last trip out. It was going to be hectic there at the turtle camp for a while, with the new peak-season masses of hatchlings coming. The fishing was in one of its poor spells, and the pump was wearing out. Each night the hatchlings were coming up out of the sand in flurries of hurried, paddlefooted little creatures the size of a silver dollar, all in a sweat to be off to wherever little turtles go. Every night fifty or more would appear inside the ring of hardware cloth that encircled each nest in the hatchery, and every morning there would be hundreds of them to be collected and put in tanks and fed on chopped fish. Each day the water in their wooden tanks had to be changed with a chattering pump that drew in the sea from the surf out in front of the tank shed. The pump broke down often, and then the water had to be carried by hand. It was constant crisis at Tortuguero when the tanks filled up with turtles. It still is. Nobody expects to rest at hatching time. But Larry and Leo had been through worse, in seasons before the Navy started coming, when the hatchlings were hauled out piecemeal by a hairbreadth schedule of flights of a four-seater Cessna airplane.

Inside the bellowing Grumman, Harold Hirth and I had eight thousand baby turtles to be put off at places scattered along twelve hundred miles of Caribbean shore. Harry, now Professor of Zoology at the University of Utah, spent three seasons at Tortuguero while a graduate student at the University of Florida.

This was goodby for another season. I watched the thin-spaced, palm-thatched houses of Tortuguero Village whip past. I felt the smoothness of air when we pulled up out of the suck of the river and the tops of the trees began to show through the ports, instead of the trunks. We raced on down the tree-fringed trough, and as the river mouth curved to meet the sea we banked seaward, past the green loom of Cerro Tortuguero, the lone mountain that stands on the far side of the pass only a little way back of the beach. It is the Cerro, the local legend says, that draws in the green turtles each July from all about the Caribbean.

It is just folklore, of course, that wild notion about the mountain being a beacon for migrating turtles. But I have spent ten years looking for a better theory to explain how they find the place, so I never argue the point. Anyway, no good navigator is likely to ignore any of the guide signs that might help him make his landfalls. For all I know, the Cerro may really be a landmark for turtles homing-in on Tortuguero. It would be pretty arrogant to scoff at the notion, so long as sea turtle navigation remains almost wholly unexplained.

The pilot held his climbing turn past Turtle Mountain and out over the ocean, and pretty soon we could see almost to Nicaragua, where the San Juan River comes down from the great lake and sends distributaries into the Caribbean. We turned back over the land and the roof of the rain forest took on the textured look it gets when you see it from a certain height. To the south the mountains behind Puerto Limón, the only Caribbean port of Costa Rica, rose blue through fifty miles of distance.

We came around into a southerly heading, and I thought we were off for Panama. But the pilot decided to give the lonesome little village one more thrill, and he put the airplane into a fast glide that took us back low over the water. We swooshed downstream treetop high, past Larry and Leo on the dock under the waving lace of the breadfruit trees. Then we turned out across the white, jagged dashes of the surf and only the ocean was under us. It was all at once the end of my eighth season at Tortuguero, and I felt the old small wrench leaving the poor lovely place there in the narrow *cocal* between the black river and the sea.

It was a Navy UF 2 we were flying in, a Grumman *Albatross* amphibian. It had been sent down by the Caribbean Sea Frontier from Roosevelt Roads, Puerto Rico, to take our little turtles around the Caribbean. The incongruous coming of the clamorous, two-motored airplane into the quiet peace of the river was the working out of many events, and of people's paths crossing in unlikely ways.

The fundamental reason for the Navy being there was the growing evidence that the green turtle is an able navigator. For some time the Office of Naval Research had been encouraging and supporting research in animal orientation. Some of the most dramatic navigation feats of migratory animals had never been satisfactorily explained. In fact, they still have not been explained. It seemed possible to Dr. Sidney Galler of ONR that when eventually they are understood, new ways of getting guidance information from the environments of the earth might be revealed; or that possibly even new *kinds* of guideposts would turn up. Our studies in the Caribbean had been piecing together a growing pattern of evidence that the green turtle has a strong homing urge, is able to hold a course in the open sea, and can make appropriate landfalls by means of unknown landmarks. If you considered the navigation problems to be instinctively solved with environmental information picked up by animal senses, the travels of the green turtle were bound to make it interesting to anybody concerned with guidance systems, as the Navy was.

I first met Sid Galler at a fisheries conference in Havana a long time ago. He had recently become head of the Biology Branch of the Office of Naval Research, and the migratory exploits of the green turtle were still mainly folklore. Dr. Galler asked me if I thought a green turtle would put up with having apparatus bolted to her shell. Not knowing exactly what he had in mind, I said I was pretty sure she wouldn't mind, if the load weren't too big to swim with.

I told him about female turtles coming single-mindedly ashore at Tortuguero to nest in spite of all sorts of injuries and incubi. A typical example is their dragging buoy logs ashore when they come in to nest. The buoys are short lengths of wood used as floats to mark turtles released in the sea for later recovery. The sea is rough most of the time off the Tortuguero nesting beach. The launch that used to pick up the turtles accumulated by the *veladores*, the turtlers, could never get very close to shore. To carry the turtles out by small boats launched through the surf was not practical. So the transfer was made by releasing the turtles into the sea towing a chunk of log on a line made fast to the upper part of the front flipper. The launch would come coasting up from Limón watching for a signal from shore that turtles were coming out. Then two or three dugouts would be put overboard and the men in them would chase down the bobbing buoys, grab the lines and drag the attached turtles aboard.

It was a fairly hairbreadth operation, and a few turtles got away each time. I could never see why a few men were not lost, too. Anyway, the aftermath of a collecting run was usually some poor turtles swimming about with logs tied to one of their main swimming flippers.

I used to figure that these were doomed turtles. But if they happened to have been females that had been caught and rigged with a buoy on their backs before they laid their eggs, their first thought —the first thought of some of them anyway—was not to try to outswim the hindering log but to go on back to shore and finish the nesting job they had traveled hundreds of miles to do. Finding a turtle going through a complicated behavioral pattern with a handicap like that gave me great confidence in the single-mindedness and load-carrying ability of the female green turtle and thus in her potential as a subject for navigation experiments. This confidence grew to enthusiasm one night when a turtle came ashore dragging a float she had towed up from Panama, more than a hundred miles away. Here was a creature, said by all the folk experts to be a long-distance migrant and open-seas navigator, which at the same time would be able to carry tracking apparatus around without apparent inconvenience, provided the right kind of tracking apparatus could be devised.

Shortly after Sid asked me about the load-carrying ability of the green turtle I got a grant from the National Science Foundation to study sea turtle migration, and set up tagging projects in Florida and Costa Rica. At about the same time an extraordinary society called The Brotherhood of the Green Turtle was formed, and the Caribbean Conservation Corporation soon grew out of it; and before long the green turtle was getting more attention than any reptile ever got before. And deservedly so; because no reptile ever so fetchingly combined features of interest to so many different kinds of people—succulence, an obvious but unexplained talent for navigation, and an evident manageability as a staple food resource for the seaside tropics everywhere.

So the *Albatross* roaring out of the hidden river was partly a sign of the open-mindedness of ONR, and partly proof that *Chelonia* is a many-sided reptile. I am going to talk a lot about green turtle virtues later on. For now, I just want to recollect how, that day, I looked back out of the bubble-port of the plane and saw Tortuguero down there sprinkled among the palms and breadfruit trees, more like one of my dreams than like any real place anywhere; and thought through the devious happenings behind Harry and me being up there with the eight-man crew of a military airplane and eight thousand baby turtles in stacks of wide, flat boxes.

We were heading for Panama to refuel. From there we would go island hopping up the West Indian arc from Barbados to Puerto Rico, leaving a batch of turtles at each of six places that had been selected as sites in a restocking experiment.

We leveled off at four thousand feet. The crew captain came back with a pot of coffee he had somehow brewed since the take-off. I took a cup gratefully, and then pushed my head out into the bubble-port once more and looked back to where Turtle Mountain stood like a dim, square cloud in the sea haze, the only high place in a hundred miles of shore. The mountain fading astern started me thinking back again through the mélange of other years and other flights in and out of Turtle Bogue, since Paco set me down there long ago in the little Aeronca airplane that used to be Francisco Vanolli's whole airline.

When I first went to Tortuguero I was looking for ways to get information to fill the gaps in the natural history of sea turtles. Some years before I had set out to write a handbook of North American turtles, and I quickly found how little was known about the big, conspicuous, edible kinds of turtles that live in the sea. This bothered me and started me roaming the Caribbean looking for whatever could be learned.

That was before it was known—by zoologists, that is—that sea turtles are migratory, and that the green turtle is among the spectacular animal travelers of the world. So one aim of my Caribbean prospecting was to find a place in which to test the stories of the fishermen and turtle hunters who spoke confidently of the green turtle as a global migrant and "a better navigator than man." I got some travel money from the American Philosophical Society, the Florida State Museum, and the University of Florida Graduate School, and on summer trips I chased rumors among the islands and around the mainland shores; and then slowly I zeroed in on Tortuguero.

The turtles had, of course, been going to Tortuguero for ages before I got there. The Indians were catching them there before Columbus came. I first heard of the place from two friends in Costa Rica, Dr. Doris Stone and Señor Guillermo Cruz, who separately told me of a wild stretch of the Caribbean beach up near the Nicaraguan border where green turtles came ashore and crawled over each other after nesting space. A little later I began to hear the same thing from the Cayman turtle captains, who for nearly a hun-

dred years had been catching turtles at the feeding grounds of the
green turtle among the Miskito Cays off Nicaragua. These men told
me plainly what our tagging efforts at Tortuguero have now finally
almost proved: that the herds of green turtles on the Miskito Cays
pastures all come from the Tortuguero nesting ground and go back
when their own breeding urge comes on them. These people said
that the Miskito Cays colony nested on a twenty-mile stretch of the
Costa Rican shore. They called the place Turtle Bogue. They said
the northern end of the Bogue was marked by a monument of
forest-covered volcanic rock, thrown out by some ancient eruption,
which stood alone and high on the low shore and guided the homing turtles in.

Now, ten years later, there were different times at the Bogue,
and I was looking back at the old seaside mountain from the port
of a fat Navy airplane bound for the far corners of the Caribbean
with a cargo of baby Tortuguero turtles. I marveled, simple-
mindedly, at how things work out, and how clean and easy it was
to get out of the Bogue with the help of the U. S. Navy.

Other years, flying out of Tortuguero was always a crisis. You
waited all morning, maybe, or even two or three mornings—with
the radio broken down as it nearly always was—for a flight you
had engaged a week or a month before to materialize. You looked
and looked through the miles of thin spray down toward Limón till
things that were not really there took shape, or you thought you
saw the airplane in a buzzard skimming a mile away, or in a
dragonfly hovering in the haze; and then you reached the last stages
of overanxious waiting when things swimming in your own eyes
became a little airplane coming. Of all the troubles that mixed with
the excitement and satisfaction of other years at the camp, the
one that undermined strong men most was waiting for the little
airplane to come, and never knowing when or even whether it
would get there. Former friends are now enemies because of that
demoralizing waiting. I know men who would not be caught dead
back at the Bogue because of those dreadful vigils.

I thought of the business of getting there in the early days, too.
The times mostly ran together, because there was less crisis about

them; but I recalled each step of the trip three years before, when the pilot was a friend of mine whom I never saw again. I remembered how when we crossed Parismina bar, the mouth of Río Reventazón, which marks the beginning of Tortuguero beach, there were cub sharks off the bar; and out where the coffee-and-cream of the river met blue sea, birds and mackerel were ganging up on sprats in dark sheets that flashed jagged white where fish slashed through them.

Almost at once after passing Parismina you could see the doubled furrows of turtle trails. They marked the sand with v's and u's or with wandering, indecisive scrolls that began at high-tide mark, went up to dry sand and then back to the surfline again. I got out a little notebook and started trying to tally the tracks. A manta ray, tilting and wallowing in the surf, distracted me, and I lost count and started watching bull turtles fighting over females that dived in haste as the airplane or its shadow passed over. It was as if the plane were a gull, and the three hundred pounds of the turtle were three ounces of bite-sized hatchling that had to dive quickly or be carried away. I am not saying a grown-up green turtle holds on to her hatchling fear of things that fly overhead. I am not saying she doesn't either.

That was a thought to set one off thinking; but we were approaching Mile Eleven, as you count back from the far end of the nesting beach, and at Mile Eleven the nesting reaches its peak of density for the whole stretch of Turtle Bogue. Two main migratory streams converge on Tortuguero to nest. One comes from the south, from Panama and Colombia, and the other comes from the Miskito Cays and Nicaraguan coast. Turtles arrive from other places too, from the farthest reaches of the western Caribbean, and a few from even beyond. But the majority each season are derived from home grounds that lie due south or north, up or down the shore. Every time anybody who is connected with the turtle camp flies from Limón to Tortuguero he looks out for coasting flotillas of arriving turtles. But none is ever seen. The nesting aggregations just turn up suddenly at the Bogue, unannounced and unobserved along the way. The dearth of observations of cruising schools of sea turtles is one of the puzzles of the natural history of the group, and I'll have more to say about it later on.

For three or four miles beyond Mile Eleven the beach was heavily cross-striped with tracks. At Mile Six they thinned out, and I had begun to wonder whether it might be a slow season at the tagging camp. But then the tracks showed up thick again at Mile Three, and stayed that way as far as I could see up toward the northern end of the beach where Río Tortuguero turned and met the sea. It was the tenth of July and the turtles were in. It was almost sure to be a good year for tagging.

I was arriving unannounced. The pilot buzzed the camp to rouse somebody to meet me in a dugout at the landing strip two miles up the shore, but the place was deserted. Larry and Leo were off hunting wari for sure. The wari is the white-lipped peccary, and eating wari is one of the better ways to extend the basic Bogue diet of beans and rice. So hunting wari is an admirable pursuit, and successful hunters are much admired at the Bogue. We clattered on away, skimming the palms all the way to the pass, where we banked sharply and glided in for a landing in the knee-high grass in the narrow, bushed-out strip through the cocoplums of the upper shore.

We taxied to the end of the strip and stopped. The pilot shut off the engine and I opened the window on my side. At once the old clamor of the Bogue surf came in, the continuous restless sound waves make rolling in at all angles as they often do down there. I opened the door and stepped out from under the red-and-silver wing. A shower had just passed, and I felt the hot sun in the rain-washed air. A ghost crab ran out of a shallow pit our sudden coming had scared him into, and made off sideways for his proper hole. I looked off down the endless swooping scallops of the shore and saw only a black vulture moping stoop-shouldered on a drifted snag.

The pilot was in a hurry to return to Limón for a flight he had to make to Sixaola. He handed my bags out and held out his hand. I shook it and congratulated him, as was the custom after completion of any flight. He started the engine, shut himself in, took off heedlessly downwind, and was quickly lost to view behind the high treetops across the river.

I moved my bags to the end of a trail that made off through the cocos to the landing on the river. I laid some palm leaves over the pile of gear, against the rain that sweeps in through the sunshine anytime down there. Before starting the two-mile walk down the beach I stood and looked around and soaked in the good, familiar, lonesome feel of the place. The sun, out between squalls, had heated the dark sand and made a kind of air that is clean and warm and not like air in any other place. The incessant sound of the surf was a landmark too, as was the stealth of a prowling beach lizard, already accustomed to the irregularity of the airplane coming. Between bursts of sound from the sea, I could hear the distant cawing of a crane-hawk and the incessant creaking of a toucan in the forest across the river. Tatters of the ocean breeze, most of which had been killed by the staggered squalls offshore, played brittle tunes in the palm leaves, and off halfway to Limón, it seemed, a dog was yammering in some far-off crisis. The dog was the only sound or sign of man. The lonesomeness was part of the place.

The barking dog recalled the Siquirres dogs that were at Turtle Bogue the first time I landed there. These were itinerant packs that used to come over from the inland towns and run wild on the beach, eating eggs and hatchlings each turtle season. Later on, the government sent in posses that shot every dog they could hit, and spread melancholy in the little village by shooting local dogs along with the migrant packs. It was a dismal time; but it is hard to think what else could have been done to save the Tortuguero turtles. Next to people, the dogs were the worst turtle plague in those days. Hateful as the sound of the old Enfields and Tommy guns was, it was they, and the new laws prohibiting turtle-turning, that saved this last of all the green turtle beaches of the western Caribbean Sea.

My reminiscing about the Siquirres dogs ended suddenly when Bertie's bad-tempered bitch bounded out of the bushes and started grabbing at my leg. I quit thinking about old dogs long dead, and kicked at this one currently at hand and missed. Then Bertie came out, big, black and shining, and no older than any other year. Bertie is the oldest resident of the Bogue. In those days the airplane landed just behind his house on the river, and he took passengers where they wanted to go in a dugout canoe. Behind Bertie was Larry Ogren. He had not been hunting wari after all. He had been at the camp since June in charge of the tagging for the season. He had a long beard, and the beard was a lot redder than I expected.

I remember that flight into the camp better than most, as I said, because the pilot was a Costa Rican whose name, like mine, was Carr; and because when he disappeared over the trees in the little plane he went back to Limón and fell into the sea and was drowned, and I never flew with him again.

Up to that year, it was fairly easy to keep Tortuguero history straight by just thinking back through the hardy souls who each season had sequestered themselves at the camp to keep the turtle work going. The first National Science Foundation grant supporting the tagging work was activated in 1955. That was the year that we first set up a camp on the beach. We have been going back ever since. Each season since then I have come and gone between the Bogue and other places where things could be learned about sea turtles. But somebody has had to stay there continuously, through each season, and each night go out on the beach to tag and measure turtles. The first year it was my old friend Leonard Giovannoli. He manned the camp alone. The idea of the Crusoe life down there appealed to him, and he became the first of the Tortuguero marooners. He had a lot of trouble with possums eating his bananas; and a couple of Carib girls who lived next door worried him some coming over to watch him bathe. But Giovannoli tagged fifty turtles one night all alone, and nobody has equaled that record. Last season a local assistant named Michak tagged eighty turtles one night, but he had a boy with him—anyway, Michak is a Miskito Indian while Giovannoli is only a gringo. After Giovannoli, there was a long run of students, mostly from the University of Florida, who peopled the camp in changing combinations, with at least one from the year before going back each year to break in the new ones arriving.

From the beginning, work at Tortuguero was blessed with the favor of Teodoro Quiroz of San José, whose sawmill at the village was for years our only source of supply, and whose nervous little radio was our only means of communication with the outside world. It was Teodoro, don Yoyo he is called in Costa Rica, who first pleaded our case before the Ministry of Agriculture and helped us get two miles of beach adjacent to the camp allotted to our use, free of commercial exploitation by the turtle industry. By the time the *Albatross* came down, the camp had grown from a shack on the beach left by Miskito Indians to a cool, fantastic, long-legged leaf-house where you could lie on a cot and see the ocean out front and the river behind, and could drink and wash from a sand well with a pump that never drew up the millipede carcasses from the bottom. We were really living pretty well by the time the Navy airplane started coming—compared to how it used to be.

The big change came about when the Caribbean Conservation Corporation was founded, and the hatchery was set up at Tortuguero to furnish stock for the restoration project. When my book, *The Windward Road,* came out, a copy luckily fell into the hands of Joshua B. Powers, an international publisher's representative in New York. Josh Powers always had a strong attachment for Latin America and the Caribbean, and for some time he had been casting about for a way to do something solid to improve the lot of the people of the Caribbean lowlands. The book brought an idea to mind. With customary energy Joshua organized The Brotherhood of the Green Turtle, a loosely knit group of influential people bound together only by the obligation to think how to save the green turtle, and thereby to insure to Caribbean *costeños* more protein in their diet, and to Winston Churchill his nightly cup of green turtle soup. The Brotherhood grew; and pretty soon Ben Phipps joined it and other things started to happen.

Ben is John H. Phipps, of Tallahassee, Florida. He is, although he says not, a philanthropist, and he has always had a strong interest in natural history, in the tropics, and in conservation. With his financial support, the Caribbean Conservation Corporation was organized. It is a non-profit group dedicated to preserving biological resources in the Caribbean. Its first undertaking was the green turtle program, in which the information gathered at Tortuguero and by the years of Caribbean reconnaissance was to be used in an effort to bring back colonies of the green turtle to old-time levels of abundance.

The green turtle was an important factor in the colonization of the Americas. It was herbivorous, abundant, and edible—even when prepared by cooks not aware that it can be made a gourmet's dish. It lived all about the tropical littoral and grazed in schools on turtle grass pastures that now are mostly vacant. It nested in numbers in places where no turtles ever come ashore today, or come only one on a mile in a year. The British Navy counted on green turtle to extend its cruising in the New World. The Spanish fleets took on turtle for the voyage back home to Cadiz. A green turtle was as big as a heifer, easy to catch, and easy to keep alive on its back in a space no greater than itself. It was an ideal food resource, and it went into the cooking pots of the salt-water peasantry and tureens of the flagships alike. It fed a host of people and to some of them it became a dish of almost ceremonial stature. In England the green turtle came to be known as the London Alderman's Turtle, because an Alderman's Banquet was considered grossly incomplete if it failed to begin with clear green turtle soup.

The one flaw in the green turtle resource was that the females came ashore to lay their eggs. At breeding time, when survival is in most delicate balance, all sea turtles leave the familiar safety of the sea, where they have grown to a size that makes them almost immune to predation, and lumber ashore and expose themselves and their offspring to the hazards of the land. A green turtle on shore is almost defenseless. She weighs on the average nearly three hundred pounds but seems almost wholly unable to use her bulk and strength in active self-defense. She is awkward of gait, myopic of vision, and single-track of mind. Once the nesting has started, she will go on doggedly through the hour-long ceremony with a pack of dogs digging out her nest beneath her, or with drunken Indians drumming on her back. It is as if she were sure that this last legacy to her race must be left, whatever her own fate might be.

So long as the dangers of this time on land remained natural ones—Indians, jaguars, and pumas for the old turtles; gulls, vultures, coatis, and the like for the eggs and young—the populations held their own. But then the Europeans came to the Caribbean, with ships to victual and slaves to feed. Through the centuries the turtle beaches were raided. Eggs were dried in strings like wrinkled beads, the old turtles were turned on their backs and either barbecued on the beach or hauled away on the decks of schooners. It is not possible to say how widely the green turtle nested in primitive times, but there were certainly several big rookeries in the western Caribbean, and probably many. Today there is only Turtle Bogue.

That was the reason I chose Tortuguero as the place for a research camp and tagging operation; and why, later on, the Caribbean Conservation Corporation established the hatchery for its restoration project there. The Bogue is simply the only place there is. Elsewhere along the shore green turtles nest singly or in small bands. There are even a few records of green turtles nesting in Florida during the past decade. But everywhere except at Tortuguero, the nesting is so spotty and intermittent that no worthwhile tagging can be done, and hatchlings and eggs for restoration programs are not available in the necessary numbers.

The only other place in the Caribbean where there is a real green turtle rookery is Aves Island, a barely exposed bank in the Leeward Islands a hundred miles off Monserrat. This feeble expanse of land seems to be the Tortuguero of the eastern Caribbean—the only place anywhere in the whole West Indian archipelago where there are big nesting aggregations. But Aves is a weak foothold. Besides being small, distant, and surrounded by tumultuous seas the island appears to have decreased in all its dimensions since it first was measured during the past century. It is apparently disappearing under the sea. We went out there one July in a boat equipped with all kinds of navigation aids, we almost missed the landfall after a rough night's run from Monserrat. We found the island by only a hairbreadth when the captain in the crow's-nest sighted birds and breakers far abeam. How the nesting turtles find Aves each July is not known. I will say more of that mystery in later chapters.

Every year a half dozen sailboats go out from Dominica to look for Aves, hoping to bring back loads of turtles. Few of them ever find the island. It is clear that only the remote and inaccessible location of the sinking islet has saved a breeding colony of green turtles for the eastern Caribbean.

So Tortuguero is the last stronghold for *Chelonia* in half the Caribbean Sea. The colony has held out at the Bogue because of the isolation of the place. It is cut off from the hinterland by swamp and rain forest. To boats it offers no anchorage offshore and a dangerous bar to cross where the river enters the sea. In its own way Tortuguero is almost as hard to get to as Aves Island is. But even so, when I first went there the whole nesting beach was being worked intensively by turtle hunters. During those years, almost the only turtles that were able to nest and get back into the sea were those that came up in howling squalls that kept the *veladores* stormbound in their coco-thatch huts.

The situation is a little better today. Several years ago the Ministry of Agriculture in San José declared the first three miles of the nesting beach a reserve for our research and tagging project. With the advent of the Caribbean Conservation Corporation, the protection was extended to five miles. Now, happily, the turning of nesting turtles and taking of eggs is legally proscribed on the whole Caribbean coast of Costa Rica. With this solid protection, and with the efforts to restore turtles to other former nesting sites in the Caribbean, the position of the green turtle seems less melancholy than it was ten years ago.

The aim of *Operation Green Turtle* is to re-establish green turtle rookeries in places known to have once been nesting grounds. Batches of Tortuguero hatchlings are released, with the hope that they will grow to maturity imprinted by the smell, taste, or feel of the place where they entered the sea and will be instinctively drawn back there at breeding time, as the salmon is drawn to its hatching place. They might simply go back to Tortuguero, of course. It is also possible that the odds against hatchling survival are so vast that our mere thousands of planted turtles are hopelessly swamped by the array of environmental hazards they face. The program has been under way five seasons, and more than a hundred thousand hatchlings have been released at twenty-two different localities. There has been no solid sign that the primary objective is being fulfilled, that turtles are coming up to nest where hatchlings were put into the sea. But green turtles may have to be six years old before they begin to nest, and it may still be some time before it is clear whether new nesting colonies are being established.

Meanwhile there have been important side benefits from the program. In some of the introduction sites the little turtles appear to be staying on and establishing resident populations, instead of setting out in the expected long-range developmental travel. Hurricanes washed away the oldest of these planted colonies, but others seem to be taking hold. Another happy trend, which may simply reflect the protection that our presence and activities have brought to the Tortuguero nesting colony, is an increase in the number of distant returns in the tagging program. The first protection ever given the Tortuguero colony came in 1955, long enough ago for the increased hatchling yield of the beach to have become breeding green turtles. It seems likely that this may account for the spilling-out of Tortuguero turtles into more distant resident range. It is certainly this factor that has brought an apparent increase in nesting at the Bogue itself. I believe more turtles are coming now to Tortuguero than came in the early years.

I know more people are. The first big influx came when the hardiest core of The Brotherhood of the Green Turtle and the Caribbean Conservation Corporation held a meeting at the camp. With a little airplane from Expreso Aereo Vanolli, we laboriously airlifted in twelve people complete with beer, ice, and air mattresses.

Ben and Mrs. Phipps were there, and Josh Powers and his son Thomas, and Jim Oliver and Chuck Bogert came down from The American Museum of Natural History. It was Jim, now Director of the Museum, who later made the arrangements with Dr. Galler and the Office of Naval Research that resulted in the *Albatross* coming to the Bogue. Hugh Popenoe and Ray Crist were there from the University of Florida, and the NBC newsman John Hlavacek showed up, just out of Castro's jail in Havana. There was a very good-looking girl from Jamaica named Elizabeth Sears. She had a toe in a plaster cast. I forget why she came or what was wrong with her toe. Gus Pascarella was there taking pictures and Billy Cruz, who now is Costa Rican representative of the Caribbean Conservation Corporation, came down from San José to "know the place," as they say in Spanish. It seemed queer his having to know Tortuguero, when he had told me all about it twelve years before. Nowadays Billy knows Tortuguero like the back of his hand.

To me, remembering Tortuguero in earlier years, that gathering was as bizarre as a conclave of pygmies would have been. The Bogue would always be to me a place of solitude, of quiet waiting for rain to stop or turtles to get there, or for the Vanolli plane to come. I remember standing outside the camp and listening to the gringo voices laughing under the electric light, and thinking back to other nights with only the wind to hear.

Not that the Bogue was always quiet, even in the old years. The Big Drunks of the Miskito Indians on Saturday nights were pretty exciting. So were the soldiers who came in once from somewhere to investigate a rumored invasion, and got separated and made a terrific noise shooting at each other in the woods across the river. One night a tapir wandered into the sawmill compound and stayed there all night knocking over stacks of boards. The next morning when they started up the sawmill engine the tapir ran about the settlement in a frenzy with a boy popping at him with the only twenty-two rifle in the town. The tapir finally charged down the riverbank and ran off across the bottom, as they are able to do. So things have happened in the lonesome little place.

But the high point of all my Tortuguero time came when the members of The Brotherhood of the Green Turtle filed solemnly out to the beach, each carrying his personal turtle tag inscribed by a jeweler in San José with the distinguished name of the owner. Each man clamped his tag to a flipper held steady by Harry Hirth and Leo Martinez; and then we set the turtles free to bear names like Phipps, Powers, and Oliver to the ends of the Caribbean and beyond. The dignity with which Harry and Leo supervised those rites was a stirring thing to see. And a proper culmination of the ceremony was that a year and a half later Jim Oliver's tag was sent back by a Nicaraguan fisherman who caught the turtle in the Miskito Cays two hundred miles away.

That was the year of biggest change at the Bogue. The next year the big two-engine Navy Grumman came roaring in. It dropped a smoke bomb, to show what cross-wind the sea breeze might be making on the river. It circled over the ocean, glided back into the narrow alley between the wooded banks, threw the river into the air for a thousand yards, and settled into the water before our dock. All the village came out to watch the incongruous fury of the coming of the *Albatross*. When it stopped, dugouts paddled out and brought the crew ashore. We all introduced ourselves and the men looked the camp over and got the lay of the land. We showed them the hatchery a hundred yards up the beach, and the tank house where the accumulating hatch of baby turtles was kept. We talked a while about the schedule for the turtle flights, and then we headed for Sibella's.

For all our years at the turtle camp we have been fed by Sibella Martinez. Sibella is a Colombian Creole whose father brought her to Tortuguero forty years ago. Our camp is located a third of a mile down the beach from her house, but we cover the distance with admirable regularity. This time, part of the crowd went in canoes and some of us walked. I was with the group that walked. As we approached the confusion of leaf-covered buildings, which Sibella's home has grown into during three decades, we could see the others landing at the dock. Jo Conner was there from the University of Florida, and my wife, Margie, and Kip Ross, a photographer from Washington, and half of the crew of the *Albatross*. As the two parties converged on Sibella's backyard-door a white horse, half-hidden under two towering sacks of coconuts, came threading its way among us. The horse was followed by a bearded gnome of a Nicaraguan who was helping Sibella's brother, Sam Martinez, dry his copra. Two dogs barked in a perfunctory way. A black pig that lay across the path in a patch of sunshine grunted at the thought of moving to let us pass, but never moved. A foot-long basilisk lizard ran up a palm trunk, stopped in a splash of sunlight and clung there, gleaming green and crested like a tiny dinosaur out of a comic strip, or out of the Mesozoic.

Seeing the basilisk there so green and bizarre on the palm tree made me think to look again at the people who had gathered to partake of Sibella's hospitality. It was an imposing clientele, with the Navy fliers all in their Kodachrome suits. You might wonder how Sibella would take such an invasion coming only half-announced that morning by a neighbor's children carrying our message. But the year before, Sibella had fed sixteen members of The Brotherhood of the Green Turtle, and never batted an eye. She has only the vacillating yield of the sawmill commissary to draw from, pieced-out by sporadic windfalls of bush meat that successful hunters share around or by supplies walked in from Colorado bar sixteen miles away; but she seems immune to the shock of not knowing how many people there will be to feed.

We went inside. After the usual flurry of people on the verge of being about to eat, we all got seated on the benches at the long table with the oilcloth cover. Sibella came in, and everybody got up again.

"Sibella," I said, "this is the U. S. Navy."

"Yes, Mister Carr," she said, and then to the Navy men, for some reason in Spanish, she said, "*Mucho gusto*," and we all sat down again.

With a practiced eye I took stock of the victuals Sibella this time had conjured up. Beans, rice, unsweetened lemonade, and bread were there as always. These were rock bottom for even the hard times when the sawmill went broke and its commissary closed, and they were the groundwork of all her fancier meals too. The bread was neither the crusty marvel the Cubans make nor the repulsive bakers' bread of the United States. It was and always is at Sibella's strong bread with body, topography, flavor, and nourishment. It is bread such as many women used to make; and what has happened to it, and to the character of people who accept the repellent bread prevalent in North America today, I am not able to imagine. Anyway, with that bread of Sibella's and nothing else, you would leave the table fed.

This time there was plenty besides. There was turtle, for instance, in two conditions. There were stewed fins, which are my favorite turtle dish and likely to become the favorite of any man not offended by the gelatinous matrix in which the fins arrive; and there was also fricasseed turtle meat adroitly spiced. These were more or less staples of the season. More festive was a splendid pot of tepiscuintle. The tepiscuintle is a rodent related to the guinea pig, only bigger and better to eat. This one was braised. Another dish contained what proved to be the stewed remains of a giant rooster I had known in life; and there was also an oddly made but savory preparation of tarpon. Plain jumping tarpon from the pass, with the meat minced away from the myosepta. You may think tarpon is not good to eat, but that is only before you have tried Sibella's.

It was a bit of a company meal. Some days get to be all the same, as I said, with only beans and rice and bread. But even so, it was and always is a surprise what Sibella could do with the old black wood stove that has staggered about her kitchen for a dozen years, and with no supermarket anywhere around.

When everyone had been fed we went back to camp. The plane captain and two of the crew that year were the kind of men who get uneasy if they are not doing something useful. They got to work fixing the pump and the generator and other things around the place; and pretty soon everything was working for the first time that season. After a while night came and we went out to watch the turtles nesting.

There are five kinds—five genera—of sea turtles in the world. They are the loggerheads (*Caretta*), the ridleys (*Lepidochelys*), the hawksbills (*Eretomochelys*), the green turtles (*Chelonia*), and the leatherbacks (*Dermochelys*). Of these only the last three nest at Tortuguero, and only the green turtle goes there in great numbers. Almost any night from July through September a walker on the Bogue beach will come upon a green turtle.

Everybody ought to see a turtle nesting. It is an impressive thing to see, the pilgrimage of a sea creature back to the land its ancestors left a hundred million years ago. The nesting rites begin, for the watcher, at least, when the turtle strands in the surf. That part is hard to watch, those minutes when she comes up with the breakers and stays there for a while, rising with a wave then bumping back softly on the sand, making up her mind. She blinks and peers, turns her nose down and presses it onto the wave-washed bottom, then looks up and all around and blinks some more. She is clearly making a decision. What her criteria are, nobody knows, and as I say, this coming to land is next to impossible to watch. The turtle is wild and skittish when she first touches shore, and even the light of a match struck far up the beach may send her back to the sea.

But I have seen a turtle landing a few times—or snatches of landings. In strong moonlight you can make the turtle out—or, eerily, on the rare pitch-dark night when the surf breaks phosphorescent like rolling fire. If on such a night a turtle by luck comes out near where you are being very still, you can see her stop with the backwash foaming flame around her, push her head this way and that with a darting motion less like the slow movement you expect of a green turtle than like a lizard or snake, then lower her head and nose the hard, wet beach as if to smell for telltale signs of generations of ancestors there before her. At this stage, anything but steady quiet on shore will scare her back to sea, maybe to come out again fifty yards up the beach, maybe not to return till another night. You have to do a lot of walking and waiting to see the coming of a turtle out of the water. I have never seen a good photograph or movie of it. We have had a lot of able photographers down at Tortuguero, but none has caught this first step in the arrival of a water reptile coming once in two or three years to dig the hostile land.

But once she has gone up into the dry feel of the windblown sand and begun to dig, if a turtle is really of a mind to lay, she can be watched, as I said, by gangs of people waving flashlights in her face, and will go on through her set maneuvers oblivious to any amount of hullabaloo. Having found the proper place to stop, generally at the edge of the first vegetation or beside the rise of a dune or log, the turtle makes trial swipes at the sand with her long front swimming flippers. From that point on she seems to sink gradually into a behavioral groove in which finally she becomes oblivious to all distraction. I remember a photographer trying to get a series of flashlight pictures of a turtle nesting, back before everybody started using electronic flash guns. The climate had somehow got into the man's flash bulbs, and for half an hour he kept shooting away with every other bulb exploding like a little grenade, throwing glass about and driving the rest of us back into the dark. But all the time the turtle went on methodically digging the big pit she rests in while she lays, then delicately she shaped the urn of the nest hole and laid a hundred-odd eggs in it. She filled the nest, covered the pit, and concealed the site with sand thrown about by her long front fins, and then made her way slowly back to the sea. Never once did she show any sign that she cared about popping bulbs or flying glass.

The incubation period of the green turtle is about sixty days. The first year of *Operation Green Turtle* we had asked Roosevelt Roads to schedule the arrival of the airplane for a date we figured would be a little way into the beginning of the hatching season. Just before the airplane got to camp, turtles began to hatch by hundreds. We soon had three thousand of them in the holding tanks, and more coming faster every night. It was time to be off on the big airlift. Before the tanks got overcrowded we were away on the first flight, to Cartagena, Colombia by way of the Canal Zone. The next flight was to Nicaragua and British Honduras. After that we left again on an island-hopping journey up through the Windward and Leeward islands. Finally we took a load of turtles and equipment from the dismantled camp directly from Tortuguero to Miami. Before it was all over we had spread 18,500 green turtle hatchlings among sixteen different places in the Caribbean, in the Bahamas, and on the southeastern coast of Florida.

Since that first incongruous coming of the *Albatross* to Tortuguero there have been four more successive years of *Operation Green Turtle*. According to our original calculations the first turtles flown out five years ago should now be maturing and ready to go somewhere to nest. But maybe we figured badly with the scant growth data available. It now seems pretty sure that *Chelonia* takes longer to grow up than we reckoned at the start. Possibly, also, the odds against hatchling survival are so high that planting mere hundreds of them to pioneer in a new site is a move foredoomed to failure by the law of probabilities. It is even possible that the whole fundamental assumption that green turtles that mature after being displaced as hatchlings will return to the place you take them is wrong. An instinctive drive may take them back to their ancestral shore instead; or possibly they just scatter about wherever the currents drop them off, and answer their breeding urge on any shore that seems attractive.

Or, maybe they are really out there, those that live on out of the first thousands, ready to come ashore in the places where we released them, and to return in numbers great enough to allow the sexes to find each other and leave behind the seeds of new green turtle colonies. Nobody knows what to expect, really.

But one thing is sure: as an offbeat venture in public relations, *Operation Green Turtle* is already a success. In a dozen Caribbean cities the flights have brought out friendliness in folk whose views on the United States range from the mildly jaundiced to the very bitter. It is mostly cheerful people who show up at the airports and gather around each season's *Albatross*. And their good will is not confined to green turtles and the amiable crews of the airplanes that deliver them. It is bound to spill over a little to gringos as a breed, and to extend itself to the whole outlandish conception of preserving live natural resources of any kind. Good will is not turtle soup, but it is an asset all the same. The *Albatrosses* have planted more than the baby turtles they have brought.

2

TAGGING TURTLES

To learn anything about the natural history of a wide-ranging sea-
farer such as *Chelonia*, the main problem is to keep the animal in
view. There are two times in the life of a sea turtle when a zoologist
can count on making contact with it: when it hatches, and when
the female goes ashore to nest. Everything else is done away off
somewhere out of sight, and has to be reconstructed by deduction
from fragments of observation.

There is one good way to take advantage of the brief contact
between turtle and turtle-student when the female comes ashore.
That is to put a tag on the turtle. As a means of learning things about
the life history of any animal that assembles in groups, as sea turtles
do at nesting time, a simple tag is an important tool. It lacks the
fascination of the gear of oceanographic research or of the apparatus
of biochemical research, but it is an effective device all the same.
Seldom can so much be learned from so little manipulation as a
tagging project demands. The simple act of recovering a tag that
has previously been put on an animal can answer fundamental
questions about the life history of the species. Even more important,
the results of tagging are bound to raise other questions to be answered by other means.

A good tag is one that can be quickly put on, that interferes little with the movements and peace-of-mind of the animal; that will stay on a long time—if the animal is one that lives a long time, as a turtle does; that is inscribed with clear directions for its return; and that offers a reward to the one who sends it back.

During the first year of the green turtle project at the University of Florida we used an inscribed oval plate of monel metal, wired to the overhanging back-edge of the shell with monel metal wire. In Costa Rica, Leonard Giovannoli and I put these tags on several hundred green turtles, and in Florida David Caldwell and I and several collaborators marked loggerheads, green turtles, and ridleys with them. As the first season progressed we thought we were building up a good backlog of marked turtles, from which the story of turtle travels would trickle in through future years. But it soon became obvious that most of the tags were being unaccountably lost before the turtles even left the nesting ground. It seemed impossible, but time after time a turtle would return tagless after an absence of less than two weeks. Such turtles could be recognized by the empty holes in the back-edge of the shell.

The green turtle, like all other sea turtles, nests more than once during her season at the breeding beach. Most of them probably nest from three to five times, at intervals of about twelve days. Where they are and what they do during the twelve-day intervals is not yet known. They surely don't go back to their home pasture. Some of these are a thousand miles away. This is one of the various questions that will be answered when tracking techniques have been worked out. One thing that is known about this period at the nesting beach is that a lot of strenuous romance goes on out in front of the shore. Some of this happens just before the female goes ashore to nest the first time. Some of it takes place betweentimes. This became obvious during that first season of the tagging program when many of the tagged turtles came back with their tags gone. The tags had apparently been ripped off violently, with the wires either broken or pulled right through the quarter-inch of solid bone and shell of the edge of the carapace. Some of them returned with the tag bent and dangling from wire through a single hole. It would have taken a strong man with two pairs of pliers to put such bends in those stiff, thick plates of monel metal.

The loss of tags was the work of the rutting male. Sea turtles in love are appallingly industrious. It is not easy to observe their conduct because observations come only in snatches, from airplanes or from shore when the turtles rise on wave crests. But the male turtle obviously makes an awful nuisance of himself. Why the female puts up with such treatment is hard to understand. To hold himself in the mating position on top of the smooth, curved, wet, wave-tossed shell of the female, the male employs a three-point grappling rig, consisting of his long, thick, recurved, horn-tipped tail, and a heavy, hooked claw on each front flipper. Sea turtles breathe air, of course —both sexes do—so both sexes naturally try to stay at the surface during the violent mating engagement. This adds to the acrobatic problems of the male, and augments his intemperate scraping and thrashing at the shell of his intended. Besides all that, the female generally stays coy and resistant for what seems an unnecessarily long while. During that time other males gather, and all strive together over the female in a vast, frothy melee in which nothing, as I said, can be seen from shore except that it is pretty exciting.

For a time we kept telling each other that no male turtle could possibly tear off the tags we were wiring on so securely. But the tags kept coming off. We began to take notice of the violent courtship encounters, and then we saw that some female turtles came ashore with a pair of deep notches on either side in the heavy bone of the projecting front-edge of the shell, where the grappling nails of the male hold the mating grip. We finally realized that it was foolish to try to fasten anything to the shell of a female green turtle at mating time because it was bound to be ripped off during courtship and mating.

It would be good to know whether the lack of barnacles on the shells of green turtles might also be a result of that strenuous courtship. The green turtle is relatively free of barnacles on the upper parts of the carapace, where loggerheads and hawksbills are often heavily encrusted. I always supposed that this was associated with the more mobile life *Chelonia* leads and with its great swimming speed. In emergency spurts a green turtle can swim almost as fast as a man can run—and with the long-distance breeding migrations it makes. Just how the fouling might be prevented I never could think. It could be simply the disability of barnacles to adapt their life cycle to conditions imposed by the habitat or changes of habitat of the green turtle host. It could be active biochemical resistance of some kind, acquired by green turtles through natural selection as a necessary refinement of their equipment for fast, sustained, streamlined locomotion. It could be that the turtles just scrape the barnacles off on rocks. Captive green turtles do scratch their backs on things. Several young green turtles that we have kept in tanks have had the habit of moving under a ledge, pipe, or anything solid that they could get beneath, and by shifting back and forth, scrape and scratch their shells against the object with exactly the rhythm and with something surprisingly like the faraway expression of a pig scratching himself against a post.

I am not saying that green turtles lose their barnacles during courtship. If they did, you would expect males to have more barnacles than females, and they don't. Anyway, it seems likely that loggerhead courtship, which I have seen in briefer glimpses, is as strenuous as that of *Chelonia*. I think it safe to say, however, that if the green turtle were susceptible to infestation by barnacles, the female would lose hers every two or three years when she goes away for the wild party they have at the Tortuguero breeding beach.

A fact that fits in nowhere, as far as I can see, is that the Surinam green turtles that Peter Pritchard, a graduate student at the University of Florida, tagged at Bigi Santi have barnacles. His tag returns are beginning to show that they may travel as far and fast as any other green turtles, and there is no reason to think the males are any less importunate. I don't know what to make of that.

So the shell tags were obviously no good. Tom Harrisson of the Sarawak Museum had learned this the year before. While we were trying to decide what change to make, Tom wrote me that in his tagging project in the Turtle Islands he had started using an ordinary cow-ear tag, made by the National Band and Tag Company of Kingsport, Kentucky. He clipped the tag to the forefin instead of to the edge of the shell, and it seemed to hang on far better than anything that had to be fastened to the shell. I decided to try the cow-ear tag at Tortuguero. The first batch came from the factory toward the end of the first season of work in Costa Rica. I rushed down to Tortuguero, where Giovannoli had been using the shell tags all season. In four days I put forty of the new tags on turtles. Renesting returns of that group showed little loss of tags, and eventually four of the forty were recovered in other countries. In a tagging project involving long-distance travel, that is a good percentage of recovery. We gave up the shell tags forever.

Tagging can reveal information on the life history of a sea turtle —growth rates, sexual cycles, local movements into and out of the locality in which the tagging is done, routes and periodicity of long-distance travel. International recoveries show the goals and something of the paths and timing of the breeding migrations. Repeated returns of tagged females to the nesting beach show how many times and at what intervals nesting occurs each season, what tenacity the females show in returning to the same place on the beach to nest, and what period elapses between the migrations to the nesting ground.

At the time I began work at Tortuguero, two other students of sea turtles, Tom Harrisson and John Hendrickson, were already learning a great deal about the green turtles that nest on the Turtle Islands of the China Sea. Nothing was known of Atlantic populations however; and nowhere was there any solid evidence to bring to bear upon the problem of migration. In fact, it was generally believed by zoologists that fishermen's tales of turtle migrations were only the tales of fishermen. It was in correcting this fundamental misconception that the five-dollar reward served so well.

If my name goes down in the canons of zoology it will be as the instigator of the five-dollar turtle-tag reward. The tag I started using twelve years ago—and the one still in use at Tortuguero and wherever we mark sea turtles—is inscribed with a number and with the offer of a reward to whomever finds the turtle outside the tagging locality and returns it to the Department of Zoology of the University of Florida. The Tortuguero tag says these things in both English and Spanish. The tag doesn't say so, but the reward is five dollars, and this is paid promptly and without any haggling. I imagine that the National Science Foundation had misgivings over the reward item in the budget of my research project plan; but they sent the money, and I never spent so little to learn so much.

In those days the reward was almost everywhere more than the cash value of the turtle. In some places it was three times more. In some places, in fact, the turtle had no cash value at all, and was only caught to be eaten locally. Almost everywhere about the Caribbean, five dollars coming so easily out of the sea was a substantial blessing, and any tag found was likely to get back to Gainesville eventually.

At Tortuguero alone 4200 mature female green turtles have been tagged. When each turtle is tagged she is measured and the eggs she lays are counted. The number of short-term renesting returns of these to the beach runs into the hundreds and there have been 175 international recoveries. Some of the data that have accumulated merely substantiate the earlier findings of the few people who have studied the green turtle nesting colonies in other places—Banks, Tom Harrisson, and John Hendrickson in the Turtle Islands of the China Sea; James Hornell in the Seychelles Islands; F. W. Moorhouse on Heron Island on the Great Barrier Reef. But much has been new and unknown, and other kinds of information are revealed as the project continues.

The local tag returns at Tortuguero soon proved that the colony nests at least three, and possibly as many as five or six times during a season. The interval between nesting emergences turned out to be about 12.5 days. It is to me noteworthy that Caribbean fishermen had already learned both these things, somehow, without the help of a tagging project.

During the second season at Tortuguero, none of the turtles that had been tagged the first season came back. This was expected, because a three-year reproductive cycle had been found in Pacific green turtle colonies. What was not expected was the return of some of the first-year turtles after an absence of only two years. Then the third year at Tortuguero came and a greater percentage of the tagged first-year group returned. Since then no Atlantic green turtle has been found returning to nest after an absence of a single year—only after intervals of two or three years or multiples of those periods. Why a two-year cycle should occur in the Atlantic population and not in the China Sea population has not been explained, but accumulating tag returns may one day explain it.

The first year at Tortuguero we marked off the nesting beach, to keep track of the site of emergence of each turtle that came ashore. In subsequent seasons the grid has been refined and each emergence can now be located to within less than an eighth of a mile. The idea here is to see how nearly a female turtle comes out at the same place each time she nests, both within a single season and on each two- or three-year migratory return. The information can be used statistically to determine whether the females show a tendency to clump—to nest close together in space and time. This is of interest because it can help answer the question of recruitment at the beach. You can't often look at a green turtle and say where she came from. But if two turtles tagged near each other on the Tortuguero beach later on are caught in Colombia, it suggests that they might have been part of a group that traveled together between a Colombian feeding ground and the Costa Rican nesting beach.

The main excitement in the tagging project is the long-range recoveries, the five-dollar tag returns. These have been the most profitable part of the program. When the Tortuguero work started, there was, as I said, no scientific basis on which to judge the truth of widespread folk stories about the travels of sea turtles. But then a tag came back from Puerto Cabezas, Nicaragua, two hundred miles from Tortuguero. The turtle had been harpooned by a Miskito Indian, and the tag was sent in to the University of Florida by Padre Feliciano of the Misión Católica at Puerto Cabezas. The first bit of solid proof of green turtle travel had come. Since then the long-range returns have come in from every part of the western half of the Caribbean and from other places to be told of later on.

Taking all the tag recoveries—both the long-distance ones and those made at the tagging beach, either the same season the tag was put on or in subsequent seasons—and looking at them from different slants, you can see some engrossing things. One noteworthy feature is the dearth of tag returns from Costa Rica between nesting seasons. This obviously means that Costa Rica has no resident colony. Its only green turtles are the Tortuguero breeding colony, which appears in July and goes away in October. The lack is partly due to a scarcity of good turtle-grass pasturage in the long, surf-pounded shore between Limón and the Nicaraguan frontier. Wave action is severe there, and several big rivers bring down silt and fresh water and for much of each year make the sea just a wide place in the coastal lagoon system. South of Limón, toward Panama, there are small reefs with turtle-grass flats behind them, but the green turtles there have mostly been killed out. So we never get tags from Costa Rica from November through June.

The bulk of the tag recoveries have been made in places scattered through the western half of the Caribbean Sea. On the tag-return map in my office the heaviest concentration of pins is off the coast of Nicaragua, between Puerto Cabezas and the Miskito Cays. The turtles were mostly caught there by the Cayman turtle captains, who traditionally net Nicaraguan green turtles for American and European markets. Lately, however, the frequency of these returns has been falling off and there have been more tags from waters southwest of Miskito Cays and nearer the mainland. The people who send these are usually Miskito or Creole fishermen who live in the mainland towns abreast of the Cays.

This shift does not mean that the habits of the green turtles have changed. It reflects a stiffening of the attitude of the Nicaraguan government toward foreign turtlers. Outsiders are finding it more complicated to get turtling licenses from Managua. Meantime, the demand for turtle products is growing and new interest in turtling has sprung up among the local coastal people. Together, these factors are changing the way pins go onto the tag-recovery map. The moral of this is that anybody concerned with either the natural history or the conservation of the green turtle has got to reckon with a lot of political and socioeconomic factors, or else get wrong impressions about green turtles.

There are other places on the map where pins concentrate. One is on the Panama coast between Colon and Bocas del Toro. Another is the Guajira Peninsula of Colombia. Nicaraguan Mosquitia is still the most-pinned space, however. Partly this is because one of the most extensive areas of turtle grass in the world is there; partly it is because, as I said, the able, energetic Caymanians started turtling in the place a hundred years ago and founded a special Caymanian culture on the green turtle. So it is not pure zoology the tag returns give you. There is some bias in the sampling they provide. Nevertheless, the reason the Cayman people began turtling there in the Miskito Cays was that turtles were abundant there; so in spite of the interplay of factors, the pins reflect a natural situation.

The spread of the tag returns throughout the western Caribbean suggests that Tortuguero is the nesting ground for that area. My failure, after extensive searching, to find any other site of mass nesting there supports the idea that the Bogue is the only west-Caribbean locality in which group nesting occurs. So does another generalization that can be made from the tagging results. This is that no turtle tagged at Tortuguero has ever been retaken nesting anywhere except at Tortuguero. This not only reinforces the idea of the importance of the Costa Rican rookery, it also is grounds for assuming that green turtles always nest in the same place. This generalization has become a useful axiom in working out the ecological geography of *Chelonia* on a world-wide basis.

Each season the nesting assemblage at Tortuguero is recruited from different, widely separated places. Zoogeographically, this has important implications. It means that the isolation of the various west-Carribean turtle populations is not real genetic isolation at all, because the populations all get back together, and presumably interbreed, at nesting time. During the season of courting, mating, and nesting at Tortuguero the turtles there may be partly from Nicaragua and British Honduras, say, and partly from as far the other way as Colombia. Of course it is possible that the different colonies are kept segregated from each other at the nesting ground by the mating preferences of the turtles. Colombian males may only court Colombian females—nobody really knows what goes on during the social time out beyond the surf. It will be a long time before we find out, too, because the only way a Colombian turtle is ever recognizable as such is by being picked up back home in Colombia.

That comment requires a bit of pondering, but not more, I think, than is reasonable to ask of a reader. The thing to keep in mind is that the only tagging of west-Caribbean turtles that is done takes place where they gather together to breed. So everything has to be reasoned backward, beginning when the turtle shows up somewhere else and is caught and its tag is sent to Gainesville. It is a fairly frustrating way to study an animal, groping backward through its life. But it produces information, slowly. Anyway it is the only way there is.

Another generalization that can be made from the Tortuguero tag returns is that the separate resident populations seem to include turtles that nest on each of the two cycles—the two-year cycle, and the three-year one. Out of the 219 of these returns to the beach, sixty-two have occurred after two years and 105 after three years. Only eleven have been retaken on two different returns. Of these, only one changed its cycle in successive returns. A turtle tagged August 1, 1960, was retaken at the Bogue on August 17, 1962, released, and then recaught on July 25, 1965. It seems possible, therefore, that the cycle changes with the age of the turtle, with the two-year period lengthening to three years as time passes, or vice versa. It will take a lot more returns of tagged turtles to get this straight.

A few years ago Harold Hirth and I made still another generalization from the Tortuguero tag-recovery data. This was that there appeared to be no definite relation between the time that elapses before a given recovery and the distance from Tortuguero of the recovery site. In other words, the turtles taken farthest from the tagging site had not always been away from the tagging site the longest. This seemed further proof that the Caribbean green turtle was not a mere wanderer that moved aimlessly away after nesting and got farther away as time passed. It suggested instead that the turtles moved periodically between regular feeding and breeding grounds. It seemed, therefore, to furnish one more bit of evidence that *Chelonia* is a systematically migratory animal. In those days that idea needed every bit of circumstantial support it could get because direct proof was, and for a long time will remain, out of the question.

It is out of the question to prove migration by tagging because this would mean tagging a turtle at Tortuguero, catching it again wherever it lived the rest of the year, releasing it a second time, and then finding it again on the beach at the Bogue. Unless the tagging were done on a massive scale, by a whole corps of people, with plenty of money for turtling gear and for chartering vessels, such a project would take forever to accumulate useful data. So still, if one is inclined to strain at gnats, all that the Tortuguero tag returns really prove is that turtles tagged there get caught far away; and that others get caught back at the beach after two or three years' absence. These and other circumstantial clues indicate periodic migration, beyond reasonable doubt; but they do not prove it. Not to the nit-picker, anyway.

To get back to the distance-time idea that I brought up, there is one way in which time interval does seem to be related to recovery distance. Proportionally more long-distance recoveries are now being made than were made during the early years of the project. About the time Hirth and I published the comment on the seeming lack of bearing of the time a tagged turtle was away and the distance of the place where she was retaken, we started getting tags back from increasingly distant places. Two came in from around on the east side of the Guajira Peninsula, for instance, technically beyond the limits of the western Caribbean; and three from clear out in the Gulf of Mexico off Campeche. There was a real shocker from Florida, from a turtle retaken near the Marquesas Keys; and another from all the way around on the north coast of eastern Cuba, in water that is not Caribbean or Gulf at all but real Atlantic Ocean. Finally, and most recently of all, a tag came back from Coche Island, at the easternmost end of the Caribbean. At the time I am writing this is both the latest and the most distant of all our tag returns. It is so far away that it has made plotting the tag-return data unhandy.

The base map has to be extended three hundred miles just to take in that one return.

These late, long-range returns do not indicate wandering by the turtles that carried the tags. Though the recoveries were made late in the project, in no case had the turtle involved been away from the tagging beach for a specially long period of time. The Coche Island one, for instance, was tagged August 19, 1964, and recaught fourteen hundred miles away on October 28, 1965. The question here is, why should there be a greater proportion of long-range recoveries late in the project than there were during its early years? The explanation could be some change in the distribution or intensity of commercial turtling, such as that in the Miskito Cays area. A more exciting possibility, however, is that the increase in long-distance returns means that the Tortuguero nesting ground is more productive now than it once was.

When I first went to Tortuguero the whole rookery was being patrolled by turtle turners, one per mile throughout the season, for the whole stretch of the nesting shore. If a female turtle completed her nesting and got back into the sea it was only because rain, lightning, or rheumatism kept the *velador* off the beach; or because the launch that picked up the accumulated turtles was laid up for repairs. Sometimes, when the launch broke down word crept up to Tortuguero and the turtlers stopped going on the beach at night. More often however, no word got there, and the turtles kept accumulating on the beach. They died there by the hundreds, many of them without having nested, and virtually all without having completed the season's nesting regimen. The way things were in those times, all the green turtle populations that used the Bogue as their nesting ground seemed doomed. And because the whole western Caribbean got its green turtles from Tortuguero, the survival outlook for *Chelonia* there seemed sorry indeed.

Even now, with new turtle laws in Costa Rica, illegal turtling still goes on, because the government is not able to furnish the intensive patrols that are needed to keep poachers off the long, wild, remote turtle beach. But the mere presence of our tagging camp during the nesting season is a deterrent to poaching. Throughout the turtle season people constantly go and come. Little airplanes fly low along the shore, and boats tear back and forth on the lagoon behind the nesting beach. On the northernmost five miles the tagging crews walk the beach at all hours. This activity makes the poachers uneasy, and they poach less than they would like to. So for the time at least, the west-Caribbean turtle populations ought to be increasing. This may explain the rise in frequency of distant tag recoveries. Perhaps resurgent populations are spreading to new areas, or spreading back into places they occupied in times before the green turtle was so heavily exploited.

I would like to believe that new nesting populations are being established by the increased productivity at Turtle Bogue. The trouble is nobody knows how a new resident colony is formed, how members of a feeding colony are stirred to abandon the ancestral feeding ground and move to new pastures. It may be by aimless straying. It could be that the move is triggered by crowding or competition on the grazing ground. None of this is known.

Even less is known about how the green turtle founds new nesting colonies. The site-tenacity of the nesting females suggests strongly that the drive to return to their natal shore when they reach sexual maturity is bred into baby turtles. Obviously, if this conservative outlook were never abandoned there would be only one big colony of the green turtle in the world. Pioneering is bound to occur from time to time, but as I said, nobody knows how. Whether it is produced by a shoving out at the edges, or by the odd, migrating female getting an urge to go ashore in the wrong place, or perhaps by changes in longshore currents that confuse a whole flotilla of traveling turtles into suddenly landing on an alien beach and nesting there, are all possibilities; but there are few known facts that help one to choose among them.

I have thought a lot about that matter, because the success of *Operation Green Turtle*, and that of any effort to extend the breeding range of *Chelonia* by transplanting little turtles, depends on the reaction of hatchlings when they are taken to a distant place and released there. Although no natural process would be the equivalent of the airplane transportation of new hatchlings to places unknown to their bloodlines, results of such transplanting projects could shed light on the problem of natural colony proliferation in a migratory animal with strong site-fixity. In *Operation Green Turtle* the fundamental unknown is whether an unswerving attachment to an ancestral nesting shore is inherited by the hatchlings, or whether they inherit only a tendency to become strongly imprinted by the physical character of the particular place in which they first enter the sea, and to travel in ways that let them locate that place when they become sexually mature.

In any tagging project the life history of the animal that is marked has, as I have shown, to be mostly pieced together deductively, by reasoning back and forth between tagging place and time, and the times and places of recapture. The process is slow and indirect. Tagging sea turtles is even less productive than tagging some other migratory animals, colonial sea birds, for instance. Banders of sooty terns get information far faster than you get it tagging sea turtles, and some of the kinds of things tern banders learn can never be learned at all by tagging turtles. There are two reasons for this. One is simply that in tern colonies the numbers of birds that can be marked in a season may run into the thousands, while in most turtle colonies it takes a lot of hard work to put on a few hundred tags. A more important advantage is that the bird man bands young birds, just before they leave for their first flight. The mark is put on at the beginning of the life of the bird, and this gives a greater potential yield of information. It furnishes contact with all ages of the species and with both sexes. At Tortuguero only the fully mature female turtles are tagged. The males never come ashore, and a technique for tagging hatchlings has not yet been worked out. I will do a great deal of complaining about that a little later on. The problem is to devise a marking system that will identify a three-hundred-pound turtle that has grown from a three-ounce hatchling, and that will furnish an address and an offer of a reward for notifying the tagger.

So up to now, all we know has had to be reasoned from the histories of females tagged after they had reached full size and sexual maturity. Little information on growth rates comes from such a program, and it tells nothing of the time the turtles take to reach sexual maturity. Sex ratios remain hidden too; and almost the only things that are learned about the habits or movements of the male turtles has to come from snatched observations out in front of the nesting beach during mating time. Some males obviously go to Tortuguero at the time the females are there. But do they travel there in the company of the females, or do they go separately? Are their sexual and migratory cycles on two-year or three-year schedules as those of the females are, or does every mature male go to the Bogue every year? Such questions can be easily answered by tagging, if the tagging is done with terns. Fledgling terns are as big as their parents, big enough when they leave the nest to carry a band about the world. And they come in two sexes, too.

My envy of tern banders is aggravated by the sooty tern so often nesting in the same places as the green turtle. There is a mystic alliance between the two. All about the world you find them on the same little islands, and every time I see them there together I feel frustrated. The turtles produce a hundred minute offspring, too feeble to bear any durable mark. They just swarm off into limbo and stay till some of them (I suppose it is some of them; it is some of some turtles that once were little) come dragging back out of the sea, as big as the dining room table, ready at last to be tagged. A pair of terns has only one child, but it is as big as they are, and it is able to carry the same big band on its leg that they do—to carry it through five years of adolescence, then to bring it back on a breeding migration, and then to take it back and forth on other migratory journeys for as long as thirty years.

It doesn't pay to dwell on the injustice of this, or to think how far along the natural history of sea turtles would be if only turtles were birds whose fledglings could carry full-sized tags. Anyway, quite a lot has been learned by just tagging the females; and as the backlog of tagged turtles grows, more information and more kinds of information are coming to light.

A good example of a recent single tag return that edged over into new fields was one put on a turtle in Surinam, and recovered in Brazil. Peter Pritchard spent several weeks of May and June tagging turtles at Bigi Santi. When I visited the camp there in June, Pritchard and I agreed that the Bigi Santi green turtles looked more like those out at Ascension Island than those of the Caribbean. That is to say, they looked like Brazilian turtles, for which Ascension is the main nesting ground. There was no solid qualitative difference you could get your teeth into, only a different conformation of the shell and forequarters. It might mean nothing, but we both noticed it and tried to define the difference. I was still talking about it when I got back to Gainesville.

Well only a little later the first return from the Bigi Santi project came in. The tag had been put on a 45-inch green turtle on May 5, 1966. It was recovered June 23 of the same year at San Luis in the Brazilian state of Maranhao, a thousand miles to the south, and far down below the sea of fresh water that floods out from the mouth of the Amazon. This not only was unique information on speed and route of travel, it was almost evidence of something I have long wondered about: whether a given feeding colony, like some winter colonies of birds, may include individuals from widely separated nesting grounds. The Bigi Santi turtle going to Brazil almost says they do. Not quite, because there is still a gap between its place of recovery and the northernmost of the Brazilian recoveries of Ascension Island turtles that we have had. But it makes you think that with time the gap will fill and this new question will be answered. Besides that, this recovery was the first ever made of a turtle that had crossed the equator. If celestial navigation is assumed to be the mechanism that guides a migratory journey, then crossing the equator greatly complicates the navigation astronomy. For a long time I had wondered whether there was any colony of *Chelonia* that has a regular transequatorial route. Pritchard's return suggests that there may be such a colony nesting at Bigi Santi.

Of all the things the tagging program has brought to light, the most exciting is Ascension Island, and the way tagging results there bear upon the almost unbelievable ability of some animals to locate tiny islands in the open sea. There will be a lot about that problem of island finding in a later chapter.

3

SEÑOR REWARD PREMIO

When the turtles tagged at Tortuguero leave the nesting ground most of them go away to some pretty remote, back-country places. The reason for this is simply that green turtle colonies have been wiped out in the regions easily accessible to man. When tagged turtles are caught the letters that tell of the captures, besides providing data for the migration study, bring nostalgic glimpses of the diverse, sequestered people of hidden Caribbean shores and islands.

The tag we use is stamped with words intended to convey the idea that a reward will be given to whomever sends the tag to the Department of Zoology, University of Florida at Gainesville. An effort is made to say this in both Spanish and English. Because the space on the tag is small, the words have to be abbreviated and juggled about to fit it, and you have to do some decoding to get the full sense of the legend. Some people give up in despair and simply copy the inscription on the envelope, beginning the body of their letter without any heading at all. Some, however, address the letter to a person named Premio, Remite, Send, or Reward; or to various combinations of the four. This used to confuse the postal officials at the University, but all of them now know that Sr. Premio Remite and Mr. Reward Send are aliases of mine. They don't know why I use the extra names, but they send the letters all the same.

When a person picks up a drift bottle on the beach or catches an animal bearing a tag it is usually not so much the chance to add to human knowledge that stirs him, but rather the sudden surge of feeling less out of touch, of being mystically chosen to receive the tag or the bottle. All finders of tags or bottles don't feel that way, but a lot of them do, and it often moves them to outdo themselves in telling about the event. Some are able to write only haltingly, some have to get a scribe or a missionary or the rare passing visitor from outside to compose a letter for them. Some write their own letters with extraordinary fluency, zest, or attention to detail.

The sampling of tag letters reproduced below hints of things not in the books about the Caribbean. Some are literal translations, some are just as they came. I have been to most of the places the letters came from. I went looking for turtles, but almost everywhere the people became an essential part of my reconnaissance, partly because they know a great deal about sea turtles, partly because they themselves are so beguiling. The letters were chosen to show the range of the charm of Caribbean people and the varied ways in which sea turtles can get into their lives.

Tasbaponnie
April 11, 1965

Dept. - Biol. - UF
Gainesville Florida U.S.A.

To Whom This May Concern, Dear Sirs

I beg to inform that on the Date sixth of the Current Month of April I caught a turtle by fishing a mile on the East of my Village, Tasbaponnie, where in after over hauling I found a Ring on one of the front fin Right hand. Which now I am Remiting to your Company acording to instructions found on Ring, which you all after Receaving will Recompense me with what so ever may be it as a Reward so as to take the Interest a next time to forward the same By who so ever Else may Come across in finding a next one, which now you all will advise me to this affair as I will await your Kind Reply to the matter, No. of pin 2604.

Regards

Yours Sincerely Friend
Alberto Julias

Campeche, Camp. Mexico
April 23 de 1961

Sr. Reward Premio
Send DERT. B 10. U.U.F.
GAINESVILLE F.L.A. U.S.A.

MUY SENOR MIO:

[Translation]

After saluting you affectionately I permit myself to communicate to you having captured a turtle with a metallic plaque, the inscription of which said the following:

REWARD PREMIO REMITE
SEND. DERT. B. 10. U.U.F.
GAINESVILLE F.L.A., U.S.A.
NUMERACION:1,243

If you are interested in this please communicate with him whose address is given above.

After having the daring to write you I permit myself to beg your pardon, and remain your attentive servant,

Marcelino Mier Camara

El Bluff, Nicaragua
August 28, 1966

Dear Prize Giver,

I am very glad to be the one that found this tyrtle drifting down to the Nicaraguan's water it was found in the Pear Lagoun Bar on thursday 18 of August at 6:00 o'clock in the morning, I caught it beside a shrimp boat in that place.

I wish that I have explained every thing the right way.

Number 3853.

Mr. Wilmore Hodgson
El Bluff, Nicaragua

Bluefields, Nicaragua
8/29/60

Dear Sir:

This turtle was caught about five miles eastward off Setnet point, by me and a friend. We were out fishing on our vacation from school with nets, when we caught him. We were very happy to find him. so we are sending the number 390 back to you as it says, to get our reward. You can send what ever it may be in care of the Instituto Nacional Cristobal Colón where we studies, Bluefields, Nicaragua C. A. Hoping to hear from you.

Yours sincerly,
Willfirth W. Perilla

It was caught around the east cost of Nicaragua.

August 10, 1964
Corn Island
Nicaragua C.A.

Hellow Sirs:

In replying to your reward of progress, I am sending you two tags that were found on turtles.

This one is mine "No. 956". I have caught the turtle four miles South East of Perl Cay. The cay is about twelve miles to the East of Perl Lagoon barr.

It was caught around 8:A.M. the 8 of July 1964.

This one is for my cousin Errol Perilla "No.1062". It was caught tree miles South of Sail Cay. The Cay is eighteen miles North west of Great Carn Island. It was caught at six o clock 6:A.M. the 5 of August 1964.

We have decided to send the two of them together to cut expence on mail and register.

Then, we are awaiting your answer as quick as possible.

On the East cost of Nicaragua, C.A.

Truly yours,
Willfrith Perilla

San Juan del Norte
Departmento Rio San Juan
Nic. 27 of April 1962

Dear Mr. Carr:

Your date 27 of March was received at this date and I am answerin your letter giving you the datas you ask for.

The turtle was capture in the Atlantic seas as none as Carribian sees write in front of Harbor head Barr about 5 miles out to see it was capture and the 29 day of Octuber year 1961. It was striken with Harpoon. As they allways catch thise turtle here.

Now I want to ask you if it is not possable for you to get me in tutch with some prople who or interested in buyin turtle and oxville and the oxville shell, I would be verry thankfull if you could get me in this' bussness. Thanking you in advance I remain your obidient servant.

Aldric Paul Beckford C.

Bluefields, Nicaragua
octubre 22, 1965

Señor
Archie Carr

[Translation]

I received the check sent in my name to the value of five dollars the 20th of the month of October. Thank you. And at the same time I want to ask you to send me a catalogue that contains photographs of curiosities of the sea, because in this part of the Atlantic there are found on the bottom of the sea some very pretty shells and snails. I should like to select some of these shells to send to you, and some other things that you would like, because it would be hard to get them there. Because as I say beautiful things come out here. So you really ought to send the catalogue immediately so I could send the things.

Su atto y S.S.
Quintin L. Marquina

Puerta Cabezas, Nicaragua
January 13, 1962

Gentlemen:

I am mailing to you as per instructions found on plate, the pin found on a Turtle fin. To my knowledge there is a reward for same, so, I am hereby asking you to please send mine to address found on envelope.

This turtle was caught at Awastara about twenty-five miles north of Pto. Cabezas, Nicaragua, approximately three months ago.

Awaiting your reply with interest, I remain,

Yours very truly,
Lester Campbell

Puerto Cabezas
January 26, 1956.-

Dear Gentlemen:

Enclosed please find plaque of your Biological Dept. I am remitting same as per requested. You may also be interested in knowing that I caught the Turtle bearer of your plaque around the Miskito Cay in the month of September 1955. I am a Miskito Indian from a small Village named *DAKURA* along the Miskito Coast, to be able to remit this to you I was forced to come fifteen miles to Puerto Cabezas, the closest point of communication. Please answer me to the address below.

Yours respectfully
Cleveland Diego

Bluefields, Nicaragua
January 14th of 1963.

Dear Sir:

I am answering your letter that enclose the money you send me, and I am pleased to tell you that this turtle was catch at Marroon Cay by setting nets. I caught it on the 17 of Octobre of the passed year at 9:00 A.M.

Nothing else for the moment, except I would like to keep in touch, I remain,

Yours respecfully,
Wilmore Hodgson

Bluefields, depto. de Zelaya, Nic. S.A.
1 de Setiembre, juebes, de 1965

:Señor:
REWARD, PREMIO, REMITE,
SEND DEPT. BIOL. U.F.
GAINESVILLE, FLA, USA

[Translation]

I address you to communicate to you that, being fishing in the Atlantic in front of False Bluff, in 35 feet of water at about twelve midnight in the fishing vessel "don Billi", of Mexican registry, captained by your servant: Quintin L. Marquina: the boat being his property, don Billi, we had the luck to fish a turtle, with respect to which I address myself to advise you of that encounter, sending the matriculation number 3476. I await an answer.

Without more for the moment
Quintin L. Marquina
Nationality, Mexican

Bocas del Toro
Rep. de Panama
1 Nov. 1955

Gentlemen:
On the 9 Sept./55 while fishing in Palmilla, Colon, R.P. I caught a turtle with a Badge (as per duplicate copy below). Sometime during the last of the said month. I sent it to Cristobal C. Zone. to be posted, with a return adress to General Delivery, Bocas del Toro, and up to the present no answer. I am notify you that if in case someone is trying to play a trick on me you can know that I am the rightful owner. If I have been tricked please send and let me know by whom, so that I can put in my claim for whatever the reward was and if in case it has not arrived to your office then you know that, that one has been found, when, and where.

Respectfully yours,
McNeill Conally

Maracaibo, Venezuela
3 de Agosto de 1963

Ciudadano
Director
Del Departmento de Biologia de la
Universidad de Florida

[Translation]

I herein address you to tell you that on the 25 of July of this month a marine turtle was caught bearing a plaque, No. 1667, belonging to that University. The turtle was taken at Castillete on the coast of Venezuela.

I should be grateful to that distinguished institution if the reward mentioned should not be sent in cash but in fishing tackle or as an insignia of some kind.

De Ud. atentamente
Jovito Fernandez

Monday/30/F/1962
Port Limon, Costa Rica

to the university of FLA
Gainesville
U.S.A.

Clamp 926

I am sending a clamp that I caught on a She turtle up the Booge Monday the ninth of July at 8 o clock the Morning.

Reward Price can be send to port Limon Costa Rica to Mr. Paul Hermay Fisherman in this port. No. of the clamp 926

Post Office
to M. Paul Hermay

Septiembre 8 de 1965
Siquirres Costa Rica

Notice.

This Reward was fond in Colorado Bar, I'am asking, please to mail reward to George Davis in Siquirres Costa Rica. Many Tanks.

I'am Your's
George Davis.

September 24, 1965
Siquirres Costa Rica.

Mr. Eugene Gourley
Student Assistant To Dr. Carr.

Dear Mr. Eugene by this you will now that I'ave, receive you letter of September 20 and was glad to hear from you. Towards tag No. 1482 of the capture of turtle bearing, this tag I most let you now that this turtle was capture on June this year, but I dont remember the date, but I reepite that it was capture in the month of June, this same year. I'am sorry to say that I dont remember the date but I hope that this will not prevent me to obtain the reward, which I think I deserv for the work that I'ave done to obtain the tag also captureing of the turtle.

Hopping that I will be well treated as you all say.

Expecting to hear from you soon. I remain your's

George Davis Davis

Maracaibo, 17 de Enero de 1963

Ciudadano:
Director Send Dept Biol U-F.

[Translation]

Atentively I direct myself to you to send you a plaque that I found encrusted on a turtle that I caught on the coast of Cojoro Venezuela. This demands that it be sent to that Institute in order to receive a reward.-

Receive a cordial embrace.

Roberto Faneite

Puerto Limon C.R.
August 8, 1963

Dept. B.J.O.U.U.F.
Gamesville, Fla.
U.S.A.

To whom it may concern, on the 7th day of August I, Benjamin Grant Brown, caught a female turtle on said turtle was a tag No. 1190.

If interested, please write and inform me what to do.

Yours,
Benjamin Grant B.

El Bluff, Nicaragua, C.A.
September 27, 1965

Dept. Biol. U. F.
Gainesville, Flo. USA.

Dear friend I take the prevellage by writing you this letter, to infirm you that I caught a Turtle and on that Turtle I have found a PRIZE. and the words that the Prize had on were these words: Send back to this Direction Dept. Biol. U.F. Gainesville, Fla. USA. With deep interest I am sending to you all and I will wait to see what sort of respond I will receive.

The turtle was caught in front of El Bluff, Nicaragua aproximately 10 miles from El Bluff, Nicaragua, On Friday 24 of September at about 10 P.M. The Turtle ways about 180 Kilos.

My direction is: The Port of El Bluff, Bluefields Nicaragua C.A. And my Name is: MOISES MCREA.

As I uttered this letter I hope that I would receive some good information, Thanking you in advance for a reply: May God Bless you:

Sincerely yours,
Moisés McRea

In sending tag-return rewards to Mr. McRea and a correspondent in Venezuela we inadvertently got the checks switched. The man in Venezuela sent back the check he received, and we mailed him a good one. The irregularity was no bother to Moisés at all as the following letter shows:

El Bluff, Nicaragua
December 9, 1965.

Dear Mr. Carr:

I wish to inform you that I had receive the CHECK that you sent to me. I realized that it wan'nt made out in my Name, but still I tried to get it change and was successful in that. I thaught then that it would'nt be any problem for you to give to the other man the CHECK that was belonging to me.

I do realized that it was a mistake that was made over there. Since then it wan'nt any problem for me to get the CHECK change, I went ahead and did that.

Thanks very much for your kind Hospitality and your Generosity, in cooperating with me, and in taking me into condiseration as to send again to me and let me know that it was a mistake that was made over there,

Please excuse me for taking such a forward step as to the changing of the CHECK that you had sent to me. As you shall celebrate this CHRISTMAS SEASON I wish you God's richest Blessing, both for you and for your family. May God Bless you in all that you do, may you be successful in the great job that you have.

The CHECK was enclosed $5.00 DOLLARS.

Sincerely yours,
Moisés McRea

The turtle referred to in the next letter was tagged on Ascension Island in the south Atlantic. The Brazilian who caught the turtle naturally supposed it had come from Florida, and the idea stimulated him, as his letter shows. Actually the turtle coming from Ascension was a lot more exciting than its coming from Florida would have been, but Sr. Renaldo had no way of knowing that.

Taxi Aerea Capixaba
Placio de Café 10°-S. 1001/2/3
Vitoria - Espirito Santo
Brasil

Presados Senhores:

[Translation]

The writer is Chief Pilot of the Capixaba Aerial Taxi. In addition, I hold the post of Chief of Operations, and as such I have always to be inspecting the places where we operate. On one of these trips, two days ago, I had the great satisfaction of helping to catch an enormous turtle, and to my great surprise found on it a ring with the following inscription: "Notify Dept. Biol. U Fla Gainesville, Flórida, USA."

The locale of the capture is a small, summer holiday station, situated on the coast very near Vitória, our capital; more precisely its coordinates are 19°35′ S, 39°48′ W.

I find noteworthy the fact that this turtle had effected so great a trip; after all, there are thousands and thousands of miles involved. Also, it is extremely comforting to us to know that, behind this small, inscribed ring is found the inflexible will of a peace-loving people and that through their studies they try to contribute toward a better world, without so many apprehensions and megatons. We Brasilians love and admire the American People, and will always be at their side in the struggle for the Peace. I hope one day, if God allows and my financial situation permits, to become acquainted with The United States, when I will have the immense pleasure of making it a visit and of conveying personally the admiration that we feel for this People and for the Great Country.

Hoping that I have complied with my duty, I conclude by wishing you a Happy New Year, replete with success and gladness.

Cordiais Saudacões,
José Renaldo

P.S. If possible, please send me some information so that we can print it in our local newspapers. The place of the capture is called "Regéncia."

The peak of brevity in the tag project correspondence was achieved by the writer of these few words, which accompanied a tag from Costa Rica.

From
this Barra Colorada
Costa Rica this is my name, Alfred Wilson

Sometimes the mechanics of returning a tag exceed the skills or energy of the man who caught the turtle, and the tag lies uselessly hoarded in a thatched rancho or dangles as an amulet for a while. Sooner or later, however, it is usually seen by someone who is able and motivated to send it in, and he does. Among the people who help consummate tag returns, missionaries have been most often involved. Anyone inclined to deprecate the role of missionaries in the world should be taken to the western Caribbean. There, on the most isolated parts of the Mosquito Coast, it is, or was, until the Peace Corps began to get there only the missionaries who help the forgotten people into the edge of the modern world. It is they, too, who return a great many turtle tags. The following letters were sent by missionaries and other helpful second parties.

Catedral Nuestra Señora Del Rosario
Bluefields, Nicaragua, C.A.
July 30, 1965

Dear Sirs:

Enclosed is a tag (no. 3093) found on turtle fished from the Caribbean Sea.

To make a short story long—I'm a Roman Catholic priest. As a missioner I was visiting a small town on the East Coast of Nicaragua here a few weeks ago. At the house where I ate, a small girl was playing with the tag. When I explained to her father what the tag was all about he readily agreed that we should forward it to you.

The data gathered is rather meager but might possibly help in your work. The turtle wearing the tag was harpooned last September. The turtle weighed about 150 lbs. The man who harpooned the turtle is called Alaric Coleman who lives in a town called Setnet Point. This is about 35 miles north of Bluefields (right on the coast). A group of Cays about seven miles from shore are called: Grape Cay, Maroon Cay, Wild Cane Cay, etc. This turtle was found close to *Still Cay* almost mid way between the coast and Corn Island. That would make it about 20 miles from shore, but this Still Cay is still considered part of the Cays above mentioned.

With the sincere hope that this information may help you in your work, I remain,

Sincerely yours,
Rev. Fr. Ward Schnur, ofm Cap

Bluefields Nicaragua
2 January 1965
Sirs:
The enclosed turtle tag, No 3190, is submitted by Mr. Cleveland Blandford, of Haulover, Nicaragua. Mr. Blandford says that he took the turtle on 16 May 1964 with a harpoon seven miles southeast of Columbilla Cay, where the water has a depth of approximately 25 fathoms.
Mr. Blandford reports that the turtle weighed about 160 lbs.
This office will be glad to forward to Mr. Blandford any communications sent to him at this address.

The Ven Laurance W. Walton
Archdeacon

Bluefields, Nicaragua
February 15, 1965
Dear Sirs:
Enclosed please find a turtle tag which was found in this vicinity. The finder, Mr. Cleveland Blandford, of Tasbapauni, Nicaragua, killed a she-turtle bearing this tag about 6 miles due East of the village of Tasbapauni. The turtle was found on Dec. 29, 1964, and weighed perhaps 200 pounds.
I hope that this information will be valuable to you in your researches. I know that Mr. Blandford will be delighted with the reward.

Sincerely yours,
Rev. Robert J. Carlson

Bluefields, Nicaragua
March 30, 1965
Dear Mrs. Harshaw [secretary to A.C.]:
Thank you very much for your letter of March 3rd, addressed to Mr. Cleveland Blandford of Tasbapauni. He is very happy to receive the check for $5.00 and wishes you to know this.
Concerning the discrepancy about turtle tag no. 3190, I am afraid

that there is no hope of clarification. Mr. Blandford does not remember clearly the details surrounding the finding of that turtle,
including the date. There is one thing that he can assure you of,
that the turtle was caught off the coast of Nicaragua between the
mouth of the Rio Grande and the mouth of the Pearl Lagoon.
Mr. Blandford promises to be more careful in the future regarding
the exact information for the turtle tags which he finds. He wants
you to know that he does appreciate the rewards.

Sincerely yours,
(*the Rev.*) *Robert J. Carlson*

2001 Hessian Road
Charlottesville, Virginia
August 21, 1965

Dear Dr. Carr:

My wife and I spent about two months in Tasbapauni, Nicaragua
this summer. Tasbapauni is about sixty miles north of Bluefields.
Two of the men there had killed turtles earlier this year that had
been tagged by your department, and requested that I bring them
to the United States. The turtle with tag no. 1409 was caught by
Mr. Ofricano Julias on March 20, 1965, one mile east of Tasbapauni.
Tag no. 2336 came off a turtle caught by Mr. Alberto Julias four
miles northeast of Tasbapauni on April 29, 1965.

Mr. Alberto Julias desires that I send him a compass with the
money for his tag if it is possible for you to send me the warrant
for his reward. Otherwise, both warrants should be mailed to the
men at Tasbapauni.

I became quite curious about the turtles that were caught so
often in the area, and would appreciate it if you could send me
information as to where the tags I have returned were attached
and the date. Any other information that your study has produced
would also be welcome if it is not troublesome for you. Please con-
firm what disposition is made as to the rewards.

Thank you for your attention to this matter.

Sincerely,
George E. Lewis II

Belize, British Honduras
1st May, 1959

Dear Mr. Carr:

Thank you very much for your letter and the cheque which was enclosed. I'm sure my uncle was very happy to receive his reward. I regret very much that owing to my sudden illness I was unable to respond to you promptly. I shall, however, do my very best to furnish you with the information you required.

First, I should like to say that the turtle was taken with a net and according to my uncle she went to the net between twilight and dawn. Another of a similar size was also caught in the same net at the time. The exact date she was caught was 8 December, 1958. The net was set in about 60 ft. of water and the place was more of a turtle-grass flat.

I am very much interested in your scientific field, and I hope that these informations will be useful to you. It is quite amazing to know that you have tagged one thousand turtles and I hope that for your endeavour you will receive many other useful informations.

Yours sincerely,
Maurice Berry

MISIONES EPISCOPALES
Bluefields, Nicaragua, C.A.

Dear Sir:

Enclosed is a tag found on a turtle killed near here by Thomas Laban of Tasbapauni. The turtle weighed 172 pounds, and was killed on Jan. 12th of this year, on the west side of King Cay (off the East Coast of Nicaragua).

I hope this information will be of value to you.

Sincerely yours,
Rev. Robert J. Carlson

January 12, 1963

P.S. Thomas Laban Strike one turtle by King Cay on the West Side January 12 so I am mention this to you all.

yours, *Thomas Laban*

Oranjestad, Aruba, N.A.
August 26, 1962

Gentlemen:

In the body of some Turtles, plates have been found with your address on them.

These turtles have been killed at the coast of Colombia in South America, in a town named Pajaro, by a friend of mine. He send me these plates to write you, because on these plates is written that you will get a reward.

The four plates have the following signalements, No. 1814, No. 1936, No. 1840, No. 1907, and Reward, Premio, Remite, on them including the address above mentioned.

If my friend is going to get a reward, please answer me as soon as possible.

Yours very truly,
Edgar Tromp

Austin, Texas 78705
August 21, 1963

Gentlemen:

Enclosed please find turtle tags No. 219, 454, 1091, 1825, 1212, 1278 and 1701.

Tagged turtles numbered 219 and 454 were caught in the cays off Rio Grande Bar (east coast Nicaragua). No date was remembered for this catch.

Tagged turtles numbered 1091 and 1825 were caught on Tyre Cay off Rio Grande Bar (east coast Nicaragua) in October of 1962.

Tagged turtle number 1212 was caught 10 miles off Tasbapaune (east coast Nicaragua) in June, 1963.

Tagged turtle number 1701 was caught 3 miles off Tasbapaune (east coast Nicaragua) on May 17, 1963.

I spent some 8 weeks along the Pearl Lagoon and talked to a number of natives who had caught tagged turtles and discarded the tags. I made it a point to tell all that I encountered (and I'm sure the word will spread to all the villages in the towns along the lagoon) that the tags were of great value in whatever sort of research you all are carrying on.

I have agreed to act as the agent for the natives involved with the particular tags enclosed and will remit any reward due for these tags to them through the Rev. Robert J. Carlson, Bluefields, Nicaragua, who, in turn, will give the money to the natives who gave the tags to me.

A word of explanation is in order. I am a senior student at the Episcopal Theological Seminary in Austin, and I spent the summer touring the Episcopal mission stations along the Pearl Lagoon. I spent enough time there to realize that the mail service is much too erratic to insure the delivery of any reward due by mail. As Padre Carlson tours these small villages each month he will be able to put any money forthcoming into the hands of those who gave the tags to me.

I hope these tags may be of some use to you in whatever sort of research project you are carrying on and, needless to say perhaps, I hope some reward is forthcoming for these people, as anyone living on the eastern coast of Nicaragua would benefit by some sort of cash reward.

Sincerely,
Harry E. Neeley

Austin, Texas 78705
October 29, 1963
Re: your letter of 10/24/63

Dear Dr. Carr:

Thank you for the check and the followup on previous correspondence. Obviously, this makes my letter of late obsolete, so please disregard it except for the request for information on tagging operations.

In regard to your query about "Mosquito Cay," there is obviously some confusion. Let me explain. Set Net Point is approximately 18 miles south of Tasbapaunie. The only way to reach it other than by boat is to walk down the beach from Tasbapaunie, swimming or wading a few tough creeks in the meantime. Set Net is a small mosquito Indian village of not more than 60 people, including men, women and children. All of the men of the village fish (turtle) for subsistence (lobster, mainly) as well as for cash. I can understand why the confusion because very few maps show Set Net. It is entirely possible that all of the turtles mentioned in your letter were taken on the particular cay off Set Net called "Mosquito" for they do catch a lot of turtles in the 12 or so cays three to fifteen miles due east off Set Net. Please bear in mind that, in the natives' minds at least, the naming and renaming of these little bits of land and palm trees called "cays" is rather flexible.

In regard to the extent of turtling operations in general I would say just from my conversations with the people in Tasbapaunie that somewhere between 200–300 turtles are caught each year just from that village alone (pop. 800 men, women and children). This is, however, a very conservative estimate. As for Set Net proper (a guess again) 75 or more.

Thank you again and don't hesitate to call on me again. I'm sure the folks who gave me those tags will be happy to get the money.

Sincerely,
Harry E. Neeley

Of all returners of turtle tags the Cayman captains have been the most helpful. They have sent in most of the tags shown on the map as recoveries from Miskito Cays. Captain Allie Ebanks has been the most active collaborator in the islands, not only because he used to catch more turtles than anybody else but because he had a feeling of responsibility for the future of green turtles. During the 1950s his letters used to show his worry over the way the *veladores* on Tortuguero beach were wrecking the nesting ground and threatening the whole future of green turtles and turtling in the western Caribbean.

The treaty referred to in one of the following letters is the agreement between Nicaragua and the Cayman Islands permitting the Cayman schooners to take turtle in the Miskito Cays, which are Nicaraguan territory.

M/V A.M. Adams
Key West
November 28, 1957

Dear Mr. Carr:

Received yours of Oct. 11. Very happy to hear from you, especially your being down in that part of the world [Costa Rica] I know it's for some good reason.

Note with great interest the various information about turtle and I hope and pray that your good efforts will yield the good fruits so greatly needed.

You mention about the Ridley. I have not seen or heard of them on the Nicaragua coast or in the Caribbean. I have only seen the cross breed between hawk bill and loggerhead and once in my time I caught one turtle that must have been a cross between a turtle [that is, green turtle: as in the case of the Spanish *Tortuga*, the unmodified word "turtle" means *Chelonia* in Caribbean English] and a hawk bill. I decided this way because the last had a turtle back and head. The cross with the loggerhead had good shell and a loggerhead head.

I think my Mexican friends have caught some of the same kinds of cross breeds that I mention, as I have talked turtle quite often to the fishermen and from their way of explaining I decided it was about the same cross breeds that I am talking about.

For your information the Adams took 200 head of turtle, all females, from Costa Rica in October, and with a good fair passage when she arrived at Key West she had lost 70 head, all caused by being full of eggs, white and yellow all broken inside of the turtle. I think it is a great sin on any government to permit that slaughter of young creatures.

Now as to their manner of navigation, I will continue in that interest along with you and it might be that we will arrive at some method before we both get too old.

Trusting you will keep your health and vigor in your profession for a long time to come.   With kind regards,

yours truly,
Allie O. Ebanks

P.S.   Just to contrast the two cargos of turtles, I am now unloading 400 head caught with nets in Nicaragua and on the one day longer passage there were no deaths.

Key West, Florida
June 26, 1958

Dear Mr. Carr:

I am enclosing 5 tags and positions of Lat. and Long. where the turtles were caught.

I hope and pray that all the effort you have made will yield the good fruits we all would like to see.

Hoping you are still keeping well and fit to keep the good work going.

Yours truly,
Allie O. Ebanks

West Bay
Grand Cayman
Feb. 2, 1959 or '58

Dear Dr. Carr:

Sorry to be so long sending the information. This was caused by me getting off the vessel for a few months and not being able to remember to take the needed information from her log when she would call through here.

I trust you are still making progress in your work altho it may not be to our interest, since Nicaragua has refused to extend her treaty with our government. We only have until August 14 this year to operate under the old treaty. Efforts are being made by this government to get some working terms before we have to go on the high seas. If not it will handicap the fishermen and make no revenue for Nicaragua, We hope they will see their mistake in due time.

Wishing all the good things of life to come your way.

Yours truly,
Allie O. Ebanks

West Bay
Grand Cayman
June 28, 1959

Dear Mr. Carr:
I hope this will find you in the best of health. As to myself I am feeling fine.
You will please find enclosed

Tag no. 734   caught in Lat. 14.10   Long 82 23   5/10/59
Tag no. 436   "   "   "   14.8   "   82 23   4/12/59
Tag no. 703   "   "   "   14.21   "   82.44   4/25/59

For your information and interest a delegation from Cayman went to Managua on April 20th. Our mission was to get a renewal of the treaty. We had a very friendly meeting with the ministers of that country. They all agreed that they could not make it 20 years but could make it 10 years. Everything was left for the two governments to draw up in documents. The British Ambassador was with us at all times. So I think he will be looking after the business end of it.

I saw an article while I was in Managua where that government and some people in Costa Rica along with your help are asking more consideration regarding the interference with laying turtles on the beach [i.e., Tortuguero beach].

We—that is, the government here—are starting a plan to raise young turtles in one of the islands. We would have to get the eggs and hatch them out and then protect them from birds and fish until they could take care of themselves, which I think is a good idea.

Now wishing you all that is good.

Yours truly,
Allie Ebanks

Colombia is a country of articulate people who take pride in the quality of the Castilian they speak. They consider it the best in the New World and it probably is, and they use it lovingly and volubly. Poets and lawyers are abundant in the country. Bogotá, the capital and intellectual center, is far back from the place where turtle tags are found, but the flair for communication gets down to the coast and even shows up in the tag-recovery letters that come from there. There is rarely a perfunctory Colombian tag letter. Most of them are filled with information and courtesy, and most are distinctively Colombian.

Riohacha, Colombia, Guajira
Mayo 19, 1960

Muy estimados señores:

[Translation]

First of all please accept my cordial salutation with my fervent wishes for your personal well being.

The press of the Capital of the Republic made conspicuous comment on the arrival to these shores of a turtle of green color, saying that, according to the inscription that it bore on a plaque encrusted on the axilla of the right fore limb, it came from your country, and that possibly the animal alluded to had been thrown back into the sea to the end of making scientific investigations and to know with exactitude the time of navigability involved in the period comprehended between the dates when thrown out and the day of its apprehension.

The inhabitants of that region, through me, want to know if the animal so many times mentioned came from the EE. UU. and the exact date when the ring or plaque was put on, for there are various hypotheses, some saying it came from Costa Rica, others from Venezuela, so that only you can take us out of uncertainty, giving us the details which in a courteous way I request.

Awaiting your amiable reply, I subscribe myself your attentive and sure servant.

Enrique Bernier Barros
20 de Julio de 1960
150 años de Independencia Nacional

P.S. The prize of five dollars for the turtle was sent to señor Miguel Bueno, resident of this place.

Tubará, Atlántico
Republica de Colombia
Octubre 10 de 1961

Señores:

[Translation]

It is a pleasure to write you to say that on the 29th of last september I caught a *tortuga blanca* ["white turtle" = green turtle] with the following numeration: 1745, proceeding from the investigatory branch of that institution.

This marine animal was caught by me personally as I am at present dedicating myself to those pursuits, using nets of Catalonian twine, which has become scarce in this country with the result that my calling is made difficult by the scarcity of said material.

The place where my nets were set is in the place called Puerto Caiman, today San Luis de Puerto Heredia, on the Caribbean Coast on a point known by the name of La Escollera de Costa Azul, at about 15 meters off the beach, and at a depth of ten meters, more or less. That vicinity has formations with deep rocks and at times of low tide the pelicans remain a long time.

The commonly-known Puerto Caiman, but today San Luis de Puerto Heredia, lies toward the east of the municipality of Tubará at eleven kilometers distance from said municipality with which it is connected by a road made by INTERCOL when it was engaged in seismographic studies for oil concessions. The municipality of Tubará is located in the northern part of the departmento Atlantico on a part of the Colina de Barlovento, at 28 kilometers to the south of the city of Barranquilla.

You may direct your answer to this letter in care of Rafael Frederico Barraza Palacios, who lives in the Municipality of Tubará.

De uds. atentamente
José Domingo Cellante Ariza, c. de c.
no. 854.946

COOPERATIVA PESQUERA DE PRODUCCION Y CONSUMO
DE BOLIVAR LTDA.

CON RADIO DE ACCION EN EL TERRITORIO DE COLOMBIA
ASOCIADA A LA CONFEDERACION NACIONAL DE COOPERATIVAS

ESCRITURA NO. 1.049   PERSONERIA JURIDICA NO.
DEL 22 DE JUNIO 1.960   000885 DE MAYO 31 DE 1960
NOTARIA LA. DE CARTAGENA MINISTERIO DEL TRABAJO

Cartagena octubre 3 de 1.961.

Señor Departmento
Biol U.F.
Gainesville Flo U.S.A.

Dear Sirs:
We are pleased to let you. Know that we have fished a "Tortuga"
weight 200 lbs. here in a very small and pour town—call "Berruga"
200 Km. from Cartagena.

The "tortuga" had a plate No. 1474 with the—following descrip-
tion: "Reward Premio Remite Sena Dept. Biol. U.F. Gainesville—
Fla. U.S.A."

The fisher-man is a very poor an honest man. His name is "José
Medrano".

The writer is Cooperativa Pesquera Bolivar. Please write informing what to do Abel Martinez Castro Ap. 17-08 aéreo Cartagena
Colombia S.A.

José Medrano Fisherman—

Desiderio R. Jaramillo Ramirez
Gerente Cooperativa Pesquera de Bolivar writir.—

Cartagena
Agosto 25 de 1959.

Sres.

[Translation]

We have the pleasure of communicating to you that the undersigned, Celestino Gomez, and Juan Cuadro Jimenez, fishermen by
profession, caught with nets at a depth of ten brazas a turtle of

gigantic size weighing 102½ kilos. This took place at 3 AM of the tenth of this month in a place known as Punta-Canoas, at a distance of about six miles from this city of Cartagena, in the Republic of Colombia, Department of Bolívar.

Said turtle had fastened to one of the front feet a metallic plaque showing a number and an inscription, thus: no 606—REWARD RE-MITE PREMIO SEND DEPT BIOL U.F. GAINESVILLE, FLA. USA. Once informed that this plaque belonged to so respected and honorable an Institution, and that by it a reward was offered to whomsoever might have the luck to catch said animal, we beg you to do us the favor of informing us what the reward is so that we may send the aforementioned plaque.

Sin otro particular quedamos en espera de sus gratas noticias.

Atentamente

           Celestino Gomez   *Juan Cuadro Jimenez*

Riohacha Abril 29 del. 960

Estimados señores:

[Translation]

Señora Carmela Reina de Bueno who resides in this city and is engaged in the buying and selling of turtles has come to this office to affirm that she bought from some Indian fishermen a turtle that had, fastened to the right front extremity, the metallic ring that I send you herein.

The turtle in question is still alive but the lady says that she cannot keep it in that state for many days because in this region there are no pens for that class of animal.

Since in the inscription engraved on the ring you offer a gratification, Sra. Carmela considers herself the right full recipient and hopes to have word from you in this respect. You may direct your reply to the address below my signature.

De ustedes atentamente,
José Maria Ballesteros
Secretario de Obras Publicas y Agricultura
Edificio Intendencial
Riohacha (Guajira) Republica de Colombia

Berrugas
Dec. 30/59
Department Biol. U.F.
Gainesville, Fla. U.S.A.
While visiting a small fishing village called Berrugas, located in the Gulf of Morrosquillo in Colombia, we saw a turtle weighting 170 lbs. and with the placard no. 936, herewith enclosed. Please answer to Angel Maria Medrano. c/o Ignacio De Lavalle— Tolu. Colombia.
We hope this information could be of some help for your investigations.

Yours very truly,
Angel Maria Medrano

COOPERATIVA PESQUERA DE PRODUCCION Y CONSUME
DE BOLIVAR, LTDA.
Cartagena
Distinguido señor:
[Translation]

Until now I have not been able to answer your letter of November 3, which I received the 12th of that month. It was a pleasure for me to deliver your gift, consisting of a check for five (5) dollars personally to Sr. José Medrano, as is shown in a photograph published in the newspaper *El Universal* of this city. Sr. Medrano, to come here from Berruga, a fishing place where the turtle was caught, had to make a trip of more than a hundred miles by land, walking 20 miles on foot from his home to take the bus in San Onofre, a coastal town of the Department of Bolivar, so that this could take him to Cartagena. I mention this to make it clear that on this trip he spent more than the amount of the check that you sent. Moreover, he had the misfortune that his sister, who accompanied him, suffered an accident in taking the bus in the market, fortunately not serious, although she had to have medical attention because of the possibility of a fracture. They have now left for their village, sending you by me a cordial salutation, and satisfied that their modest contribution has served to further the investigations that you are carrying out in your department of biology.

For us it would be very interesting to know what age you calculate the turtle to be, and what its weight on reaching maturity was. Any other fisheries information would be received by this Cooperative with much pleasure, and would enable us to interchange information to mutual advantage.

Also I should like to tell you that Sr. Medrano was questioned by the undersigned as to how he captured the turtle, and he showed the small steel point shaped like a lance with barbs that is inserted into a wooden pole, and which when it is stuck into the turtle comes loose from the pole, remaining fastened only by a heavy line. This is the way the local people fish, for lack of modern equipment. The cooperative has been developed with the aim of promoting economical ways to mechanize and technify fishing. The undersigned hopes that on his return from Chile where he is going on a fellowship to take a course in Fishing Techniques and Industrial Procedures, he may be able to observe objectively and at close hand the program of your investigations, and then to see if it is possible to visit the turtle beach in Costa Rica to get information directly from that place.

I should like to have information on modern methods of fishing in that place and on nets, especially, for the capture of turtles.

Saludando a Vd. muy cordialmente,
Desiderio R. Jaramillo Ramirez
Gerente, Cooperativa de Pescadores de Bolivar

Sometimes a tag falls into the hands of an old friend. This letter came from Dr. Frederico Medem of Cartagena, Colombia, an able biologist and authority on South American herpetology, especially on crocodilians.

November 4, 1963
Dear Archie:

Today I want to inform you shortly about a *tagged Green Turtle* which appeared in Cartagena.

The moment I had to go out to the field, the Navy called and asked me to come over and to have a look at una tortuga grande que tiene una ficha metálica. It was a big female of *Chelonia mydas,* caught October 7 or 8 near Boquilla, Cartagena. A *Capitan de la*

Armada bought and transported her to the *Base Naval*. The animal was in rather good condition and bore the tag No. 2957 on the right fore-flipper. The capitan, who was about to go to Puerto Rico, wanted to take the turtle and the tag personally to this Island. I asked to take measurements, notes, etc. but the war-*canoa* was leaving at least, so I was told. I told the Tte. Ardila, who made the contact, that the most important thing is the tag and gave him your name and address. I hope, they send the tag and the data. The female was about 1000 mm. long and her weight was five *arrobas* or more, I guess. I told them to put her in a soft place and not to leave her in the truck and to put salt water as a natural refreshment on her.

That's all.

Sorry not to give you more data and also photos which I wanted to take later but could not.

I still lament the loss of the frog and Anolis collection.

Best Wishes.

Sincerely yours,
Frederico Medem

Besides the letters about recovered tags, the sea turtle research attracts another kind of communication. This comes from the people to whom fate takes the drift bottles that I will tell about in another chapter. The drift bottles are dropped into the sea off Tortuguero, Costa Rica, as a way of learning something of the currents there. The bottles used are furnished by the Woods Hole Oceanographic Institution. They are plain eight-ounce beverage bottles of heavy glass, tightly stopped with a cork pushed down even with the lip. Each bottle has sand and a card inside. The sand is ballast to make the bottle float with the top just flush with the surface, to minimize wind drift. The card is self-addressed, for return to Woods Hole. There are blank spaces to be filled in with the exact location of the find and the name and address of the finder. One side of the card is colored a bright orange to draw the attention of a passing boat or beachcomber.

Mostly the folk who find bottles just fill in the cards and mail them to Woods Hole, where Dean Bumpus graciously sends them on down to Florida. Once in a while, however, the person who comes upon the bottle is exhilarated by the event and can't bear to see it close with the impersonal filling-in of a card. Sometimes, also, the information furnished is incomplete, and I have to write back for more. In any case the resulting letters are likely to be rewarding, as the two that follow show.

Sabana Bight
Guanaja, Isla de la Bahia
Rep. de Honduras C.A.
March 6, 1965

dear Sir I take my pencil in my hand to drop you these few line to make you know I have found your card I was so glad whin I found it I made Sure it was a few dollors But when I look it over I See what it was now I am a little boy just 12 years in May 30 So I am a orphant Boy am very poor would yo take pity on me and send me a few dollars I dont have no one to give me enything I am goin to School But half naked But I trust in god that some day I will be a man and Better my condition So may god Bless you while I
Remain you
Edwin Forbes
excuse for Ritn you with Pencil

473 Polack Street
Stann Creek Town
British Honduras C.A.
14th March 1965

Hello Gentlemen:
I do hope that you may still have this card in mind, and kindely grant upon me my request, However, Let me convey to you of how i found this card. But first let me interduice my self, my name in full

is Philip Anthony Velasques a Carib Descent, a citizen of Stann Creek Town, British Honduras, Central America, Well Gentlemen, about this Card. I will give you full information about it. On Sunday the 14th of March 1965 at the hour of 1:30 P.M. I was out sailing in my boat, and landed about 500 yards from off Commerce Bight pier which is about 1½ miles from Stann Creek Town, When Suddenly I saw a white Bottle driffing on the Beach, near the said pier. At the time the atmostfare was faire, The wind was then blowing North, North Easterly. But it was shifting mostely on the East. As i have on my watch then, I stay for a while stearing at the Bottle, Before i ever pick it up. And I Broke it, Read it and fill it up. However, I will go on further. To explane, That previoues before Sunday, about Thirsday Friday and Saturday Dated the 11th and 12th and the 13th March 1965. The Wind was blowing Very Stong, and the sea was rough. To me on thoose 3 days Since Then were then rough dayes. I presume that the rough waves pushed the Bottle here to This sure caven quicker. Why it is me That find it, In concluding I would mension further That at This Time of the year, The Wind mosley blew North North Easterly. However, I have been Longing to go to the United States of America To join the United States Navey. An if you would be kind enought to Take me across I will go for That kind of Study and Learn Well. Because of the fact That to learn is To help Orthers, and to help Orthers means That you will be deadecating your life to Save mankind from the distress of Bad Winds and hurricane, And if you would just considered to send for me I will do just that for the World, and More, Thanks, I will be on The Look Out for Your Early Reply.

Respectafully Your's
Philip Anthony Velasques

For full information I am a Carib Desent a citizen of British Honduras, a native of Stann Creek Town, A Batechelor at the age of 25 years, A Law abiding Citizen, A member of a jury I am never been to prison before in my Life. I am a hard Working man, a seaman for a number of years, a farmer, and a Labourer and a honest young man, All That is me. So you can try me. Thanks again.

Philip

Cahuita, Costa Rica
March 4, 1967

Dear Friend.

It is with great pleasure I return thank to you all for your prize that you had given out for the bottles that were sent out. It may seems somhow simple to some others but to me is was somthing great not for the reward but to know what was the arts and intress that you all had to send out those bottles. It was realy somthing great for I my self would realy like somthing about the same but would just sit and ponder it to my self and would never think of doing such.

Well if there is any more about such I am willing to take part just to gain a little more experents about the sea for I am living very near and instead of siting and pondering I will keep in toch with you all.

Sincerely
Stanley Dixon

I am asking you all not to be nettled with me for not answering you letter in spanish I read spanish very well but I don't write it.

The image of Stanley Dixon sitting and pondering is one of the rewards of sea turtle research, and a thing I shall often sit and ponder.

4

A HUNDRED TURTLE EGGS

When a green turtle comes ashore she lays roughly a hundred eggs. Compared to the numbers of eggs laid by wholly aquatic animals such as mackerel or lobsters a hundred is not very many; but it is more than a lizard lays or a setting hen sets on. The eggs are big, round, and white, and they seem a great many when you see them all together.

All sea turtles lay more than once in a season. The usual green turtle comes ashore at least four times during her sojourn at the nesting beach. She often lays more than a hundred on her mid-season trips ashore and fewer on her first and last trip. But the average is close to a hundred per nest; and there is a great deal of biology packed into that figure. The biology is still mostly unknown, but it is clearly there. The whole race and destiny of the creature are probably balanced at the edge of limbo by the delicate weight of that magic number of eggs. One marvel of the number is how great it is; but another is, how small. When you think of the unpromising future that confronts a turtle egg and the turtle hatchling that comes out of it, you wonder why sea turtles don't give up their stubborn, reckless old way of leaving their new generation on shore, and instead carry one big, well-tended egg in a pouch or release myriads of turtle larvae to join the plankton, and swamp the laws of chance with teeming millions of largely expendable progeny.

The answer is, of course, that the turtles have hit on the formula for outwitting predators, or at least for surviving in spite of them. The formula is simply one hundred turtle eggs. For the green turtle, predation combined with the other kinds of environmental resistance the race must meet is measured, in a manner of speaking, as four hundred eggs per season. Any fewer, and the resistance prevails and the race wanes. Any more, and the eggs are too heavy to carry in one turtle's belly, or too costly to fill with the right amount of yolk.

I should not perhaps have got started talking this way about turtle eggs, because there is no end to it, really. But I feel strongly that everybody ought to know that the size of a complement of turtle eggs is no mere accident and not simply the payload that a lady turtle is able to swim with. It is a number packed with ecology and with evolution. There are so many factors involved in setting it, in fact, that I think it may be worthwhile to try to make an inventory of them, to see how they work, and how they get so interwound with each other that thinking about them makes you finally feel that almost everything the race of the turtle does, or that happens to it, is to some degree reflected in the number of eggs the female drops into the hole she digs in the sand.

Predation is the most obvious factor. If there were no predators there surely would be fewer eggs laid. So one reason the green turtle lays a hundred eggs is that most of them, or most of the hatchlings they produce, and even probably a few of the grown-up ones are bound to be eaten by predators. A fully grown sea turtle has few important enemies. Big sharks attack them once in a while, and on shore jaguars and tigers sometimes kill them. But the main mortality is in the nest and among the hatchlings. The whole world seems against the hatchlings both during their trip from the nest to the surf and for an unknown time after they enter the sea.

If you were able to get a complete list of the animals that prey on turtle eggs and young it would surely include most of the carnivores and omnivores, both vertebrate and invertebrate, that live near a turtle-nesting beach. The predators range in size from ants and crabs to bears and Bengal tigers. Some of them live along the beach itself, some in the coastal scrub. Some come from far back in the interior, showing up for the turtle season as the Siquirres dogs at Tortuguero used to do, and as the Rancho Nuevo coyotes do to this day.

At Tortuguero nowadays the most important non-human predators on the beach are dogs and buzzards. The dogs are the worst. They move in on a laying female and take the eggs as they are laid or prevent her from covering them. They are stronger at digging than buzzards are, too, though buzzards dig better than many people might imagine. Most people, in fact, probably don't imagine that buzzards dig at all. The other regular turtle eaters on the Bogue beach are opossums; the few domestic pigs that range the northernmost miles; and, down on the remote central section of the shore where tracts of swamp forest border the beach, the ravening hosts of wari, or white-lipped peccaries. These sometimes travel out to the beach from the inland forest at nesting time and hatching time. This is of course a catastrophe, especially if it happens in early October when in hundreds of nests the little turtles rest in tight bundles in little cavities only an inch or less beneath the surface, waiting for the time that seems to them proper for bursting out into the unknown world. The gangs of wari range from twenty to a hundred or more. They are a direfully efficient scourge of all small animals. Where peccaries pass there are almost no small ground-dwelling animals to be found. Wari are so devastating that when I am asked why the green turtle chooses Turtle Bogue to cling to, out of all the thousands of miles of Caribbean shore that look like good turtle beach, I think first of saying: because peccaries find it hard to get there across the lagoon.

By chance or by adaptive arrangement, a turtle nest is safe from most natural enemies during the greater part of the sixty-day period it takes the eggs to hatch. The egg-eaters are a menace while the eggs are being laid and for a day or two afterward. After that, however, there follows a peaceful period when no animal seems able to locate turtle eggs in the nest. Why this is, nobody knows.

But then comes the time of hatching and emergence, and because there is usually a strong peak in nesting intensity, there is also a peak in hatching intensity: for from three to eight weeks there may be little turtles on the beach by the thousands. For them, the danger begins, as I said, when they have risen together in the nest almost to the surface of the sand. They lie there for a while as if awaiting some signal, for the thin crust over the nest to reach a certain temperature, perhaps. Whatever it is they wait for, it usually materializes at night, most often after midnight, and apparently most frequently of all during or after drizzling rain.

When they come out they waste no time about it. Their trip across the sand to the surf is both fast and direct. So for the turtles of each nest, this time of maximum peril in the whole life of the species is not really a long time at all. It is only a minute or two, or a little longer if the way to the sea should be blocked by many obstacles. Still it seems to a human observer a foolhardy violation of common sense to leave your young ones far back from the sea on the hungry shore, behind dunes or debris which (the chances are) cut off the way to the sea and hide it from view. The little turtles come out into a world anxious to eat them. They have simply got to go fast and straight toward the ocean even though they can't see it, never saw it before, and know of its existence only as a set of signals to react to instinctively. It seems a little odd, the mother turtle leaving the new generation in such a predicament. Her doing it is certainly one reason she has got to lay so many eggs. Serves her right, you might feel like saying; but before getting indignant about it you have got to look at some other factors that the turtle, that is, the race behind her, had to take into evolutionary consideration.

I have no doubt that, back in the days before turtles evolved the way they are, if somebody had suggested to their race that they ought to have fewer offspring and take better care of them—not leave them behind on land, but tend them in the sea, perhaps in the admirable way a porpoise does—the ancestral turtles would have been amenable. That this never happened doesn't necessarily mean it would have been impossible, that natural selection could not possibly have built child-care into a turtle. What it means is that except for the recent ruin humanity has brought them to, turtles are a satisfactory product of natural selection which, in spite of seeming flaws, are really doing all right. They are a surviving and thus evidently successful animal, in spite of what seems to a man the desperate plight of their young on shore. This just adds a bit more proof to the proposition that the hundred eggs a turtle lays is a package pregnant with meaning and history. In other words, ravening as the turtle predators are, they have not killed off the turtles.

But just swamping the predators, overflooding the menace of enemies at the nest, on the beach, and in the sea, is not, as I have said, the only factor that keeps turtles laying a basketful of eggs at once. There are other subtler ways in which many eggs laid together are clearly destined to produce more new mature turtles than eggs laid singly would produce. Some of these factors are hard to demonstrate, but Harold Hirth and I once set out to do so; and we learned enough to be sure that the nest of a sea turtle is more than a hole full of independent embryos or hatchlings.

Until recent years most people, if they ever thought about the matter at all, believed that in a turtle nest the individual hatchlings, as they emerged from the shell, dug their separate ways up to the surface, through the inches or feet of sand or soil that make the roof of the nest. People should have known better. Anybody familiar with a sea turtle beach knows that baby sea turtles come out as a sort of a little eruption. For years it has been known also that various kinds of fresh-water turtles do the same thing, and that in some nests the hatchlings stay in the nests through the winter or through pro-longed periods of drought and then quickly break through to the surface when they somehow feel that things are right outside—or perhaps just a period of rain or thawing makes it mechanically possible for them to break the drought-hardened or frost-hardened roof of the nest. These overwintering turtles are not separate agents that just happen to have timed their actions in the same way. They are really a sort of little team, a simple-minded, co-operative brotherhood, each member of which is to some degree better off because his siblings are there. They all contribute, in small vital degrees, to the job of getting the group out of the group predicament of being buried in the earth. Then, after they get out they go on working mindlessly together to lower the penalties of being succulent on a hostile shore.

This is not moonshine. It is elementary, fairly sound, and decidedly fundamental natural history. You can see it happening. Larry Ogren, Harold Hirth, and I were able to watch the things that go on in sea turtle nests by digging up to a nest from one side and replacing the wall with a pane of glass; or by simply reburying eggs at the usual depth, in a box of sand, lodging them at one end of the box against a glass-pane. In a paper that Dr. Hirth and I wrote we gave this account of what we saw in nests of green turtles.

> The first young that hatch do not start digging at once but lie still until some of their nestmates are free of the egg. Each new hatchling adds to the working space, because the spherical eggs and the spaces between them make a volume greater than that of the young and the crumpled shells. The vertical displacement that will carry the turtles to the surface is the upward migration of this chamber, brought about by a witless collaboration that is really a loose sort of division of labor. Although the movements involved are only a generalized thrashing, similar to those that free the hatchling from the egg, they accomplish four different and indispensable things, depending on the position of the turtle in the mass. Turtles of the top layer scratch down the ceiling. Those around the sides undercut the walls. Those on the bottom have two roles, one mechanical and the other psychological: they trample and compact the sand that filters down from above, and they serve as a sort of nervous system for the hatchling superorganism, stirring it out of recurrent spells of lassitude. Lying passively for a time under the weight of its fellows, one of them will suddenly burst into a spasm of squirming that triggers a new pandemic of work in the mass. Thus, by fits and starts, the ceiling falls, the floor rises, and the roomful of collaborating hatchlings is carried toward the surface.

The turtle siblings thus appear to operate as a survival group; a group, the members of which, by instinctive, generalized, and

wholly non-altruistic actions help one another survive. Konrad Lo-
renz, the famous German student of animal behavior, once listed
all the kinds of such co-operative "companion" relationships that he
could think of. In his classification, the sea turtle nestmates would
come closest to what he called "brother and sister companions," but
they really don't fit any of his categories very well. The hatchlings
in a turtle nest are all offspring of a single female parent, who knows
or cares nothing about their fate, and of one or more father turtles
who are even less concerned, if possible, than the mother is. There
is no parental care and no teaching or guarding by any mature
turtle. The little survival band is not trained or prompted by any
coach, nor does it consciously work toward any common end.
It is just a lot of baby turtles getting restless and becoming annoyed
with one another, but in useful ways. Their petulance at being
crowded, jostled, and trod upon makes them flail about aimlessly.
It is the aimless flailing that takes them steadily up to the surface
of the ground.

To demonstrate the real utility of this mindless teamwork (or
"proto-cooperation," as such relationships were named by Dr. Clyde
Allee back in the twenties) you only have to bury single eggs at
nest depth and then keep track of their fate. Their fate is dismal.
In our tests, out of twenty-two eggs that hatched singly, only six
of the hatchlings reached the surface of the sand. All these were too
weak to continue across the sand to the water. As more eggs are
added to the experimental groups, arrivals at the surface increase.
Maximum success was achieved by clutches of eggs far smaller than
the average one-hundred-egg clutch laid by sea turtles. We found,
in fact, no increase in emergence-success in groups greater than
ten. A ten-turtle team seems just as able to reach the surface as a
group of one hundred.

There are other social advantages in the big groups, however.
These have not yet been investigated carefully, but there seems no
doubt that the unconscious co-operation continues during the trip
from the nest to the surf. Once the hatchlings are out on the beach
the bonds that integrate the band loosen, and each hatchling is
more completely dependent on his own senses to take him across

the sand in the right way to find the sea. Even here, however, the hatchling that is one of a hatful of nestmates seems to have a slight advantage over one that comes out alone. In tests with young hawksbills, hatchlings that were allowed to crawl singly across the beach stopped more often than siblings released in groups and seemed to lie still longer during stops, and perhaps to orient less surely toward the surfline during bursts of travel. Single turtles, thus, are on the open beach longer and are more likely to be caught by a ghost crab or a night heron, or, if emergence has been by day, to dry up. When a nestful of hatchlings comes out all at once, or in a few smaller contingents, periods of hesitations are fewer and shorter simply because the turtles keep bumping into one another. If a sprinkling of hatchlings has stalled for a time, and a nestmate comes charging up from behind and touches one of them, the one touched springs into action, the action spreads, and the whole group scrambles away off toward the sea as if you had wound them up like toys and set them down together. Here the advantage of being one of a group is simply that each member may remain less long sunk in recurrent spells of lassitude. There is also some evidence that the path of members of a big group of hatchlings trends more directly toward the sea than that of turtles traveling separately. The main body of the group is nearly always well oriented. When a single hatchling strays in a way that takes him across the stream of traffic, he usually corrects his heading to conform with the group course. These observations have been casual and are not supported by data. They came back to mind clearly, however, when William Hamilton, of the University of California, told me of finding that migratory groups of birds are able to guide themselves better than birds migrating singly.

Those advantages are almost surely part of the reason that a green turtle lays a lot of eggs instead of only one. There are no doubt many more reasons, even less easy to see at work or to prove by statistics. There is some indication, for instance, that eggs heat up slightly from their own vital functioning. John Hendrickson found the temperature to be higher inside turtle nests than outside, and so did Harry Hirth at Ascension Island. By simple rules that apply to volumes and surfaces, a big bunch of eggs should warm itself more than a single egg does; and being a little warmer may be some help in incubation.

After the hatchlings enter the sea they may regroup somewhere and somehow take more advantage from being a group again. Nothing can be said about this because nothing is known about baby turtles once they have entered the sea.

So far I have talked a good deal about possible reasons why sea turtles lay so many eggs, but have said nothing about why they don't lay more. The lowness of the number one hundred has got to be explained, too, because there are definite advantages in producing a great many offspring. I doubt that it is just an accident. A number of factors are probably at work to keep the number from rising. One way to increase the number of eggs would be to make them smaller. To do this the amount of food for the embryo would have to be reduced. This would be bound to cut down the size of the hatchling and thus to turn it out into the world less well equipped to scramble, to resist drying up, and then to do whatever is required of little turtles to get through their first hidden year in the ocean.

An increase in the number of eggs with no accompanying decrease in their size would almost surely overburden the female. The female green turtle may have to swim a thousand miles to her nesting ground, and once there, to fast throughout the period of time it takes her to complete the assembling of say, four successive sets of shelled eggs for the four nestings of her season at the breeding ground. Here again, nothing at all is known about the amounts of energy involved, but it would obviously be unreasonable to suggest that a sea turtle should haul more eggs around.

Even if the female turtle could carry more eggs to the beach, she would probably have trouble housing the bigger clutch in a proper nest. A proper nest means one with proper conditions of temperature and humidity, as well as one with a roof thick enough to hide the eggs. The nest a sea turtle digs is not just a pit. It is an elegantly flask-shaped, slightly lopsided, spherical chamber that communicates with the surface by a narrow neck. From the care with which the turtle adheres to the standard pattern in making this cavity, and from observations of hatchlings emerging both from such bottle-shaped natural nests, and from artificial nests of straight-sided cylindrical shape, there seems to be some advantage in the flasklike conformation. In the natural nest the emergence-group appears to be a little less troubled by heavy cave-ins that cover them in loose sand, slow down emergence, and break the group into smaller units that come out at different times or not at all.

One of the important functions of the nest is to provide the eggs and young with a way to avoid desiccation, flooding, and temperature fluctuations. The nest must be deep enough to damp down the daily changes in weather and to keep the eggs in continuously moist, continuously warm sand, and yet not so deep that high tides in the sea flood it and drown the embryos in salt water. All these considerations would seem by logic to be involved in determining the size of the nest and logic also suggests that the size of the nest to some extent influences the volume of eggs that the race produces. And yet if you watch a sea turtle make her nest you might conclude that the only factor influencing the size and shape of the nest is the digging reach of the turtle that makes it. Every female sea turtle makes her nest just as deep as her back leg is able to stretch. There are two ways, therefore, that she is able to control the micro-climate of the nest. One is by choosing the right kind of beach, and the right place on the beach; the other is by varying the depth of the body pit, the broad shallow basin she makes to rest in while nesting. The nest proper is dug in the bottom of the body pit, and the depths of the body pits that green turtles make vary markedly. This gives the turtle the necessary leeway in locating the nest at the most appropriate level, despite her stereotyped insistence on digging the nest down as far as she can possibly stretch her back leg. How sea turtles divine proper beaches and nest sites is not known. That they do divine them seems obvious from the fewness of the badly placed nests one finds, and indeed, from the very existence of sea turtles.

Two of the stubborn problems of green turtle biology are how

#2   11-25-2012 12:43PM
Item(s) checked out to MERTEL, ELIZABETH

TITLE: The sea turtle : so excellent a f
BARCODE: 3 2052 00519 1716
DUE DATE: 12-23-12

TITLE: Sea turtles
BARCODE: 3 2052 00448 4062
DUE DATE: 12-23-12

TITLE: Endangered sea turtles
BARCODE: 32052008639133
DUE DATE: 12-23-12

Renew online at www.toaks.org/library
Renewal by phone at 449-2660 or 449-2688

the baby turtles are able to locate the sea, and where they go during the months after they enter the surf.

To worry about the former of these may seem at first glance like nit-picking. Why not suppose that the little turtles look around and see the ocean, and walk out to where it is? But the answer is not that easy. The question has had a great deal of attention. The water-finding process seems to be essentially the same in marine and fresh-water species, and zoologists have made extensive observations of the behavior of hatchlings of various species in an effort to decide what the cues are that lead them to the water. All these studies seem to agree that the main sense involved is sight, and that some quality or quantity of the light out toward the sea is what leads the hatchlings in the right direction. Beyond that, little has been learned; and saying the guide-sign is some aspect of the illumination over the sea is not saying much, really.

Sea turtles are among the most confirmedly aquatic of all reptiles. In body form, musculature, and behavior they are all drastically modified for successful life in the water. But they have retained one old reptilian feature that ties them to the land, and that is the shelled egg that has to be lodged on shore. The inconvenient, hazardous nesting venture on land complicates life for both the female turtle and her young and is surely influential in determining how many eggs must be laid to insure survival.

When a female turtle returns to the water after nesting, she never follows her incoming trail, so she cannot be guided back by the sign she laid coming in. When the return must be made from a place where the water is hidden by vegetation, topography, or debris, you have to conclude that a fairly fancy guidance process is being used. It seems likely also that the sea-finding ability of the female going back after nesting and that of hatchlings newly emerged from the nest must be the same, and that both differ fundamentally from the orientation of the adult in its long-range migratory travel. A light-compass sense and even perhaps a true navigation process are among the mechanisms that guide the migrating turtle. In the trip from the nest back to the water, however, orientation seems to be basically a tendency to move toward a special kind of illumination or away from the lack of it. The sea-finding feat and the long-range navigation are probably composite sensory processes in which a fundamental signal is repeatedly supplemented or reinforced by local signs. Of the two, the return to the sea is more easily studied experimentally, and it can serve as a helpful model for understanding high-seas navigation.

The trip of little turtles to the water begins when they break out of the nest. This may be located on unobstructed beach sloping evenly toward a sea that lies in full view. More likely, however, the location of the nest gives the hatchlings a first view of nothing but sand and sky. In either case the little turtles have got to find the water, and unless they are eaten they nearly always do. After a few short false starts they begin to crawl, and almost at once swing into the general direction of the sea. They move around, through, or over obstacles, and go up or down slopes with unswerving "confidence" in whatever sign it is that marks the ocean for them. They can find it by daylight or at night, in all weather except heavy rain, with the sun or moon hidden, or shining brightly in any part of the sky. The main guiding cue is not yet wholly understood. Although sea finding quite evidently involves light, it is certainly not a simple tendency to move toward light. Otherwise the hatchlings would be expected to go directly toward the sun or moon, which they only rarely do. On the other hand, they sometimes do get distracted by an artificial light source, or even by some especially intense patch of natural light such as a hole in cloud cover provides. Most often, however, they move confidently toward the water, no matter what the condition of the sky may be.

After the soft dune sand is left behind and the turtles reach the hard tidal flat, the main guidepost can be supplemented by local signs. Besides the fundamental light-response, a chain of other signs and responses may affect the course or speed of the progress to water. White breakers in strong moonlight and fiery surf on phosphorescent nights both bring accelerated effort. At night a lantern beside the direct path to water often, but not always, distracts a train of hatchlings, and by day a shiny or white object may do the same. The hardness and smoothness of the ground sometimes causes

Hatchling black turtle (Chelonia agassizi) from Michoacan, Mexico.

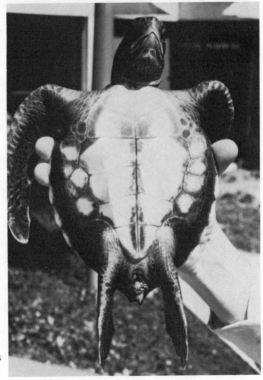

Yearling black turtle from Michoacan, Mexico.

Young loggerhead found in sargassum on the edge of the Sargasso Sea.
Bob Hueter photo

Miskito Indians delivering turtles for tracking tests to R/V Alpha Helix in the Miskito Cays.

The turtle poacher.

Male Pacific ridley from Mazatlán, Mexico.

Mature female Kemp's ridley.

Young ridley and green turtle from Yankeetown, Florida.

Young olive ridley taken on the windward side of Martinique.
This is the first record of the species for the island. The turtle
was very likely hatched in Surinam. Anne Meylan photo

The arribada *at Nancite, Santa Rosa National Park, Costa Rica.* David Hughes photo © National Geographic Society

them to move momentarily faster. When they come to a strong seaward slope the turtles may accelerate their pace somewhat, and if a reverse change occurs they slow down. If a log obstructs the way, they move along beside it to the end and then at once turn seaward again. No normal feature of beach topography either disrupts or replaces the response to the basic signal, whatever it may be.

When sand wet by the highest waves is reached, another surge of speed and confidence is often shown, and some of the turtles may even break prematurely into short bursts of swimming strokes. The touch of the wet sand may be the cue that brings on this premature change of gait. When a wave slides up the flat and lifts the turtles, the flying swimstroke is instantly taken up by all the hatchlings; and during the time that they are alternately lifted and stranded by the coming and going of the sheet-flow, some confusion is evident among them. As each wave-wash comes back, however, they begin swimming forward a little toward the surf.

This sudden "learning" to swim, seems to illustrate what students of animal behavior call the releaser effect. It appears to require no practice period at all. The capacity may develop in the end of a single wave, and along with it there appears to come a current sense too, that causes the turtles to align themselves with the swash and backwash. This response allows them to continue on a seaward course in spite of the changing direction of flow of the surf. It must be their occasional bumping on the bottom that indicates to the hatchlings that the water is in motion, and that it goes first one way and then the other.

As the turtles reach deeper water they keep swimming seaward, dashing forward under water for a few feet, emerging to breathe and look around, then going down and moving ahead again. When they reach the breakers their heads go down as each crest grows white. Presumably they dive for the bottom and go under the plunge of the surf. This stage of the journey has not been observed closely, but a complex innate behavior is bound to be involved. In waves approaching shore, the relation between translation, plunge, and backwash, and between these and the position of the step in the bottom is complicated and variable. It is not really known how a turtle hatchling gets through a breaking wave. It is a normal obligation for them however, and the fact that they do get through even the powerful surf of Pacific beaches suggests that they have strong adaptive adjustments to wave dynamics.

Various field experiments and observations show that the orientation process in the sea-finding ability of sea turtles is not based on compass sense. That is, the little turtles are not hatched out with an instinctive urge to go north to get to the sea, or south, if that should be the way the water is. After blindfold tests had virtually proved that the hatchlings needed their eyes for finding water, we carried out some crude experiments with females that had just nested, and were therefore ready to return to the water. These were moved to various places between the sea and a lagoon that lay three hundred yards away through a coconut grove. In all the situations in which the ocean sky was clearly in view, the turtle went toward it when released. Nearer the lagoon shore, however, where trees hid the sky over the sea, the direction choice shifted and all the turtles tested went into the lagoon. Likewise, hatchlings taken just before emerging from a nest at Tortuguero on the Caribbean, flown across Costa Rica to the Pacific shore, and there released and allowed to emerge from an artificial nest back in the dunes, went directly to the strange ocean, even though it was completely hidden from their sight.

The ability of the female to find the water after nesting appears to be the same as the juvenile sea-finding sense, and not a new capacity acquired later in life. This seems indicated by tests with year-old turtles. Tortuguero hatchlings, reared to ages of nine and fourteen months without seeing the ocean, found the water readily when released on the beach. Some of these had been kept under natural light at Tortuguero and others under artificial light in the laboratory at the University of Florida, where the period was spent in two-gallon tanks in which swimming was limited. In some twenty-two trials with such turtles all found the sea without major setback, even when a variety of obstacles blocked the course to the water and hid it from view.

Further indication that the sense is generally distributed throughout all age groups came from a test we made with a big, mature male green turtle. One of the many things that had not been known about green turtles was whether the sea-finding sense is shared by the male. It might be thought that the capacity would be superfluous in males, because they never go ashore a single time if they live a hundred years. So one day when Captain Gibson of Yankeetown telephoned me to say he had caught a big bull turtle off the north of the Withlacoochee River, and that it was the biggest green turtle he had seen there in twenty years, I went over and bought it from him.

The turtle was a big one and very fat. He weighed 360 pounds. I would give a lot to know where he came from, and how he came to be on the inshore flats with the yearlings that spend summers there. We put the turtle in a truck and carried him over to Daytona Beach. We moved him back among the dunes, untrussed him, and then stood back to see whether he had the gift of looking at the sky and seeing the ocean in it, or whatever it is that the babies and female turtles do. The old bull shifted and pivoted his bulging body a little, and then sure enough, he swung oceanward and seemed about to move off toward the unseen surf. He never moved a foot along the way, however, simply because he was too fat to walk. He could drag along an inch at a time for half a dozen inches, but then had to stop and heave, completely exhausted with the work of moving his bulk for the first time on land. He had never been on shore since he left the beach as a three-ounce hatchling. He had no idea how inexorable a force gravity can be. He hardly even knew there was any. Nevertheless, in spite of the immobility of the old turtle, each time we twisted him a little toward the land he laboriously shifted his heading back to face the sea. It was pretty clear that if he could have moved at all he would have moved as straight to water as a female returning from her nest is able to do.

It finally became obvious that little more was going to be learned about the sea-finding sense by simply watching turtles of different backgrounds go back to the ocean under different conditions of weather, time, and topography. More searching tests would have to be arranged, to show what features turtles see in the beach land-scape, and what kinds of light they find most attractive and most useful as signs for sea finding. Accordingly, Dr. David Ehrenfeld of the University of Florida began a series of experiments in which he equipped turtles with spectacles with changeable lenses. The lenses were filters that let in light of controlled wave length, or that modify the light in other ways—diffusing it, depolarizing it, or simply cutting down its intensity. In this way he was able to begin analyz-ing the natural light on the seashore in a systematic way, using the turtles themselves as indicators to show what features of the light may point the way to the ocean.

Most of Ehrenfeld's early work was done with the adult females returning to the sea after nesting. When the turtles were blind-folded by putting cardboard squares into the spectacles, they trav-eled in hesitant circles, or blundered off on a course that got them hopelessly tangled in the sea grapes and cocoplums far up the beach away from the sea. So the experiments clearly reinforced the conclusion we arrived at some time ago, that green turtles rely mainly on vision to find the water. It is, of course, possible that they also can hear the surf or feel the vibrations caused by the pounding breakers, or that they can smell or taste water vapor or particles in the air; but all non-visual senses together, if used at all, are not adequate to guide the turtles to the water when they are blindfolded.

When the cardboard squares in Ehrenfeld's turtle spectacles were replaced by special filters that only allowed some of the colors that make up ordinary white light to pass through, the turtles performed differently, depending upon the color they were allowed to see. A filter that let in light of green wave lengths seemed to make no dif-ference to them. They crawled to the water as quickly and directly as if there were no filters at all. Blue filters caused a little trouble, but the difference in performance was so small that it probably was insignificant. When the blue or green filters were replaced with red, however, the sea-finding ability dropped markedly; the turtle took a long time to reach the water, and often followed a devious route in getting there.

At that point it could be concluded that either there is something about green and blue light that tells the direction of the sea, or turtles see better in green and blue light and are simply using it in their inspection of the contours of the beach or of other features not yet identified.

Another possible source of seaward guidance is polarized light. The effect of this has also been studied by David Ehrenfeld. When light is reflected from any smooth, flat surface such as the ocean or a highway, or when it is passed through certain transparent substances, a part of it is changed physically. It has been proved that this changed, or "polarized," light can be detected by honeybees and some other animals and is used by them as a celestial landmark in finding direction. To see whether turtles also use polarized light, depolarizing filters were placed in the spectacles. The filters made no difference at all in the ability of the turtles to find the water. It seems pretty clear that turtles do not rely on sea-polarized light in sea finding.

In October 1965, Dr. Nicholas Mrosovsky, a British experimental psychologist who had previously worked with fresh-water turtles, came to the research station at Tortuguero to study the sea-finding problem in a different way. Instead of altering the natural light coming from the environment, Dr. Mrosovsky chose to supply the turtles with his own light of brightness and colors determined by filters at the light source.

Working on the beach with portable battery-operated equipment, Mrosovsky gave baby turtles a choice between heading in the direction of the sea, or turning at right angles to it in order to go toward a colored light placed at beach level. He found that blue and green lights could compete with the light from the sea in attracting the baby turtles. Red light was considerably less attractive. In another experiment Mrosovsky allowed the hatchlings to move toward either of two colored lights. In these tests the turtles showed a consistent preference for blue or green light over red, even when the red light was the brighter.

In more recent experiments Ehrenfeld tried to see whether he could find any grounds for choosing between two sea-finding hypotheses suggested by his work with the mature turtles. Were they using some quality of light from the sky to find the sea; or were they relying upon the silhouette of the land to supply the information necessary to guide their movements? This time he took along a homemade but very sensitive portable spectrophotometer capable of measuring the brightness of the light of any visible color, and coming from any particular portion of the sky.

A testing arena was set up several yards from the sea, on the site of that used by Mrosovsky for his experiments. This was a circular arena 42 feet in diameter surrounded by a wall 18 inches high. Twelve young palm trees were planted at regular intervals around the arena. The wall and palm trees were intended to hide the treeline and beach contours without blocking the light from the sky. At various times throughout the day and night, Ehrenfeld moved his spectrophotometer out to the center of the testing arena and measured amounts of red, blue, green, and polarized light coming from the sky over the sea and over the land. Immediately after taking these measurements he released batches of hatchlings in the center of the arena and recorded the directions they chose.

The results seemed to answer the questions they were supposed to test. The spectrophotometer showed no consistent differences between the light in the sky over the sea and that over the land, and the turtles in the walled arena were surprisingly disoriented. Some of them headed directly inland, even when the ocean was lapping against the far side of the arena wall. Many did not bother to move at all. When the wall and trees were removed, and other batches of young turtles were put into the arena, virtually all of them headed directly for the sea, even though it was still not visible.

From these experiments it seems that whatever the guidepost may be it is not located high in the sky, but low over the horizon. The hatchlings do not raise their eyes to the sky for guidance toward the sea. A brief glance, or series of glances, about the landscape is apparently sufficient. Just what feature of the exposure or illumination provides the guidepost has still not been clearly determined. The tests gave some preliminary information on the color vision of green turtles, however. Although apparently not blind to any of the colors visible to man, they seem, at least while on land, to be most sensitive to green light. All of the conclusions reached so far are based on preliminary experiments and need further confirmation. Even this seemingly trivial aspect of sea turtle life will have to have a great deal more study.

Another puzzle in the natural history of little sea turtles, and one that surely hides factors of great importance in determining the size of the egg complement, is the disappearance of the young for their first year of life. At most of the known nesting grounds the water in front of the beach is wholly unfit habitat for the hatchlings. The extreme exposure to predation by traveling bands of surface fishes, the lack of any conceivable source of food on the wave-washed bottom, and the constant sweep of alongshore currents all make the home waters an unlikely place for little turtles to stay in; and exhaustive searching has failed to find them there at any time after the hatching season.

During the first year of life, green turtles are almost surely dependent on animal food. Since they are unable to catch and dismember prey of any size, it seems possible that during the first months after hatching they may move from place to place as increasing size permits them to feed on invertebrate animals of increasing size. In any case it is pretty clear that no appropriate kind of food is available in the open water off the nesting beaches where the little turtles enter the ocean.

To what degree predation limits the range and habitat of the green turtle during the first year is not known. Young sea turtles of all kinds are eaten by gulls and most other big sea birds, and by all the kinds of predaceous fishes likely to occur in alongshore waters: jack, kingfish and other mackerel kind, snook, sharks, and a great many others. I have seen most of these strike at newly sea-borne green turtles, and examination of stomach contents suggests that the predation by some of them is efficient, exhaustive, and probably a regular and catastrophic factor in the life of sea turtles. In some places the appeal of young turtles to snook and sea bass is the basis for a strong, illegal traffic in loggerhead hatchlings that are used as bait.

It is, in fact, hard to see how enough hatchlings escape predators to keep the race going. They obviously do, however, and this anomaly may one day help the effort to trace out their movements during the first year of life.

Meanwhile, observations made on young turtles kept in tanks may have a little bearing on the problem. For example, an intimate relation with bird predators is suggested by the sensitivity of hatchlings to shadows that pass overhead. Both in confinement and when swimming in the sea beyond the surfline, a little green turtle may dive instantly when any object passes over it. As I suggested in an earlier chapter, it may be this same horror of overhead objects or motion that makes it next to impossible to get a good look at grown-up female green turtles from a low-flying airplane.

Another trait that appears to be an escape mechanism is the ability of baby turtles, newly arrived in the sea, to vary their regular cruising locomotion with extraordinary bursts of speed. I first noticed this while watching several hundred young green turtles that had just been put into a circular pool on the grounds of the Lerner Marine Laboratory on Bimini. In their routine, restless crossing and circumnavigating of the pool most of the turtles moved with the steady, birdwing strokes of the foreflippers that one is accustomed to seeing green turtles use. Once in a while, however, a single turtle in the pool would detach itself from the circling mass and streak diametrically across to the opposite side at what appeared to be from five to ten times the usual speed. In these sprints the flippers were moved too fast for the motion to be seen. They appeared to vibrate, rather than to stroke the water. The dashes I saw were all made by separate hatchlings that found themselves on a side opposite that where most of the others had gathered. Thus, the examples of superspeed seemed motivated not by the urge to escape anything but rather by a sudden frenzy to rejoin an aggregation of their fellows. The bursts may nevertheless be, under natural conditions, an adaptation to escape predators. While they would probably not elude a jackfish, I believe that bigger, less agile enemies such as sharks could be hopelessly outmaneuvered by the dashes.

Those same little turtles in the pool at the Lerner Marine Laboratory posed another problem that has yet to be answered. I have described some aspects of the strong seaward orientation and drive that take little turtles across the beach after they come out of the nest. Obviously, this initial sea-finding sense must be set aside and some other orienting mechanism brought into action at some time after the hatchlings enter the water. If it kept on operating, the turtles would simply continue to travel toward the open sea until whatever difference it is that they see between sea-light and land-light was no longer strong enough to serve as a stimulus. In an effort to learn something about this transitional stage in the orientation life of hatchlings, some time ago we started making crude tests to see how the sea finding was affected when hatchlings were placed in water in outdoor tanks located at various points about a seashore. Young sea turtles kept in water swim almost constantly during daylight hours, and this initial restlessness lasts for days or weeks. The tests proved little except that compass sense and navigation are probably not involved in sea finding, which we already knew. They did, however, support the experiments that have shown the sea-finding capacity to be based on visual response to illumination. Indoors, in evenly illuminated tanks, the turtles swim aimlessly around the walls or push doggedly against them. If lighting is uneven they usually tend to congregate at the end with the greatest illumination. If a group of new hatchlings is suddenly released en masse in open water they rarely swim about aimlessly, but tend to follow straight courses, and the courses usually bear away from the land and toward what generally appears to a man to be the most broadly illuminated outlook.

A dramatic illustration of seaward orientation by swimming hatchlings was the performance of seven hundred Costa Rican hatchlings in the circular tank, previously referred to, on the grounds of the Lerner Marine Laboratory. This was not a proper arena for orientation experiments. The tank was surrounded by trees, buildings, and other objects. The confined hatchlings could not see the water itself however, and as a matter of curiosity I was moved to record the clumping tendencies and direction preference of the little turtles. For three days their distribution in the pool was observed at nine in the morning, at four in the afternoon, and at midnight. During the daylight hours there was marked pileup on the seaward side; and at night the concentration was even heavier—in fact almost total—on the landward side. The daytime massing was clearly produced by a concerted positive, active, sometimes frantic, swimming toward the seaward wall. At first I thought that the grouping on the opposite side at night must be some sort of exciting nocturnal back-azimuth orientation, but after meditation I saw there was a more prosaic explanation. During most of the period of the tests there was a steady sea breeze blowing. In the daytime, the turtles swam stubbornly across the pool against this wind. At night they stopped swimming and slept at the surface and were passively swept backward against the landward wall, where they piled up in floating windrows. Once understood, this was a convenient regimen. Each twenty-four-hour cycle the crude experiment was automatically set up again by the wind.

It is not known to what degree this tendency to swim toward the ocean may be simply an extension of the urge of the hatchlings to walk toward it when they emerge from the nest. Other tests have shown that the innate sea-finding capacity is not lost when turtles are kept away from water for as long as a year after hatching. Since the mature female has a similar sense, it appears likely that the ability is kept throughout life.

So a lot more work will be required to show whether and, if so, when, the compass sense or some other navigation sense appears in the young turtles. A well-planned program of field and laboratory experiments will be required to determine the cues and senses by which newly sea-borne hatchlings are guided, and to learn when the drive toward the sea is suspended or replaced by other orientation responses. Answering these questions will be a step forward in the effort to solve one of the baffling puzzles in the natural history of sea turtles: the disappearance of the young during their first year of life.

The negative results of a great deal of searching of the shores of the Caribbean, the Gulf of Mexico, and the Atlantic coast of the United States have made me unwilling to believe that little sea turtles merely follow shorelines when they move away from the nesting beach after hatching. Throughout this area I have systematically canvassed net fishermen for clues. Along those coasts hundreds of miles of small-meshed nets are regularly set or dragged during the months of the turtle-hatching season. Only when nets are used adjacent to the nesting beach are little turtles caught. That they are caught there proves that they do not simply avoid nets elsewhere. That they are not caught on other sections of the shore suggests that they must move farther out to sea.

Other scraps of fact support that assumption. The coloration of the young green turtle is unlike that of the loggerhead, hawksbill, and ridley. It suggests that of free-swimming pelagic fishes: dark above and white below. This arrangement supposedly constitutes obliterative coloration for a creature that swims in the upper waters of the open sea. The white underparts make it less visible to a predator viewing it from below against the sky, while the dark back merges with the dark depths of the water to hide the turtle from water birds overhead. The green turtle shares this coloration with the leatherback, which is the most aquatic of all turtles and, indeed, the most completely pelagic of modern reptiles except the sea snakes or, perhaps, the Loch Ness Monster.

The feeding habits of little turtles kept in tanks may help one to visualize their habits during their early life in the sea. The smallness and weakness of their jaws must keep them in places where bite-sized, or biteable, food is available. In captivity they show a preference for animal food over plants—at least over the plants we furnish them. In tanks no more than two or three feet deep they feed equally well at the bottom or at the surface. In deeper water, however, they have trouble finding and manipulating food on the bottom. In water four feet deep baby sea turtles of all kinds would probably starve if fed only food that sinks. The natural habitat of young sea turtles, therefore, must be either very close to shore—which appears to be almost surely not the case—or at the surface in some part of the sea in which there is a reliable supply of floating food.

Although the body size of available prey may be an important limiting factor in the range and habitat of little turtles, if you watch them in a tank you see that they supplement their weak biting power and small gape by skillfully tearing at their food with the single, sharp, thornlike nail that projects from the foremargin of each front flipper. This same nail, incidentally, is later used by the male in his grappling-hold on the female during mating; and also by the nesting female, to clear away vines and break roots during her excavation of the nest.

There appears to be a fundamental difference in the sleeping habits of the young and mature green turtle. At night, confined hatchlings stop their frenzied swimming and float quietly on the surface, with their long foreflippers drawn in and laid smoothly along each side of the back, presumably to keep them from being bitten by small fishes, crabs, or other surface associates. The mature green turtle appears most usually to sleep on the bottom with its shell shoved under a ledge of rock or coral. Whether the green turtles sleep during their high-seas migrations is not known. If they do, they must float at the surface like the juveniles, because their routes of migration take some of them through parts of the ocean in which the water is thousands of feet deep.

Theories to account for the disappearance of little sea turtles are in one way like those that seek to explain how green turtles navigate: they are all preposterous. The most likely idea at present seems to be that the hatchlings for a time become plankton, that they drift more or less passively in the open sea. If this is the case, then it would seem reasonable to look for them downstream in the current that washes their natal shore. If the hatchlings on entering the water just swim out to sea for a certain distance and then relax, they must be picked up by any alongshore currents that are there and be carried wherever the currents go.

The trouble with this theory is that nobody knows where the currents go. The little alongshore drifts and eddies inside the major swirls like the Gulf Stream are very sketchily known, at least in the Caribbean. If you look at a chart that shows ocean currents, you see off our turtle beach in Costa Rica arrows that point to the northwestward. These show how the Equatorial Current, having just squeezed itself through passages among the easternmost Antilles, flows on up through the Yucatán Channel between the Yucatán Peninsula and Cuba, and into the Gulf of Mexico. It does some circling there, and then funnels out between Florida and Cuba and emerges in the Atlantic Ocean again, this time as the Gulf Stream. Looking at such a chart, and figuring from the trend of the major surface currents of the region, it might seem logical to search for the baby turtles in the place where the current comes close to shore in Yucatán or Cuba. A great deal of searching has been done there but no baby turtles have been found. Most of our tag returns, however, have come from localities in, or not far out of, this main northwesterly current. This may have some bearing on the problem of the disappearance of the hatchlings. But what? A lot of returns come from the other way too, from Panama and Colombia and even from Venezuela. But all of these tags are from mature turtles. Both the northern and the southern tag-recovery sites are the grazing grounds of the grown-up, herbivorous animals. I have never seen a baby green turtle on these flats anywhere, and nobody I have talked with has seen one there. So the lead that the current at first appears to offer peters out, and you have to go on back to Tortuguero and take up the trail of the lost hatchlings once again.

At Tortuguero the Equatorial Current is always a good way offshore, but it appears to vary in its offshore distance from season to season and perhaps from year to year. Inshore from the main stream, there is a southerly countercurrent, which also varies markedly both in strength and in distance from shore. The big rivers that enter the sea between Puerto Limón and the Honduran frontier set up still other local swirls that might influence the exodus of the little turtles from their hatching ground. With all these variables conceivably involved, it is not possible to say, just by looking at the charts, where currents would take the hatchlings.

To try to learn more about local Tortuguero currents during late September and early October—the time when the hatchlings are emerging in greatest abundance—we started dropping drift bottles into the sea there at that season. For three years now we have put out bottles at different distances off the beach, hoping that later on returns would suggest what might happen to small turtles whose only ambition was to keep swimming out from shore, toward whatever kind of look it is that draws them to open ocean.

We have had some returns, and as we ought to have expected, they prove next to nothing. In the first place, a lot of the recoveries are made on the strip of shore only a few miles north of our camp, where no baby turtles are ever seen after the nesting season. Most of the long-distance turtle-tag recoveries from the Tortuguero program have been made among the Cays of Miskito bank off the coast of Nicaragua. The bank is the biggest turtle pasture in the hemisphere—possibly in the world. We never had a bottle return from there, but this probably just means that there are few beaches there for bottles to stand on, and hardly any people to find them if they did come ashore.

Many of our recovered drift bottles were picked up in British Honduras, a place where green turtles occur although not nowadays in abundance. It is a place too, in which I have spent a lot of time talking with the Caribs about the problem of the little turtles getting lost. There are able amateur marine naturalists among the black Caribs there, but none of them has suggested a solution to the puzzle. The only little green turtles they see are the ones the Navy airplane takes every October from the hatchery of the Caribbean Conservation Corporation.

It should be no surprise if drift bottles fail to reveal the habitat or travels of the lost hatchlings. Drift bottles tend to stay where they go ashore. Little turtles never go ashore at all. The most that can be hoped for from the bottles is a clue or two, some hint that might suggest some section of shore, or some eddy of ocean, where a close search might seem to be worth making.

I told of some of the signs that suggest that young green turtles are pelagic—that is, that their habitat is for a time the open ocean. There are some objections to this notion. The spry awareness little turtles have of the untrustworthy character of sea birds, and the obliterative effect of their white bellies and black backs could help explain how the hatchlings avoid being eaten at sea. But there would remain the puzzle of knowing how they are able to find anything to eat out there. There is only one place I can think of where, at the surface of the open ocean, there might be a concentration of small, soft-bodied, simple-minded animals that baby turtles could find with no more active finding power than they appear to have. That place is among the floating rafts of sargasso weed, which drift in tropical currents and accumulate in vast volume in the Sargasso Sea.

Sargasso weed, or gulf weed, as it is also called, is the common name given any of a number of species of brown algae that grow on rocky tropical shores. The plant has a long stemlike portion with flat leaflike blades branching from it, and spherical floats as big as peas that help keep it up at the surface where the sunlight is. The plants break loose in rough weather and drift about with surface currents. Unless wrecked or thrown ashore by wave action they live on indefinitely. A lot of plants get caught in the Gulf Stream and are swirled into the central north Atlantic, where they accumulate in the quiet center of the current system that circles that part of the globe. This is the place known as the Sargasso Sea. It is a region of little rain and wind, a high-evaporation rate, and very clear, salty water, which stands at a higher level than that of the surrounding ocean.

It is estimated that some ten million tons of sargasso float in that tranquil sea. The weed accumulates there, partly because more of it drifts in on the Gulf Stream than drifts out the other side on the Equatorial Current, and partly by vegetative reproduction. Algae were pioneers in the art of sexual reproduction. The sargasso algae, however, are for some reason unable to procreate sexually. They simply grow and reproduce by breaking off branches of themselves. The individual plants probably never die, unless they are smashed by waves. Rachel Carson suggested that some of the sargasso weeds out there in the Sargasso Sea today might have been seen by Columbus. In his time the place was feared by mariners as a trap for ships. It was fancied to be a solid field of clinging plants that hindered the progress of ships. This was, of course, an error of the times. The weed is not that dense. There is quite a lot of it out there, though, and together with the peculiar conditions of climate and hydrography that prevail in the place, it makes the Sargasso Sea one of the distinctive regions of the earth.

The Sargasso Sea is often referred to as a biological desert. What the people who call it that have in mind is the generally skimpy plankton and fish faunas in the water there, which is warm, clear, and poor in nutrients. The sargasso weeds themselves, however, are by no means sterile. They have a very diverse fauna of small creatures, most of which are strongly adapted by evolution to life in a gulf-weed raft. A sargasso raft in fact, is an organized biological community, integrated by a variety of ecological bonds. One only has to look at the sargasso fish, for example, to see the reality of the sargasso raft organization. The little fish is a classic case of concealing form and coloration. Sprigs of weed sprout from it, sargasso berries are painted on its sides, and it even seems to be encrusted with the same tracery of small limy worm tubes that decorate real sargasso weed.

The raft fauna ranges in body size from that of a multitude of tiny larval creatures that live there to the big, rambunctious dolphin that seems strangely drawn to lurk about in the drifting weeds. There are pipefishes there and sea horses, filefishes too, and various kinds of crabs, octopuses and sea slugs, all molded by natural selection in ways that let them find enhanced survival for their race in rafts of sargasso weed.

A big gulf weed, therefore, wherever it may be found, is not just a drifting plant. It is an integrated company of different kinds of animals, vertebrate and invertebrate, grazers, scavengers and savage predators, to all of which the weed is a source food, an asylum from attack, or a buoyant craft on which to cruise the warm currents of the world. And because these are precisely the requirements of a baby green turtle fresh through the surf, and off to wherever it is they go, why not suppose that the hatchlings join up with the sargasso fauna for a while?

Bob and Gene Schroeder of Islamorada, on the Florida Keys, have kept hundreds of young green turtles in live-cars. When they throw sargasso weed into the cars, the turtles scramble busily about the weed, eat some of it, forage through it for hidden bits of the ground fish the Schroeders feed them, and at night sleep supported by the rafts. They seem, in short, to be instinctively at home in a sargasso raft. Only a few sea turtle hatchlings have ever been found in sargasso weed. One man found nine baby loggerheads in one raft in the Gulf Stream of Florida, and one or two loggerheads have been reported in weeds on a few other occasions. No green turtle hatchlings have as yet been found in sargasso, at least not by anybody able to identify them, or excited enough to tell about the discovery.

I ought to make it clear that I have never been able to locate a place, or anybody who knew of a place, where little sea turtles of *any* kind could be caught. Not even one little sea turtle. I never even heard rumors of the existence of such a place, and this is a very significant thing, because all about the world fishermen are mostly zoologists at heart. Hardly any other aspect of the lives of sea turtles is left out of their folklore.

In the years that studies of sea turtles have been going on at the University of Florida, the smallest green turtles we have been able to find, predictably and in numbers great enough to be studied with profit, are in the dinner-plate-to-washtub size—the ten- to fifty-pound weight group. I have got into the probably unwise habit of referring to these as yearlings. Nobody really knows how old sea turtles are when they reach these sizes in their natural environment. Their growth in captivity varies so much that it sheds little light on the growth to be expected in nature. Ten pounds, for good years, might not be far off. It is at about that size that they begin eating turtle grass, and soon afterward they turn wholly to grazing. After that, the growth rate probably goes up sharply, because food is unlimited and grazing can go on steadily, with little work spent in foraging.

It is at this stage that the Atlantic green turtle returns to the view of turtle students and fishermen, as an adolescent grazer living in loose bands on flats of turtle grass, manatee grass, Cuban shoal grass and a few other marine spermatophytic plants.

One of the things that originally turned my interest toward sea turtles was the regular seasonal arrival of such a colony of young green turtles off the west coast of peninsular Florida near Cedar

Key, only a short way from where I live. The Cedar Key turtles are not there the year around. They usually come in April and leave in October or November. Nobody knows where they come from, or where they go when they leave. They show up first toward the southern end of the territory they occupy, in the vicinity of Anclote Key, off Tarpon Springs. Turtle fishermen there say that when the young turtles first show up they come in from the south, and are usually in small but definitely associated groups. It is hard to know how much stock to put in those observations, but it is obviously foolish to ignore them. These west coast green turtles are caught commercially. Most of the boats are from Cedar Key, Yankeetown, and Crystal River and most of the turtling is done in the shallow water between those towns. No records are kept of the numbers of turtles taken in the fishery. Some of them are killed locally, some are sent to nearby restaurants, and a few are sometimes shipped to more distant markets.

For eight years we kept the west coast colony under fairly regular surveillance. During that time, no turtle that weighed less than three pounds turned up. There were one three-pounder and two more only a few ounces heavier, and several that weighed between four and five pounds have been caught. The great majority weighed over ten pounds, and the average weight for the colony is about thirty pounds.

When the National Science Foundation made its first grant for support of my sea turtle work, I set up a little tagging project at Cedar Key, with David Caldwell's help. Tagging on any commercially exploited green turtle feeding ground is expensive, because you have to buy the turtles by the pound, then pay a reward if they are retaken, buy them again, and so on. We managed to get tags on fifty-three green turtles. Of these, nine were retaken. None was ever found outside Florida, and none was recovered more than three months after the time it was tagged. All the recovered turtles had been originally caught off the mouth of the Withlacoochee River and hauled by truck to Cedar Key, thirty miles to the north, where they were tagged and released in the bay. All of them were retaken back on the Withlacoochee flats.

The west coast turtles are caught by setting big-mesh nets across sloughs and channels in the shallow grass flats. The turtle men know the areas where they work in great detail, and most of them can be trusted to tell you exactly where a given day's turtling took place. If Captain John Gibson said he caught a green turtle on a certain set, the information could be trusted. One morning we tagged one of Captain Gibson's turtles. It had been taken to Cedar Key and laid out belly-up on the fish house floor. We bought the turtle, tagged and measured it, and let it go two miles off Cedar Key. Late that night John Gibson took the same turtle on the exact same set on which it had been caught the first time. What struck my fancy, almost as much as the arresting example of apparent homing ability, was Captain Gibson's complete lack of astonishment over it. To him it was just the thing to be expected. All the turtle fishermen at Cedar Key and Yankeetown can tell you tales of homing turtles. There has been a green turtle fishery off Cedar Key for a hundred years. Through that century turtles have from time to time been lost and some of those recaught and somehow recognized by the men who caught them. And so, stories of extraordinary homing feats are common, as they are in every place where green turtles are caught and kept in crawls.

Our few tag returns were the first direct evidence that the talk might not be moonshine. The recovered turtles could have all been just blundering randomly about when taken again, but I doubt it. One of them, for instance, made the trip back to the mouth of Crystal River twice. Originally caught there, it was moved to Cedar Key and released. Twenty-nine days later it was retaken a few miles to the south of the Withlacoochee. Again it was tagged, kept in a crawl at Cedar Key for several days, then released. Sixty-five days later it was caught again at almost the exact site of the first recapture. That time it was butchered before we were able to buy it again.

If that apparent homing tendency was real, the kind of homing involved was a curious one. The turtles were not going back either to a nesting and hatching ground of their race or to a feeding ground used at maturity. The place where they were retaken was a temporary station, almost surely a summer way-stop in a developmental

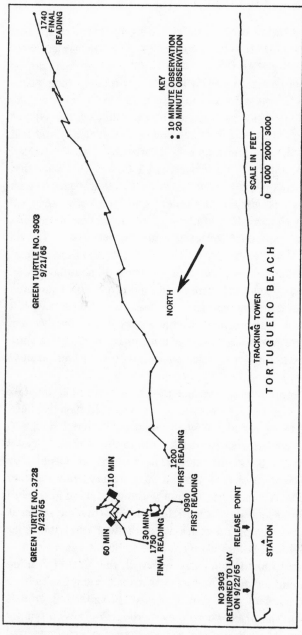

Plots of the movements of two female green turtles off Tortuguero, Costa Rica. No. 3728 was allowed to nest before being rigged with a helium balloon and released. No. 3903 was rigged and released before she had nested. The former loafed about in front of the shore. The latter struck out on a straight southeasterly course, but the following night returned and nested at the point indicated.

migration of some kind. Their "homing" thus is really just a return to the place where the migration was interrupted. This is an interesting thing for them to do, but it does not tell us where the Cedar Key turtles come from, or where they go when they leave in November.

The Cedar Key turtles are not hatchlings. The smallest of them are at least several months away from hatchlinghood; and it seems certain that their hatching place is a long way off. Although green turtles still come ashore singly to nest along the lower east coast of Florida, this happens so seldom that the nests there cannot be considered the source of any green turtle population anywhere. Certainly the Cedar Key colony cannot be thought of as the issue of the odd, lone females that straggle ashore on the east coast between Palm Beach and Melbourne.

The maximum size of the turtles of the west coast itinerant colony is about 125 pounds. This is just under the weight of the smallest of the mature females that come up to nest at Tortuguero. As this would lead one to expect, none of the Cedar Key turtles is ever found to have eggs in the oviduct. It seems evident that the yearling turtle colony of the Cedar Key flats comes from a hatching place somewhere far away. I get a very uneasy feeling when I look at a bunch of young turtles on the deck of Captain Gibson's boat at Yankeetown, or laid out on the fish house floor at Cedar Key, and think that they may have hatched out of eggs laid on the beach where our tagging camp is in Costa Rica. Not being able to test that feeling is distressing. I don't know which is worse really—not knowing where the Cedar Key turtles come from, or not knowing whether the females that nest at Tortuguero are grown-up hatchlings that hatched out there. Both uncertainties are aspects of the same refractory puzzle: where do sea turtle hatchlings go after they pass through the breakers of their natal shore?

Although there is not a scrap of solid evidence to prove it, logic suggests that the Cedar Key turtles come from Tortuguero. In a roundabout but quite real way, the west coast of peninsular Florida is downstream from Tortuguero. A prevalent pattern of travel for migrant sea animals is down the current for the feeble young, and back upstream or across current for the parents, which are stronger at swimming and supposedly better navigators too.

A diagrammatic example of this sensible-seeming pattern is the Ascension green turtle migration, discussed in detail in another chapter. When I first thought of Ascension as a good field laboratory for testing green turtle navigation, it was the specklike size of the island that attracted me. Scheduled, convergent mass migration from anywhere out to such a little island would be prima facie proof of an advanced navigation ability. I was at first not sure whether it would turn out to be the turtles from Brazil that make up the Ascension nesting colony, or those from West Africa, or perhaps both. I ought to have known this, however, because of the relation of the island to the Equatorial Current. This flows directly from the bulge of West Africa out to Ascension. The coast of Brazil lies directly down the two-knot westward stream of the current. It is inconceivable that newly hatched turtles could breast the thousand or more miles of steady current and go from the hatching beach to a feeding ground on the African coast. If you assume they do, you have to suppose also that they hatch out with the capacity to keep heading the right way in the current the whole long time it takes to land. They could never travel that far against contrary currents without repeated complicated position finding to make corrections for current displacement. So on purely logical grounds, Africa seemed much less likely than Brazil as the year-around residence of the Ascension colony. To get to Brazil from Ascension a baby turtle needs only to swim a few yards out from shore. From then on, the current would take over and the only responsibility of the hatchling would be to keep from being eaten.

Reckoning the distance from the island to Brazil as twelve hundred miles, and the average speed of the current as two knots, it might take the little turtles around three weeks to get to shore waters. The time would be less if the young turtles paddled a little. The paddling could be guided by compass sense alone, with no need to find position, but only to know in a general way where west is, and to keep going in that direction. But even if they did no swimming the turtles might reach Brazil without starving. We have kept

newly hatched turtles that long at Tortuguero without food. They
weaken perceptibly after a week of fasting, however. It is probably
necessary to assume that the Ascension hatchlings find some kind
of food at the surface, during the crossing to the mainland shore.
Unless the food is that found in sargasso rafts, I have no idea what
it could be.

Looking back over the preceding paragraphs it seems to me that,
despite the frequent declarations of ignorance and uncertainty about
baby sea turtles, there is a dangerous air of false security there. It
lies in the implication that because the mature Ascension turtles
live in Brazil, it is to Brazil that the hatchlings go. Obviously, no
such thing is known. They may go to some very different place.
Their parents live in Brazil, and the currents about their native
island almost surely sweep them in the direction of Brazil. But if
you search and converse along the whole coast of Brazil you find
no more baby turtles there than anywhere else. So the Ascension
hatchlings either grow to dinner-plate-and-washtub size on the way
to Brazil, which is inconceivable; or they go on past the bulge of the
mainland into the common limbo of all little sea turtles, and then
come back to Brazil when they are big enough to graze the pastures
there.

One of the few certainties in the search for the juvenile habitat
of the Ascension green turtles is that it is not the waters around the
island. If they did remain in the neighborhood, it would have to be
close inshore against the rock or in the half-dozen small coves with
sand beaches. Besides being swept by a steady westward current,
the island rises abruptly from great depths. There is no food there
for an air-breathing, bottom-feeding animal, and predaceous fishes
known to feed on green turtle hatchlings are abundant. Anyway,
for two hundred years people have fished and netted and puttered
about the shore waters of that island, and nobody ever reported
seeing young green turtles, or green turtles of any kind, except at
nesting time. So it is certain that the hatchlings do not stay where
they are born. And because Brazil is the nearest and most accessible
land, because grown green turtles live there in abundance, and
because our tagging results show that the Brazilian colony goes out

to Ascension to nest—one turns confidently to Brazil as a place in which to search for little turtles. And at that point the blank wall rears up again, because the little turtles are not there.

The situation in the west Atlantic and Caribbean is even more confusing, if there can be degrees of complete confusion. If the Florida yearlings are adolescent hatchlings from the Costa Rican rookery, then where have they done their growing? And after that, where do they spend the time it takes them to reach maturity? Do they become the turtles of Miskito bank, far back upstream toward Tortuguero? Green turtles of various size groups are found there, although never yearlings. Or is the Florida colony a lost outpost of strays, cut out of the normal life of some race by the current, and now too far downstream ever to get back into the migratory cycle again?

While we are waiting for somebody to find the habitat of young sea turtles it would be very helpful to be able to mark hatchlings in a way that would make them recognizable when they reach maturity. It is, as I said, not even known whether the big female turtles that go ashore on a given beach hatched out on that beach a decade or more before. The strong site tenacity the females show in going back to a place for repeated nestings makes it reasonable to believe that they must have been born where they themselves nest. But this can be proved only by recoveries of mature turtles that were marked as hatchlings. And though it sounds like a simple thing, a permanent tag for a baby turtle is frustratingly hard to devise.

The trouble is finding a mark that will resist the changes a turtle undergoes when it grows from a three-ounce hatchling to a three-hundred-pound adult. Holes punched in the edge of the shell or flippers fill in, or erode through to the margin. Notches sawed in the shell-edge open into wide emarginations as the shell grows, and then disappear completely. Branding the upper or lower shell makes a mark that might last if the size of the turtles stayed the same; but they grow so fast it soon becomes impossible to tell the brand from a barnacle scar or a coral-scratch or, later on, from the marks made by the courting male. It is the same with tattooing. You put on a fine, clear, pigmented mark and in three months the particles of

Green turtle left to die after calipee was removed.

Young green turtle of lost-year size washed ashore with sargassum on the east coast of Florida.

Black turtle, La Paz, Baja California. The dark pigmentation is characteristic of East Pacific populations.

Young green turtles in tank at the Lerner Laboratory orienting toward the nearest open sea.

Opposite: Young green turtles from the Atlantic and Pacific oceans (left, Tortuguero; right, French Frigate Shoal), showing deeper body and heavier pigmentation characteristic of East Pacific populations.

Young lab-reared green turtles that had been released among dunes at Daytona Beach, Florida. The turtles had never been near a beach prior to the test.

Female green turtle, Ascension Island.

Green turtles mating, Tortuguero, Costa Rica.

Green turtle entering the sea after nesting, Ascension Island. Both the turtles and the waves are big at Ascension.

Dr. Karen Bjorndal with green turtle grown in the Union Creek experimental impoundment of the Caribbean Conservation Corporation and Bahamas National Trust, Great Inagua, Bahamas. Alan Bolten photo

ink have all spread apart or are hidden under thickening upper layers of shell or skin. And the fastening on of mechanical devices is completely impracticable. Any external tag is soon either overgrown or popped off by the increasing thickness of the tissues it perforates. A radioactive tag of some sort came to mind early in the sea turtle study. This was quickly ruled out, however, because of the risk of ill-feeling among people about the Caribbean, when they should learn of the plan to install radioactive slugs in an animal so esteemed as human victuals. It could be done in a harmless way, but it would make for prohibitively bad public relations, in a project that depends on pan-Caribbean good will.

When plans for radioactive marking of hatchlings dissolved, the idea of a magnetic tag came up. Why not get a lot of tiny magnets made of some of the new alloys that make stronger magnets than iron does, and somehow install these inside thousands of baby turtles? Of course, nobody without a magnetometer would be able to tell a tagged turtle from an untagged one; but with the right detection apparatus, it ought to be possible to move about among turtles in a crawl, or lying belly up in a fish house or turtle cannery, or on the deck of a Cayman schooner, and pass the instrument over the outside of the turtle and detect the presence of any field of magnetism that a magnet inside might be throwing out. The idea seemed promising. It was hard to figure a way to code the magnets so that an individual turtle could be recognized, but at least it seemed a way to identify a Tortuguero hatchling, for instance, if you found it as a twenty-five-pound Florida yearling, or if it should come ashore still later to nest on Tortuguero beach.

I looked around and had no trouble locating an engineering company willing to furnish the magnets. They designed and made us 20,000 beautiful little magnets of a fancy alloy. They put them up like tiny sausages, in chains of ten, in tight-fitting tubes of teflon. Each magnet was a thin, shiny section of wire, only eight millimeters long. It could easily be injected into a baby turtle by inserting an ordinary hypodermic needle and then pushing the magnet in through the needle with a sterile plunger. They were lovely little magnets, and we stuck a lot of them into baby loggerheads, green turtles, and hawksbills, and the turtles seemed not to mind at all.

But this scheme went to pieces, too, when the contractor called one day to say that the magnetometer he had designed for the work had turned out to be able to detect the magnets at a distance of only five centimeters. An instrument sufficiently sensitive to detect the feeble field of our tags would cost nine times the original estimate, and even with that, the turtle being inspected would have to be given a very close going-over. The body of a sea turtle changes its form and dimensions drastically, and the little magnets seemed likely to shift about inside. Finding one of them in a turtle the size of a calf, which might be the only marked turtle among twenty other untagged ones, seemed just too shaky a prospect to work hopefully toward. Especially when you pondered that the detection was a blind search for a grown-up hatchling that had been one of a handful tagged, among millions of its year-group that got no recognition mark at all.

I don't know what to make of the fact that, as different as the habits of the five kinds of sea turtles are when they mature, the young of all of them remain equally hidden from view. I have talked mostly about *Chelonia* in this chapter, but only because more is known about it than about the others. The habitat of all hatchling sea turtles is unknown. It is a dilemma, therefore, whether to theorize about five kinds of lost hatchlings, or to try to trace them down one by one. I suppose both have got to be done at once.

It may prove nothing at all, but the farthest from any possible nesting beach that baby turtles have been recorded was a hundred and thirty-five miles. The turtles were three baby loggerheads. They were taken from the stomach of a white-tipped shark by the research vessel *Atlantis* in the open sea due east of Cumberland Island, Georgia. Maybe the shark ate the turtles away out there where he himself was caught. Maybe, however, he ate them in close to the hatching beach and then swam out to sea. There is no way of knowing; and if one did know, it would do little to help solve the puzzle of lost baby turtles, generally. If the shark ate the little loggerheads where he was caught, what were they doing out there, and where in the world were they going?

Wherever it is that hatchlings seem to lose themselves, they cannot be really lost. They must be in some pretty good place which, though not thought of by zoologists, is nevertheless altogether reasonable and proper for little turtles to be in. Until that place is found, there will be a big gap in the natural history of sea turtles. There will be unknown enemies of turtle hatchlings out in unknown places, and unknown ways to foil them. Famine and storms will be out there where the hatchlings are, and good things to eat, too, and calm seas for foraging. So long as this vital, vulnerable stage in the lives of sea turtles remains hidden from view, nobody can hope to know why a sea turtle lays a hundred eggs.

5

ARRIBADA

The lights went out. A switch snapped and the screen lit up with an aerial view of a long, straight beach, bordered by broad surf, like lace between the ivory sand and the deep blue of a wind-whipped sea.

Then the scene changed and an airplane stood on the beach, and another was coming in for a landing. When the second plane stopped a man got out, walked a short distance, then began to dig up turtle eggs. Some more men appeared from somewhere and joined him beside a monumental heap of turtle eggs they had dug out of the sand.

It was the most turtle eggs I ever saw in one place. They were little eggs, obviously not those of a green turtle or a loggerhead and the next scene showed why, because suddenly a turtle was there busy with her work of digging a nest. The turtle was an Atlantic ridley. She not only was *Lepidochelys kempi*, which some people said didn't lay eggs at all, but she was out there in the full sunlight of a brilliant Mexican morning, violating the inflexible sea turtle custom of nesting after dark. So the turtle on the screen was not only the first Atlantic ridley I had ever seen digging any beach, but she was doing it by day, as if this were the only proper time for a sea turtle to lay her eggs.

The scene on the screen cut to another turtle digging, then to a pair digging side by side; then to a turtle scraping sand to fill a finished nest. Then there came some exasperating footage of a man standing on a turtle to ride; and another man started catching eggs in his hands as a laying turtle dropped them into the nest. For some reason, people who watch sea turtles nest seem always bound to do those two things: catch eggs as they are dropped, and ride on the back of a turtle. I wasn't surprised when those men did it, but I was pretty impatient for them to get it over with. Everything those turtles did was to my eyes a marvel; every slight mannerism was the material of dreams. The playful attitude of the Mexicans seemed irresponsible.

They kept at it though, for quite a few feet of precious film. Several more turtles came up from the surf together, and other men tried to stand on them, and for what seemed an unending while they all had a hell of a time of it there, riding the worried, simpleminded little ridleys, anxious to be about their fabulous nesting bee. Finally, when I was ready to rend my garments, the cameraman tired of the horseplay. He turned his lens down the shore. And there it was, the *arribada* as the Mexicans call it—the arrival—the incredible crowning culmination of the ridley mystery. Out there, suddenly in clear view, was a solid mile of ridleys.

I don't know how many turtles the film actually showed. Dr. Henry Hildebrand, who found the film I am telling about, made a careful estimate of their numbers and decided there were ten thousand turtles on shore. Counting those clearly in view on the beach, and reckoning the average time it took a female to finish nesting, and the length of time there were turtles out on the beach that day, Henry calculated that the whole *arribada* had forty thousand ridleys in it. I have not gone through the sort of calculations he did, but just looking at the film I see no reason to think he overestimated. The customary metaphor to use in telling of great abundance of beasts is to say that one might have walked across a lake (or stream or plain) on their backs, or could have walked a mile without touching the earth. In the film you could have done this, literally, with no metaphoric license at all. You could have run a whole mile down the beach on the backs of turtles and never have set foot on the sand. And because sand was flying, and because ridleys are frisky, petulant nesters, as compared with green turtles, the scene was charged with feverish activity. The ridleys seemed more like overwrought creatures searching for something lost than like turtles about the business of procreation.

One male turtle in the film, for instance, was so taken up with the spirit of the occasion that he followed a female—one out of the ten thousand females—far up the beach, making fervid, unwelcome, and futile efforts to mount her all the way. Sea turtle mating normally occurs only in the water. Seeing it in the film like that heightened the air of unreality of the mad, unprecedented scene.

It was in Austin, Texas, that I first saw the ridley film, in a darkened classroom at the University of Texas. I recall clearly the trouble they had with a shade, and somebody having to go to look up a film spool of a different size, after the room had been darkened, and the tension about what I had been told I would see had already grown too tight for comfort. It was the time of the Austin meetings of the American Society of Ichthyologists and Herpetologists. For a couple of years Henry Hildebrand, who is Professor of Biology at the University of Corpus Christi, had been tracing rumors of turtle nesting along Gulf beaches of Texas and the adjacent coasts of Mexico. His sleuthing finally took him to Tampico and to Andrés Herrera, a Tampico engineer who it was said had an old film of fantastic numbers of sea turtles on the beach. This was, propitiously, just before the ASIH meetings. The rumors about the film turned out to be true, and the meetings were a good place to get maximum reaction from a showing of it.

Henry called me to arrange a preview, to make sure it was really ridleys the film showed and not just wishful thinking. I figured that his carefully understated account of what I would see must be aggrandized by his enthusiasm over finding it. It just had to be. Still, a film showing even a single ridley nesting was worth going to Austin to see, and I went. That was how I came to be in the dark classroom in Texas when the Kodachrome *arribada* went ashore at Rancho Nuevo, and the world suddenly seemed to me a place in which anything can happen.

The film was short. It was shaky in places, faded with time, and rainy with scratches. But it was the cinema of the year all the same, the picture of the decade. For me really, it was the movie of all time. For me, personally, as a searcher after ridleys for twenty years, as the chronicler of the oddness of ridleys, the film outdid everything from *Birth of a Nation* to *Zorba the Greek*. It made Andrés Herrera in my mind suddenly a cinematographer far finer than Fellini, Alfred Hitchcock, or Walt Disney could ever aspire to be. At the Cannes Festival the film might not receive great acclaim, although it might. To any zoologist, however, especially to a turtle zoologist and most specifically to me, the film was simply shattering. It still is hard for me to understand the apathy of a world in which such a movie can be so little celebrated.

I am not exaggerating a bit. Not only was the film itself astounding to see, but in my case the timing of it was utterly eerie—the way it was teasingly led up to, after decades of search and blank mystery.

Back in the 1940s, when I began seriously searching for the breeding ground of the ridley and uneasily listening to fishermen who said it never bred, Andrés Herrera was one of a few people on the Gulf coast of Mexico who knew of the *arribadas*. He had never seen one, but he had heard enough to be pretty sure that, wild as the tales about them were, there was substance to them. He happened to mention the stories once in Mexico City, where they were heard by a photographer for RKO Pathé. The Pathé man became excited by the rumor and prevailed upon don Andrés, who had a light airplane, to fly him up the coast to try to make movies of the horde of turtles. It was said that they came ashore there on any unforeseeable day between April and June and on some unpredictable mile on ninety miles of uninhabited shore. The men agreed on a date, and when it came the cameraman went down to Tampico and Sr. Herrera flew him the one-hundred-odd miles up the coast to Soto la Marina and back. They saw no nesting turtles anywhere.

They knew the odds against them were heavy, however, and were ready to stick with the project for a while. The next day they tried again, and no *arribada* was there. Day after day they kept it up, and they found no turtles anywhere along the whole lonesome shore.

During the twenty-fourth flight, the Pathé man got sick. That night he said he had about had it; he was not going to look for the *arribada* any more. Maybe he began to figure the *arribada* was just a myth. I don't know. Anyway, the next day he stayed behind in Tampico. He lent Sr. Herrera his camera, though, and Herrera flew up the coast again. That was the time he made the greatest movie of the age.

It really was an extraordinary sort of progression toward a climax, all the way around. For Andrés Herrera it was a grand, gratifying way to wind up his twenty-five days of flights. For the RKO man it was a sort of a climax, too, though one with a bit of reverse English to it. I am not sure how he felt about the matter, really. For Henry Hildebrand it was solid reward for his patient ransacking of the Gulf coast of Texas and Mexico for facts behind rumors. For me it was a reverberating answer to a twenty-year-old question.

I have made a lot of rash statements in my time. One of these was that the ridley sea turtle, after the giant squid, the abominable snowman, and a few other creatures, was the most mysterious of living animals. When the answer to the riddle of the ridley came, it came in a crescendo appropriate to the mystery. It is too bad that the ridley is only a turtle. It is a crying shame that the ridley mystery was only a puzzle of zoology, a thing that never really impinged upon the lives and peace of mind of people in general. That is too bad and a great waste, because when the answer to the puzzle came, it came with an impact not often felt in natural history. To me Andrés Herrera is a man who ought to be knighted, or to get a Nobel prize, or some kind of a prize. And he would, too, if the ridley were only DNA, or an Unidentified Flying Object, or something more negotiable.

But crashing as the ridley climax was, it was not wholly out of the blue. From the time I gave the puzzle a thorough airing in *The Windward Road* until Andrés Herrera's film came to light, some scraps of progress had been made. It was an inching, tantalizing progress though, so ragged and slow that it brought no joy at all. In a report on the dragging progress of that period I wrote these wistful words:

> It once seemed to me that the mystery would have to wait until somebody stumbled on masses of ridleys ganged up in an overlooked place, perversely carrying out their sex rites in secret. But instead of coming in a burst of light the answer is just trickling in as time goes by. We finally know for sure that ridleys come in two sexes. We know how big they are when mature, and what the hatchling looks like. We know they are able, at least occasionally, to reproduce their kind. The mystery has dwindled, and what remains to be done is fill gaps and clear up stray uncertainties.

That was the way things seemed to be going. A big mystery ought to have a dramatic unwinding. The ridley mystery seemed destined to dribble ignominiously away before a slow accumulation of little facts.

One of the first solid signs that the nesting ground of the ridley might soon be found was three ridley shells on the wall of a *cantina* on the southern Gulf coast of Mexico. The *cantina* was a little thatch-roof pulque place south of Alvarado, in the state of Veracruz. The shells were nailed to the front of the shop, and even seen briefly from our passing car they were clearly ridley shells. They were all painted red; and the three of them there unaccountably in a neat row had an air of occult significance, like the three golden balls that hang in front of a pawnshop. What the three turtle shells meant to the owner of the shop I didn't know. To me, they were a sudden sign that the old ridley mystery might one day really end.

I slammed on the brakes as we passed the shop. The station wagon careened to a stop, and our smallest child started piping to know what red turtles were doing on the wall of a store.

"I don't know," I said. "But I aim to find out."

"Why don't you go see?" he squeaked, and I said I would.

I moved the car off the road and got the family out and safely engaged in feeding sandwiches to some burros that waited outside the shop. Then I went inside, ordered a beer, and started talking to the *dueño* about the turtle shells.

"Where did the turtles come from?" I said, as casually as I could, to keep from awakening any feeling on his part of unnatural interest on mine.

"*No son de tortuga,*" he said. "*Son de cotorra.*"

The sentence is almost untranslatable. *Cotorra* means parrot in Castilian. *Tortuga* means turtle, but along most Latin American coasts it is used also restrictively as the equivalent of *Chelonia,* the green turtle. In those places all the other kinds of sea turtles have special names, some very local, some widely current like *carey,* which, everywhere that Spanish is spoken, is the name of the hawksbill turtle.

"Very well," I said. "*Cotorra.* But where did the shells come from?"

From that point on the talk went well. The man was a mine of information about turtles. He was one of the true *conocedores,* the knowers of turtles, that you come upon once in a while. He happily started telling me many things. Some of what he said was nonsense, but a lot of the things he said have turned out to be true.

He told me, for instance, that the shells had once housed female turtles, and I could see that that was probably so. He also said they were fully grown females. When I asked how he knew that, he said because they had been caught on the beach where they came up to lay their eggs—and no creature ever lays eggs until it is grown, he said, which is very sound. The importance of that was not just the logic in it, but the man's being the first human I had ever met who claimed to have seen ridleys on a nesting beach. So right there in that little *cantina* the puzzle was unwinding. Here was a shore where ridleys came and laid eggs, like any proper turtle. Here, at last, after twenty years of looking, I was in a nesting place of the ridley. The nesting place, at least, of three ridleys.

It might seem overanxious of me to have so quickly taken as fact the man's claim that the turtles nested in front of his shop. The year before, however, two students from the University of Kansas had bought two baby ridleys from fishermen a little farther north along this same stretch of coast. They were the first ridley hatchlings that anybody—that is, any communicative naturalist acquainted with the ridley mystery—had ever seen. Their having been found on the Gulf coast of Mexico was not positive proof that they hatched out there, of course. Conceivably, they could have drifted in from a distance on alongshore current. But they were the first baby Atlantic ridleys ever to be made known to zoology, and for me they made the coast of Veracruz a place I was bound to go back to.

Those hatchlings were, in fact, the reason we were there, my family and I, when I found the ridley shells on the *cantina* wall. We had driven up from Costa Rica. Along the way we had stopped at every coastal town accessible from the Pan-American Highway and at each stop I had gone through a routine ransacking of the place for turtle clues. I searched the fish markets, walked the beaches looking for tracks, poked about garbage dumps after shells and bones, and quizzed all the fishermen I could stimulate to talk, to hear what they would tell. All the way up the isthmus the two little Veracruz ridleys were in my mind, and it was their image that drew me across to Coatzacoalcos, and from there on northward up the road they were building along the southern shore of the Gulf of Mexico.

Even before the Veracruz hatchlings were found, glimmerings were appearing in the dark of the ridley mystery. For instance, in the old, lean days when no pregnant ridley had ever been seen, people used to suggest, only half in jest, that the ridley bears its young alive. This is pretty desperate thinking, because turtles are among the most conservative of animals. No other turtle bears its young alive; and none ever did. Turtles would not be caught dead bearing live young. So it was very exciting indeed when one day David Caldwell, who had been working as research assistant on my sea turtle project in Florida, found a fisherman at Cedar Key who had caught a female ridley carrying eggs. The eggs had no shells and were the size of marbles, but they were obviously about ready for the white and shell to be laid on. Besides having these eggs, the turtle was a good deal bigger than any other we had seen at Cedar

Key. She weighed ninety-three pounds. Most of the ridleys of the colony we were tagging in the Cedar Key–Crystal River area weighed from twenty to fifty pounds. They were clearly juvenile, non-breeding, itinerant turtles that were recruited from elsewhere, from somewhere far away. That is to say, this only egg-carrying Atlantic ridley that we had seen or heard of was also much the largest. So finally, we got from her some notion of the size of the grown-up ridleys. While this was no great advance, it might be a help in the slow search for the breeding ground.

Substantiation of the evidence that ridleys probably started breeding at weights of around ninety pounds was this curious incident described in a letter from Mr. F. G. Wood, Curator of Research of Marine Studios, Marineland, Florida:

On June 8, 1955, [*Mr. Wood wrote*] a male loggerhead in the circular tank was observed mating with one of the female ridleys. We have no male ridleys. The loggerhead was a great deal larger than the ridley, which was estimated to weigh about 100 pounds, but the disparity in size didn't appear to present any difficulty.

Two days later, on June 10, a number of turtle eggs were seen on the drain cover in the center of the circular tank. This is not an unusual occurrence. On previous occasions, however, whenever the egglaying had been observed the turtle doing the laying had in every case been a loggerhead.

This time, the possibility of ridley eggs occurred to us. The eggs on the drain were destroyed by triggerfish before any could be retrieved, but we were prompted to move the female ridley into the flume that same day. A couple of days later we transferred her to a 16-foot cypress tank behind the lab which contained only small loggerheads.

Eggs were seen on the floor of this tank on August 3. I find that the number of eggs was not recorded, though it is my recollection that there were not more than a dozen or so. I pickled two of them in formalin, rinsed the rest in fresh water and buried them in a box of sand. During succeeding weeks we checked an egg from time to time, found no indication of development, and eventually opened and discarded the last one. Whether because they were infertile or because of their initial immersion in sea water, none of the eggs that have been recovered from the floor of the circular tank has ever been viable. The eggs were approximately spherical, and the two that I pickled were 37.5 mm and 38 mm in diameter.

While that case of cross-mating proved nothing, it suggested a lot of important things. It showed that female ridleys were not uninterested in sex, even with a ponderous and bumbling loggerhead as a partner. It proved that ridleys probably hatch out of a standard reptilian shelled egg. Even these things had not been known before, and the misalliance substantiated our idea of the size at which Atlantic ridleys begin to breed. Also, a ridley being willing to mate at the time her eggs were ready to be laid suggested that the timing of sexual cycles in ridleys was like that of other sea turtles, all of which copulate just before, or just after, the female goes ashore to nest. Finally, that the Marineland affair occurred in June suggested the season at which natural reproduction ought to be looked for. All this may sound like trivial stuff, but to a sea turtle man of the middle 1950s it was pretty exciting.

In one way, however, Mr. Wood's observations of the dalliance of the Marineland loggerhead and ridley tended to confuse the issue. They might be taken by some people as substantiation of the common superstition that the ridley was not a true species at all, but a hybrid between other kinds of sea turtles. This belief in a hybrid origin was one of the blank walls I often came to when I used to try to get fishermen to help me figure out where ridleys came from.

Belief in the existence of crossbred turtles was widespread. It still is. It is usually the ridley that is thought to be the half-breed. In some places the ridley is known as mule-turtle or bastard-turtle. But some of the talk of turtle hybrids goes on where there are no ridleys, and I used to spend a lot of time trying to learn the basis for this. In an article on the sea turtles of the Cayman Islands, Bernard Lewis of Jamaica called attention to a notion of Cayman people that there is a kind of hybrid turtle there they call McQueggie, or sometimes McQuankie. Mr. Lewis wondered whether there might be some relation between it and the ridley. So did I, although there was no known record of the ridley in the Cayman Islands.

On three stopovers in the islands I traveled around canvassing Caymanians about McQueggies. Nearly everybody I talked to agreed that such a thing existed but nobody knew where a McQueggie could be seen.

"They only come one, one, one," was what nearly everybody said.

Leonard Giovannoli and I once made a house-to-house canvass along the north side of Grand Cayman, stopping wherever there were people to ask about McQueggies or about any arrivals on this exposed shore of sea turtles other than the hawksbill, loggerhead, green turtle or leatherback. Finally, out on the coast east of North Side Town a man told us that a neighbor who lived a little farther along the shore had recently caught a McQueggie and might still have it alive. We went there and found the McQueggie in the backyard of a fisherman's cottage. It lay back-down in the pigpen. Its plastron was off, its meat was gone, and a pig was blissfully chomping on its entrails. To the surprise of the owner and the disgust of the pig, I shouted triumphantly, jumped into the sty, hauled out the grisly corpse, and turned it back-up on the sand, where Leonard and I huddled anxiously over it. It was the shell of a half-grown loggerhead. The only distinctive feature was that it was an unusually clean, brightly marked shell, with no algae or encrusting barnacles and with the brown ground-color redder than is usual. Otherwise it was no different from the carapace of any other yearling loggerhead.

A lot of people had gathered around. They were all believers in McQueggies, and I asked them to tell me if this was one. Without exception they agreed that it was. There seemed no doubt at all that on that shore, at least, a McQueggie was nothing more than a brightly marked, young loggerhead.

In tracing the rumors of hybrid sea turtles, the closer you got to Florida the more insistent the talk became. Cuban fishermen were full of the rumors. At least they were before Castro, and I imagine they still are. All rural seashore Cubans would tell you of *injertos*, which means literally grafts, among the sea turtles there. There was a special kind of graft they called *champán*. Dr. Aguayo, of the University of Havana, discovered that this was nothing but an old hawksbill with the scales of its shell thin and laid on side-by-side, instead of overlapping like shingles, as they usually are in hawksbills. Out at the marine biological station at Playa Baracoa, Leonard Giovannoli, David Caldwell, and I were with considerable ceremony shown four *injertos* that had been brought in by fishermen. These turned out to be only yearling green turtles, with nothing peculiar about them, as far as we could see.

So it slowly became clear that most of the folklore about hybrid turtles, the talk of McQueggies, McQuankies, *bastardos, injertos,* and *champanes,* was without substance. There might be grounding for it somewhere, but it was not going to be easy to find.

Along the coasts of Florida it was the ridley that was thought to be a hybrid and was called mule or bastard. And as long as nothing solid could be found to take its place, the hybrid theory of ridley origin was impossible to shake off. Zoologists could doubt the theory that the ridley was a cross, but they had nothing to offer in rebuttal. I spent a lot of time on the hybrid stories in those days—not because I had much hope that they would explain the ridley puzzle, but because I wanted to know whether sea turtles really do hybridize. I never saw a hybrid. They may cross occasionally, but it is bound to be very seldom.

When chasing McQueggies and the like began to seem an unprofitable approach to the ridley problem, I began traveling about the shores of the Atlantic, Gulf, and Caribbean on a more or less random search for hidden ridley nesting. One place I visited was the Azores. Paul Deraniyagala, the Ceylonese herpetologist, had suggested that the Azores might be the breeding place of the ridley. Young ridleys drifted into coastal waters of the British Isles occasionally, and Deraniyagala suggested that the waifs might have ridden the current northward from an Azores nesting ground. Only one ridley was known from the Azores, but it was a very small one, in fact, the smallest ever seen until the Veracruz hatchlings were found. It was obviously not many months from its hatching time and place.

So I went out to the Azores, but I found no sign of nesting ridleys. There were only deep, troubled, water and steep, rocky shores, with little sand beach suitable for turtle nesting. I talked with a great many fishermen and whalers, who said that a few times a year sea turtles are caught in nets about the islands. The people knew little of sea turtles, really, but a few were able to state convincingly that more than one kind occurred there. One man even said he knew a kind of turtle that was not loggerhead, carey, green turtle, or trunk-back. That was probably the ridley. But everybody agreed that the islands had no nesting colony of any sea turtle. I got little new information but I did manage to lay the ghost of an Azores nesting ground for the ridley. To my own satisfaction, anyway, I laid it. The little ridley that had caught Deraniyagala's eye had just come in to Corvo on the Gulf Stream from somewhere in the New World. So did the others that stranded in the British Isles and on the coasts of France and the Netherlands.

From the Azores I went on to Portugal and Spain, and everywhere pressed fishermen to tell me what sea turtles they knew of, and where they nested. Then I continued the search along the bulge of Africa, and from there up and down the Equatorial Current to the bulge of Brazil. I learned things about sea turtles, but nothing about the Atlantic ridley.

I heard of the Kansas students finding ridley hatchlings in the southwestern Gulf of Mexico and immediately went down there and started walking beaches, talking with fishermen. I found no other hatchlings nor any tracks on shore, nor bones, nor shells of ridleys. But in the short extent of coast, from Tuxpan to Alvarado, for the first time in two decades of turtle dialogues, I found people who claimed that a fifth kind of sea turtle—a kind other than the hawksbill, loggerhead, green turtle, or leatherback—sometimes came ashore to nest. They called the fifth kind *cotorra*—or *lora*, which also means parrot—and they said it was very rare. I learned that much, but saw nothing at all. Then I had to go away.

It was the next year that I came upon the three red ridley shells nailed to the wall of the *cantina*, visible from far down the highway like a sign to tell of the thing I had sought for so long. So I went in, as I said, and talked with the *dueño* of the pulque shop, and learned the things I spoke of.

For several miles up and down the shore from the shop people agreed that the *loras* or *cotorras* came out to nest every year. The nesting season was said to be May or June, but everybody said that only one or two *cotorras* showed up each year on any given mile or more of beach. The *cotorra* was very scarce, they said.

I came to accept that pronouncement without reservations. On that trip, and on two others squeezed in between green turtle trips to Costa Rica, I reconnoitered the whole Gulf coast of Mexico from Coatzacoalcos to Tampico. The only other ridleys I ever found were two that had been butchered at Anton Lizardo when they had come out to lay. I heard a recurrent rumor, however, that great schools of turtles came ashore to nest at a place in southern Veracruz called Montepio. Though vague, this talk was so widespread and consistent that it seemed worth investigating. I had to return to Florida to resume teaching my classes at the university so I prevailed on my old friend Leonard Giovannoli to go to Montepio and look around. To get there in those days you had to go a long way in an outboard-powered skiff. Leonard went, and he brought back only a photograph of one dead ridley, and the assurance of the few people who lived at Montepio that *cotorras* nowadays come ashore one by one, and some years not at all.

When there seemed no other way to learn more about the rare ridleys of Veracruz I turned my attention to Padre Island, Texas. In doing that, I jumped right over the place where the answer lay, the Tamaulipas coast between Tampico and the Texas border. Padre Island is a long, narrow sliver of offshore bar that runs from Corpus Christi to Brownsville. I had never been to Padre Island and had not heard of anybody else having explored it as a possible site of ridley nesting. Actually Henry Hildebrand was already gathering information and rumors there, but I knew nothing of that. The first time I went there I found no turtles, tracks, or folk who knew of any nesting. The place, in fact, seemed a desert as far as sea turtles went, without even the trails of loggerheads that ought to mark such lonesome shores in June. A number of people I spoke with, told me categorically that turtles no longer came ashore on Padre Island. I went home depressed again about the ridley mystery.

It was the solution coming in such fits and starts that got to be so irksome. It was fine to know of a place where ridleys nested. It was obvious, however, that the nesting that was going on in Veracruz was not sufficient to furnish the abundant ridley population of Florida and of places far on downstream in the Florida Current and Gulf Stream.

Then in 1958 Kay Eoff, of Brownsville, Texas, at that time a graduate student at the University of Florida, found a man who traveled the Padre Island shore frequently in a beach buggy to fish for redfish, and who said that once in a while he saw turtle tracks there. I went out to Texas to talk to the man. That time I came upon the shells of five big female ridleys displayed for sale in a gift shop in Port Isabel, at the southern end of Padre Island. The turtles had been caught by Mexican shrimp boats. They represented more fully grown Atlantic ridleys than I had seen in all my years of searching. I bought two of the shells, took them down to the shrimp docks, and showed them to the crews of one boat after another. The men seemed perfectly familiar with the kind of turtle the shells came from. They called it *lora* or *cotorra*, as the people in Veracruz did, and to my astonishment they said it was the only common species thereabout and that it was often caught in trawls, close inshore, in spring and early summer. Another thing they said was a thing you never hear when you talk about ridleys in Florida. They said that when the turtles were butchered the females often had shelled eggs in them.

That made a great day's ridley hunting. I took the ridley shells proudly home to Florida. When I got there I found Larry Ogren waiting with an article by John Werler that I had completely overlooked. It told about a ridley nesting on Padre Island. The man who found it was Jesse Laurence of Corpus Christi, Texas, where he was County Engineer. I at once telephoned Mr. Laurence, and he looked up his records and sent them to me together with some photographs to substantiate the identification. It turned out that he had found not one nesting ridley, but two, on jeep trips made along the beach two years apart. The notes he made were as follows:

(1) June 3, 1948, Padre Island, Big Shell Banks, 6/10 mile south of Old Yarbrough Pass, which is 25 miles southwest (along Padre Island Beach) of Gulf Beach Park. The latter is 23 miles southeast (down Mustang Island Beach) of Port Aransas Pass. A turtle weighing about 80 pounds laid about 100 eggs in a hole 6 to 8 inches in diameter, 15 inches deep, belled out at bottom, and located 50 yards above high tide. Eighteen of the eggs she laid were dug up and incubated in a bucket of sand. After 58 days these produced two little turtles.

A photograph of one of these, clearly a ridley, was reproduced in a newspaper account, a clipping of which Mr. Laurence sent me. This was the first published record of nesting by the Atlantic ridley.

(2) May 23, 1950, Padre Island, 22 miles south of Gulf Beach Park, about a mile inside Little Shell Banks. A turtle weighing about 100 pounds laid about 100 eggs, of which 27 were taken to Corpus Christi and put in a basket of sand. Five of them hatched, beginning July 25 (after 62 days).

Mr. Laurence made the trips on which he found the nesting ridleys to get engineering data for a proposed road from Port Aransas to Port Isabel. He saw no other turtles or tracks. A surprising feature of the observations was that both turtles were nesting in the daytime. Of the hundreds of nesting turtles I had seen, none had been on the beach earlier than twilight or later than gray dawn.

Those Padre Island records extended the known nesting territory of the ridley by several hundred miles, and brought it across the frontier into the United States. But there was still no indication as to where the main ridley population of the Gulf of Mexico and western Atlantic Ocean came from. I took stock of the ridley mystery, saw that it still persisted, and suggested several factors that might be contributing to its durability. One thing I named was the lightly cut nesting trails that the little ridleys make, which are easily obliterated by wind and rain. Another was the habit of nesting in remote, undisturbed, and virtually inaccessible places such as Padre Island and parts of the Gulf coast of Mexico. Still another thing, I said, might be the bizarre custom of nesting by daylight, which would remove the female from the view of any turtle-nest hunter who had the usual preconceptions. Up to that point my theorizing was sound. All those ridley customs did indeed help keep their secret hidden. But then I listed another reason, and this pulled my score way down. I said that maybe another reason people rarely saw ridleys on shore was that they always nested scatteringly, and they never formed nesting groups in any one place but mixed dilutely in with other kinds of turtles. After saying that, the very next thing I learned about ridleys was what I saw in Austin when Henry Hildebrand showed Herrera's film of the *arribada*.

Earth-shaking as the denouement of the ridley mystery was, it by no means put the puzzle on the shelf. Instead, it has engendered a whole new set of new problems. Solving them may take longer than finding the *arribada* took. Since that momentous day in Austin when I saw the Herrera film, several people have tried to arrange to intercept an *arribada* and see the fantastic sight. Henry Hildebrand has been down there repeatedly. Three times I have been flown along the coast just offshore to look for the masses of ridleys that are bound to form offshore just before the *arribada* chooses the mile of beach it nests on. Nothing has come of our efforts. However, I did find four other people who had seen *arribadas* during the past three decades. All of them concurred in the details as shown in the Herrera film, as further documented verbally by Sr. Herrera, and as published by Henry Hildebrand in his article in the Mexican journal *Ciencia*.

There can be no doubt that the Atlantic ridley, alone among sea turtles of the world, characteristically congregates, or until lately congregated, to nest in numbers perhaps as great as forty thousand. The assemblages form any time from April through June, usually during a time of high wind and heavy surf. They always take place during the daytime, and always occur somewhere along a ninety-mile stretch of the Tamaulipas coast of Mexico north of Tampico. The most frequently selected site is the region of Rancho Nuevo, in the Municipio de Aldana, where most of the nesting activity is concentrated on some single mile of shore. Nesting may be so heavy there that the turtles crawl over each other, throw sand in each other's eyes, and dig up each other's eggs.

One of the bizarre attendant circumstances mentioned by every-body who has seen an *arribada* is that the arriving turtles are met by coyotes. The coyotes come in *arribadas* of their own, in packs the people who have seen them say are bigger than anyone ever saw before. Coyotes occur in the hinterland all along the coast, but they gather on the beach only when ridleys come. The people believe the coyotes have some sense that tells them the time and place for intercepting a ridley *arribada*.

During the nesting time, it is eggs the coyotes are after. Nobody I have talked with says he has seen a coyote molest a nesting turtle. After the nesting the coyotes go away; but later on, at hatching time, they come back again. For two weeks or more they patrol the beach and prey on the helpless hatchlings, as dogs and buzzards do on the green turtle beach at Tortuguero.

What I have heard of the Rancho Nuevo coyotes seems curiously similar to the coming of the Siquirres dogs to the Tortuguero, back in the days before the patrols from the capital came down and machine-gunned and poisoned them. The dogs, like the coyotes, were alleged to arrive at the beach from the backcountry before —not after, but just *before*—the green turtles came in from the sea. You hear the same about the coyotes' interception of the ridley *arribada* at Rancho Nuevo. I suppose that, if really true, the timely coming of the Siquirres dogs was the less-astonishing divination. The green turtles arrive at a predictable season, and their nesting spreads fairly evenly along twenty miles of shore. So it could have been that the dogs, back inland across the swamps and rain forest in Siquirres, somehow had got themselves set on a schedule of feel-ing in their bones when the right time to trek to the seashore came. It could have been a feeling they acquired by having made the same journey with profit the year before at the same time, with older dogs, perhaps, whose own elders had in their turn learned the proper time and place to go. How it all got started is hard to figure, but at least there is no blank wall of unprecedented mystery there. But if Tamaulipas coyotes really do decide in advance the time and place to meet an *arribada*, they are very clever indeed; because that jubilee can happen, as I said, anywhere along ninety miles of shore, on any of at least one hundred days.

But the prescience of the coyotes is only a bagatelle compared with the unaccountable redundance of the ridley *arribada*. Why should turtles gang up to nest in such numbers? Knowing only what I know of the hazards and rewards of such assembling, the *arribada* seems an ecologic monstrosity. No other kind of sea turtles nest in such concentrations. The nearest thing to them would probably be green turtles on some of the Turtle Islands of the China Sea, or better, those on Aves Island in the eastern Caribbean off Martinique. Aves is only a few hundred yards long and less than eight feet above sea level in its highest elevation, but each August gangs of green turtles come up every night to nest. They crowd in so densely that it is next to impossible to camp on the island at that season. The turtles upset your tent, walk across your body, and trundle your gear about the island. They also dig up the eggs of their fellows. Because Aves is the only remaining nesting ground of the green turtle in the eastern Caribbean, such competition would seem like racial suicide.

But there may be a reason for the intemperate crowding of the Aves green turtle colony. Their island is apparently disappearing beneath the sea. I shall have more to say about the shrinking of Aves in another chapter. The Tamaulipas coast, however, is not shrinking at all. The ridleys there are not being squeezed mechanically into a diminishing nesting space. The mad-looking massing of turtles there is apparently just their idea of a proper breeding party.

The only other aquatic reptile I know of that gangs up in such numbers is the South American *arrau*, *Podocnemis expansa*, one of the side-necked turtles of the Amazon and Orinoco rivers. Unfortunately, it is not clear why the *arrau* masses, either. But in its case the migrations that bring the hosts together take place up and down a river. The assemblage may thus simply mark the site of some beach or bar, which racial experience has proved is favorable for nesting under the conditions of weather, water level, and predation pressure that prevail at nesting time. It is not that way with the ridleys in the *arribada*. They have almost a hundred miles to choose from, and they come ashore at a different place every year. There may be some specially attractive feature of the spot they select for the emergence of a given year, but to a man the point of emergence is indistinguishable from a dozen other places along the shore. That is to say, the Orinoco side-neck turtles move along the river till they come to a good bar that they somehow know of, and they nest there; and because good bars are scarce the nesting colonies are enormous. Or at least that appears to be what they do. The Tamaulipas ridleys are almost certainly doing something different. Their initial coming together must be at sea. The vast conclave must form somewhere else, either just offshore or away off at a distance. They are obviously not drawn into the aggregation on their single nesting mile by the physical character or contours of the shoreline. The choice of a landing place may in fact not be a choice at all, but a chance drifting into the coast, as a group of drift bottles put out together may tend to be picked up by a current and carried ashore somewhere, still together. Not much is known about the local currents off Tamaulipas. The Gulf Stream is known to generate accessory eddies in that part of the Gulf, however, and maybe the *arribada* comes in on one of these. Even so, the main puzzle would remain unexplained. It would not be clear how, much less why, the original massing occurred, either out in front of the nesting mile, or off in whatever place the great group comes from.

Everybody Henry Hildebrand talked to about *arribadas*, and all the people I know who have seen them, agree that the turtles come out with the heavy surf of a *norte*, a strong wind from the northeast. The explanation most people offer for this is that the waves help the turtles get on shore. This seems unlikely to me. If the association between the north winds and *arribadas* is real, which it appears to be, I should more happily accept Henry Hildebrand's explanation of it. Henry suggested that the custom of coming in with the wind evolved as a means of insuring maximum obliteration of the nesting trails, by the blown sand, the high waves, wind, and tides. With coyotes and the like standing hungrily around every season for millenniums, any tendency that would help hide nests would have sur-

Antonio Suarez (starboard side) and the author engaged in lively conversation about explotación completa, *off Escobilla, Oaxaca, Mexico.* Laura Tangley photo

Calipee drying. This amount of dried material came from perhaps four mature green turtles.

Two-week-old leatherbacks, Tortuguero.

Leatherback at dawn returning to sea after nesting at Bigisanti, Surinam. Henry A. Reichart photo

The author (in bow), Marjorie Carr, and Larry Ogren in Tortuguero Lagoon, October 1961. The elevation at left is Cerro Tortuguero.

Flatback turtle (Chelonia depressa) *at Crab Island, northern Australia.* Colin Limpus photo

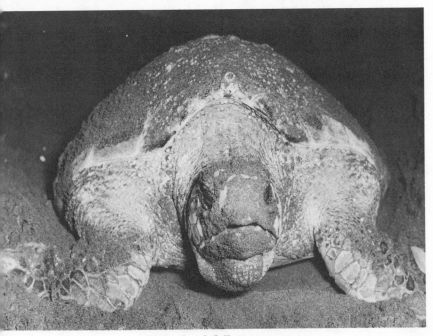

Nesting hawksbill, Tortuguero.

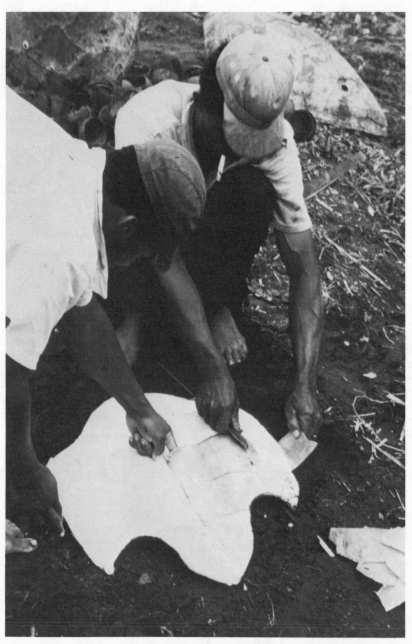

Careyeros *removing shell from a hawksbill plastron, Tortuguero.*

Hawksbill in sargassum at Los Roques, Venezuela. Anne Meylan photo

Hawksbill being dispatched with a club after being harpooned. Hawks-bills are less pacific than green turtles and sometimes cause great disturbances when boated.

Spray of hollyhock leaves, flowers, and bird. This is an example of superb traditional Japanese tortoise shell craftsmanship. Practiced by some Japanese families for hundreds of years, this tradition is cited by Japan in justifying its refusal to stop importing the shell of the critically endangered hawksbill. Florida State Museum photo

vival value, and with time would be bred into the race by natural selection.

Another thing local people say about the *arribada* is that the turtles come in on a full moon. A full moon means a spring tide, and the high water would extend the reach of the waves still more, and would more completely hide the nesting trails. Nearly everywhere you find sea turtles of any kind nesting, the local opinion is that the time to find them is on a full moon. And yet everywhere I have had a chance to test this pronouncement it has turned out to be untrue. Still, the ridley is a curious animal. Its *arribadas* could be timed by the phase of the moon.

None of these circumstances help solve the main question, which is, why do the great gangs form? One explanation might be that they are a way to combat predation, to swamp and override predators with an embarrassment of prey, and so to send a few young on into the sea despite the attendant bands of coyotes and whatever other enemies gather on the beach, in the air, or in the ocean out in front.

That is the idea that comes to the minds of most people when they ponder the problem. It came to mine, too, and still does from time to time. But always I put it away because I don't really know how to think straight about it. In another chapter I have said quite a lot about the complex and delicate way turtles must balance their potential for producing young against the forces that destroy the eggs and young. All the factors I spoke of there, and a lot more that I know nothing about, come into the picture when you start figuring whether it might be profitable strategy to saturate the eaters of eggs and young with more than they are able to eat.

A distraction in the case of the *arribada* of the Atlantic ridley is that the closely related Pacific ridley appears to follow a directly opposite plan. The east-Pacific ridley spreads its nesting all the way from Ecuador to Baja California. The females come out on almost all the clean beaches there, wherever they can squeeze among the people. They put their eggs, not in the one basket of a single mile of shore, but in thousands of separate nests through two thousand miles of coast. It would be interesting to know whether and to what

degree these two very different nesting patterns are actually shaped
by the evolutionary need to combat nesting dangers—that is, were
really influenced in their evolution by special kinds or combinations
of enemies.

Even if an *arribada* is just a tactic to overcome predation, it is
not easy to explain how it works. There is too much natural history
left to be learned. The predators are not just a static population of
chronically hungry coyotes, each avid to eat exactly the number of
eggs or little turtles that it takes to fill him up. There is more than
that to be figured in. For instance, as abundant as the coyotes at
Rancho Nuevo are said to be, they are really only a meager few
when compared with the hungry hosts that gather outside the surfline at hatching time. For the hatchlings that get past the breakers
there are the fish predators to face. Redfish, sea trout, and snook
are voracious consumers of little sea turtles, and these abound along
the Tamaulipas coast. There are sharks there, too, and snappers that
tear happily up from the bottom to strike at the black-bellied hatchlings paddling out to sea. A great diversity of roving mackerel-kind
moves into any bonanza of baby turtles it may learn of, and presumably follows the hatchlings till they thin out on the wide surface
of the ocean.

I am getting to my point. It is that though swamping terrestrial
predators by concentrated reproductive effort might be a feasible
ruse, glutting the ravenous hosts in the sea is another thing. In spite
of the inroads of the coyotes, the number of little ridleys that enter
the sea out in front of a mile the *arribada* nested on two months
before must be staggering. It must, in fact, be of the order of 100
times 40,000, which I make out to be four million little turtles, that
go into the sea along one mile of shore during a period of a few
days. The question to ponder is whether this massing of succulent
prey may not draw in a lot more fish predators than even the unnatural concentration of hatchlings is able to overawe and give in-
digestion to. I don't know. But it is a thing to think about.

Another possibility is that the *arribada* crowds in to the Rancho
Nuevo area simply because it has been concentrated there by har-
assment and persecution elsewhere, and the coast became the best

place left for a nesting gathering. The Rancho Nuevo colony may be a last supergregarious strain of a species that has been wiped out of all the rest of a formerly extensive nesting range. The Mexican coast north of Tampico and south of Matamoros is very thinly inhabited. Until lately there has been hardly a house in a hundred miles. There are scattered commercial fishermen, and a few sports fishing camps are being established; but the country has been as thinly overrun by man as any section of the Gulf or Atlantic from Coatzacoalcos to Nova Scotia. In spite of the coyotes the *cotorra* has until very recently been freer of persecution on the southern Tamaulipas coast than it would have been anywhere else in the Gulf of Mexico.

The flaw in this reasoning is that there is no evidence that persecuting a turtle colony will concentrate the survivors, or even that people stealing their eggs or killing nesting females makes the colony move away to a safer place. What happens instead, I think, is that you persecute the colony and after a while it just dies out. The persecution never drives the turtles off en masse, to reassemble in a safer place, as persecuted human refugees would do. I doubt that troubles elsewhere have herded the vast bands into the safe place the *arribadas* nest in.

I don't mean that ridleys didn't probably once nest in greater numbers elsewhere on the Mexican coast. They almost surely did. I mentioned earlier that all along the southern Gulf coast of Mexico you hear talk of hosts of *cotorras* coming to Montepio in southern Veracruz. But it is olden times the people are talking of, and the Montepio "colony" is nowadays only a sprinkling of solitary nesters. There were almost surely *arribadas* at Montepio in days gone by. Their waning may have come with the growth of the Tuxtlas, the two attractive little towns in the hills inland from Montepio. San Andres Tuxtla, especially, has grown apace in recent decades. Mexicans have immense reverence for turtle eggs as an aphrodisiac. They are, in fact, more religious in their faith in this alleged property of turtle eggs than any people I know anywhere, unless it be the Colombians. The people of the Tuxtlas have multiplied lately, and tourists come down from the plateau in growing numbers, hungry for *mariscos* and avid after aphrodisiacs. The visitors and the local folk all eat turtle eggs, and in due course new hosts of Mexicans are born, and they eat eggs too, and in their turn are stirred to procreation. So it may be that the Montepio ridleys have just waned away on the counters of *cantinas*.

One way to understand the meaning of the Rancho Nuevo *arribada* would be to find out where the turtles in it come from. This is not easy to do, because mature Atlantic ridleys are not found anywhere in numbers. David Caldwell and I tagged or measured three hundred ridleys in the Cedar Key–Crystal River colony. Only the one I referred to earlier as having been found with big, unshelled eggs in the oviducts was mature. Around on the Atlantic side of the peninsula of Florida, between Canaveral and Fernandina the ridleys run a little bigger than at Cedar Key. But there too they seem never to be sexually mature.

Lacking any known home territory for grown-up ridleys, one might hope to trace the origin of the *arribadas* by plotting sightings of traveling schools at sea. The trouble there is, such sightings are so rare they add up to nothing useful, at least, in the Atlantic and the Gulf of Mexico. Ridley fleets are seen on the high seas, but only along the Pacific coast. The ridleys there are another species, *Lepidochelys olivacea*. Their cruising in schools only introduces another puzzle.

Since my old friend Jim Oliver came upon a lot of ridleys fifty miles off the Pacific coast of Mexico, and stopped a United States ship of war to catch some of them, I have heard of similar encounters many times. You will hear of them, in fact, practically any time you talk with seamen who travel between San Diego, California and Guayaquil, Ecuador. If you cruise not too far off the Pacific coast of Mexico and Central America, in July, August, and September you will very likely see a school of turtles. There is no proof that these are always ridleys. I have found, however, that in every case in which the observer knows sea turtles or brings back a photograph from which an identification can be made, the ridley is the species in the school.

The bands are apparently not really schools, in the sense of a school of fish, for example—a close-knit aggregation formed by the sociability of the members. What most people report is that they cruised for a long time, sometimes for hours, and were never out of sight of turtles. In other words, most of the reports are very like Jim Oliver's and his is still by far the best account in print. Every time I write anything about ridleys I quote from it, and am going to do it again now:

> While I was enroute by ship from San Diego, California, to the Panama Canal Zone an unusually large number of marine turtles was encountered throughout the day on November 28, 1945. The species was subsequently identified as *Lepidochelys olivacea* (Eschscholtz). On this date our location was approximately 50 miles off the coast of the Mexican State of Guerrero. Our course was southeasterly at a speed of 15 knots. The sea was exceedingly calm with virtually no wind or swells. The turtles were first called to my attention at 9:30 A.M., but I was not able to observe them personally until after 11 A.M. At this time 24 individuals were within sight. The turtles were floating idly on the surface with the upper one-third of the carapace, and rarely the head, protruding above the surface. Individuals were usually at least 500 yards from the nearest neighbor so that there was no close aggregation. All seemed to be adult or subadult, ranging in estimated carapace length from 18 to 30 inches. A large bird, probably the masked booby, was utilizing the turtles as a place of rest; birds were standing on approximately half of the turtles. The number within sight at any one time remained fairly constant until about 3 P.M., when progressively fewer were seen. Several schools of porpoises and about 15 sea-snakes, *Pelamis platurus,* were observed during the same period of time.
>
> At 1 P.M., a small motor launch was put in the water in an endeavor to collect some of the turtles. The method used was to approach to within 10 to 15 yards of the turtle, to shoot it in the anterior part of the carapace with a forty-five calibre gun, and then have a swimmer grab the turtle by the carapace to bring it to the boat. The turtles were easily approached, making little or no effort to escape until the boat was nearly upon them. When we approached one turtle that had a bird on its back, the bird flew away when the boat was within 15 yards range. The turtle seemed completely oblivious of the bird's departure, but when the boat closed

to six yards, the turtle raised its head from the water, sighted the
boat and hurriedly started to swim away. The shooting served to
stun the turtle so that the swimmer could reach it before it escaped.
Once the swimmer had secured the turtle by the carapace and
turned it upside down, it was easy to handle. Even a large turtle
seemed relatively helpless in the water when on its back. The turtles
made little effort to bite, although in their efforts to escape, the
claw on the front flipper inflicts a dangerous wound. One made a
two-inch-long cut in the wrist of the swimmer, while another tore
an inch-thick piece of wood out of the gunwale of the motorboat.

I have never seen one of these big schools. I saw about a dozen
Pacific ridleys together once, in the channel off Isla Ratones, Honduras, and three other pairs copulating nearby. They were close in to
the nesting beach, evidently just hanging around the place together
to attend to reproductive chores. During early August 1960, when I
was in Mexico, I heard that commercial and sports fishermen were
seeing great numbers of mated pairs of sea turtles off Guaymas and
Mazatlan. Figuring the turtles must be ridleys, and hoping to see
courtship and mating and to compare density of the offshore gatherings with that of nesting tracks on shore, I made two cruises off
Mazatlan, covering some two hundred miles of coastal waters in all.
On the first trip we saw three mated pairs of ridleys, and between
eight and fifteen miles out single turtles were abundant. They were
not massed in schools, but for miles at a time they were more numerous than any sea turtles I had ever seen at sea before. On the second
cruise, four days later, there were even more turtles. During a two-
hour period, some sixty turtles were sighted between twelve and
twenty miles offshore. These appeared not to be traveling but
merely loafing and foraging off the chosen nesting site. All were
alone and all probably had just come to the surface to breathe after
a period of feeding when they were sighted. Even this much concentration was hard to reconcile with the feeble show of nesting activity that was going on along the beach. These turtles, nevertheless,
were probably a nesting colony.

The big bands that people see in deep offshore water are very
different. They are surely going somewhere, although where they

are bound for nobody knows. The east-Pacific ridley has never been found nesting in groups of even a fraction the size of the Rancho Nuevo *arribadas*. It appears instead to nest separately, or in sprinklings of a half-dozen to a few dozen along a mile of shore.

This gives a puzzling twist to the problem. The Atlantic species masses to nest but is never sighted at sea in schools. The east-Pacific ridley groups to migrate but scatters along the shore to nest. It is, of course, possible that *arribadas* of the east-Pacific turtle occur, unseen, in some remote part of the coast but it is hard to think where it could be. From Baja California to Ecuador nesting goes on nearly everywhere, and yet you hear no word and see no sign of great gatherings. I doubt that there are any Rancho Nuevos hidden anywhere along the east-Pacific shore. Of course I once would have said the same thing of the Gulf coast of Tamaulipas.

The greatest nesting concentration in Central America is probably along the Honduran coast between San Lorenzo and the Nicaraguan frontier. Here, and formerly on Isla Ratones in the Bay of Fonseca, the maximum nesting density is perhaps as much as a hundred turtles per mile of beach. There are gaps in my firsthand acquaintance with the shores of Pacific South America, and even with those of Panama, Costa Rica, and southern Mexico. But in all those places I have done much conversing with the local *conocedores*, and everywhere heard the same story; that the ridley—*caguama* it is usually called on the Pacific coast—comes ashore only one-by-one, or a few in any given kilometer.

I once made a fairly detailed ridley survey of the Mexican coast north of the state of Nayarit. During an August and September I traveled with my family by car from abreast of Hermosillo down through Sonora and Sinaloa to San Blas in Nayarit.

It is 650 miles from Kino Bay in Sonora down the coast to San Blas. Part of the way, the road runs along the eastern shore of the Gulf of California, but farther south it goes along beside beaches of the open Pacific. In all this territory the only sea turtles I found were the green turtle and the ridley. The leatherback and hawksbill were known to the local people, but only as casual visitors. Nobody appeared to know anything at all about the loggerhead. The only turtle said to nest regularly anywhere was the ridley. There were a few rumors of nesting by other sea turtles, but whenever I could run the stories down they turned out to be based on some confusion of names or localities. At Kino Bay green turtles were abundant, but the fine ocean beach that runs for miles from Puerto Kino to the craggy promontory at Kino Nuevo was completely unmarked by turtle trails. Nobody there knew anything at all of sea turtles nesting.

The northernmost nests that we found were around Mazatlan. From there on south, all sections of the shore appear to be regular ridley nesting ground, but everywhere the nesting is curiously thin-spread. Nowhere is there traffic to compare even with that at some loggerhead and green turtle rookeries—much less to suggest that the east-Pacific ridley is a close relative of the *cotorra* of the Gulf of Mexico. At Los Serritos a few miles north of Mazatlan, at the peak of the season and with the moon and tide just as the local folk said they ought to be to give the egg-laden turtles a hankering for land, only four ridleys nested in three nights, on two-and-a-half miles of beach. During the same time at the nearby beach at Sábalo, no turtle came out on one mile of shore. On a mile-and-a-half of beach near San Blas three ridleys nested in a period of three nights, and at Matanchen, near the same place, a mile yielded only one nest on one night. At a place called Tamborito, just north of Teacapan, a careful search of more than a mile of beautiful, dune-backed shore, described by the local people as a good place for ridleys, showed no trace of turtles at all. At the one house nearby, the farmer told me the only tracks he had seen in a month were those of two ridleys he had found nesting a week before when his oxen had strayed on the beach. That is the sort of dilute nesting that seems everywhere to be the habit of the east-Pacific ridley. Some of the dearth may simply reflect the toll of centuries of egg hunting and turtle turning. In much of the world it will never be known what mankind has done to limit sea turtle range and abundance, and what is a natural condition. This is especially the case on the fine high beaches of the Pacific coast of Mexico.

The trail a ridley makes on the dry upper sand of the nesting beach is shallow, narrow, and evanescent. To an observer making an aerial survey of a shore sparsely frequented by ridleys, the beach might seem completely devoid of nesting activity. A ridley is so relatively little and light and the sand of many of the shores used is so loose that the trail digs down no farther than the uncompacted surface, and the tracks may disappear completely during the hours following the nesting emergence. Thus, a track count made from the air, or even afoot, will usually log only trails from the night before, while at rookeries of the other sea turtles an accumulation of all tracks made since the last heavy rain can usually be seen. Even taking this lack of visibility and durability of ridley trails into consideration, what I saw in Sinaloa and Nayarit seemed to indicate that nesting activity there was very thinly spread.

It seems to be the same in Central America. During the height of the ridley breeding season in Costa Rica, my wife and I found a single female (10 August 1957, at 11 P.M.) on two miles of beach between San Isídro and Carizal. In Guatemala, in early September 1959, although ridley eggs were common in the markets and people at the port of San José were talking of turtles nesting on beaches near the town, there were no tracks in a mile-and-a-half of beach that I walked. When Charles Bogert and I visited the Guerrero coast in 1952, ridleys were nesting both at Playa Encantada, south of Acapulco, and at Pie de la Cuesta north of it. There were eggs in the *cantinas* but they were scarce and expensive. Because the people were killing all turtles that emerged, the discarded shells gave a rough idea of the amount of nesting that was going on. Both they and the dearth of tracks on the beach indicated that nesting was everywhere scant and scattered.

After the shock I got from the Herrera film, I am never going to make any dogmatic utterances about ridleys. I have to say, however, that it is hard to think where any great nesting aggregation of east-Pacific ridleys, of a size comparable to the migratory flotillas that Jim Oliver and others have seen at sea, could be hiding themselves away. The incongruity is heightened when you consider the situation with the Atlantic species, in which the huge nesting conclave is preceded by no high-seas gatherings—at least not by any that ever are reported.

So it is another peculiar feature of the *arribada* that it just suddenly condenses out of the sea at Rancho Nuevo, with nobody ever seeing cruising schools converging on the place. I have done a lot of talking about this with the crews of shrimp boats and trawlers that work in the coastal waters north of the *arribada* country. They know ridleys, and they catch them in their nets, as I have said; but they never tell you of seeing schools of turtles.

Sightings of massed sea turtles anywhere in the Atlantic are very rare, and in the few such cases I have heard of, the kind of turtle involved has not been known. The one published record of a sea turtle school is that of Terrance H. Leary, who saw leatherbacks loosely grouped off the Texas coast. During World War II, when coastal waters were closely watched for enemy submarines and mines, schools were reported occasionally along the inner edge of the Gulf Stream between Florida and Virginia, but I was never able to make out what turtle was involved.

Very recently a similar sighting was made by Gary Athey, a physicist at the Naval Oceanographic Office in Washington. Here again there is doubt as to the species of turtle, but Mr. Athey's notes on the aggregation are excellent. The turtles were seen from an airplane flying at an altitude of 1000 feet, some 25 miles off the coast between Cape Hatteras and Cape Lookout. Mr. Athey was tracing the edge of the Gulf Stream with a radiation thermometer. The turtles were in the edge of the stream, where the temperature ranged from 17 degrees to 17.5 degrees Centigrade. The grouping of the turtles was not a patchlike school but a ragged string of about 200 of them separated from each other by distances averaging about 600 feet. They all were heading southward, parallel with the coast and thus presumably against the current of the Gulf Stream. When Mr. Athey telephoned to tell me of seeing these turtles he had identified them as "small loggerheads." When sent a silhouette chart comparing the five sea turtles in dorsal view, he decided they could just as well have been ridleys.

Although better documented than most such observations, Mr. Athey's are similar to those that airline and Air Force pilots have reported. In each case, whatever kind of turtle was involved, it is hard to understand what the schools were doing in the places where they were seen. If Athey's turtles were ridleys, they might possibly have been heading for the Tamaulipas nesting ground. Why they should swim upstream to get there, instead of moving over to the coastal water, is not clear. The current runs at a steady two knots, and bucking it seems a poor way to swim to a nesting fiesta in Mexico.

It is conceivable, of course, that all such flotillas are not really schools at all but gatherings about some especially heavy concentrations of floating food, such as jellyfish, Portuguese men-of-war, or sargasso weed.

The greatest concentration of positively identified Atlantic ridleys that I ever heard of (away from Tamaulipas) occurred in just about the most unlikely place that anybody could imagine. It was Martha's Vineyard, Massachusetts. It took place a long time ago, and ever since I first heard about it I have waited anxiously for it to come to mean something. So far, though, it remains a freakish happening that seems only to becloud, not just the question of the origin of the *arribadas*, but the whole life cycle of *Lepidochelys*. Nevertheless, I think I ought to tell about it. Maybe a reader will see some hidden meaning in it.

I was told about the Martha's Vineyard ridleys by William Schevill of the Woods Hole Oceanographic Institution. Bill is an old friend of mine. Although mainly interested in whales and porpoises, he has for years been my faithful collaborator in ponderings of ridley ways. Some years ago Bill wrote to say he was sending me a pickled ridley that had been picked up on May 12, 1956, at the foot of Gays Head cliffs, on Martha's Vineyard. Unless dead ridleys are very buoyant, this one must have come in quite close to the beach before dying, and must have crossed some very cold water in doing so. Cogitating on the degree of cold tolerance implied by its arrival, Bill got himself interested in the strangely numerous ridley records for Massachusetts waters that seemed to be turning up at the time. This interest led him to the discovery that a number of yearling sea turtles caught in Buzzards Bay some years before, and exhibited as loggerheads at Woods Hole for two summers, were actually ridleys. That was a time when, after sixty years of not having believed in the reality of the ridley as a separate kind of turtle, museum curators had been persuaded that it was in fact a valid species and had begun dragging out their old sea turtle specimens, re-examining them, and often finding those labeled loggerhead to be really ridleys. Finding the Buzzards Bay turtles seemed to Bill to be a continuation of the tendency for all old Massachusetts sea turtle records to turn out to be based on misidentified ridleys.

"It seems as if this is real ridley country," Schevill wrote. "Maybe they breed on Penikese or Cuttyhunk."

The latter remark was a joke. I had been looking for ridley nesting for years. In a later note Bill had this afterthought.

> Just talked to Mr. McGinnis of MBL [Marine Biological Laboratory]. He says that about 20 years ago a whole fleet of such turtles came into Woods Hole, carcasses littering the beaches. He fished half-a-dozen sea turtles out of his barrels. All ridleys. Says he has a few more. What is this, a Yankee turtle?

Bill went on to say that Mr. McGinnis, even after talking it over with old-time colleagues, could fix the date no more closely than "about 20 years ago." He remembered that the time of year was midsummer; that the stranded carcasses, although there "by dozens," were only a small fraction of the original school; and that the live turtles had passed *outward* from Buzzards Bay into Vineyard Sound.

These were pretty eerie observations. I could see no shred of sense in a flotilla of ridleys turning up so far north, and much less in their being found swimming seaward out of an inland bay. I wrote Bill this and though his answer was, as his answers often are, a bit tainted with levity, at least it shed light on the odd course the turtles were taking when discovered. His explanation was as follows:

> So as not to confuse you unduly (a little is ok), perhaps I should let on that our tidal circulation in Buzzards Bay and Vineyard Sound may be considered as somewhat clockwise; so that it is quite reasonable to imagine a chunk of water containing, for example, a

passel of ridleys, coming in from the sea between Block Island and the Vineyard, being inhaled into Buzzards Bay (where the flood begins some three hours earlier than in Vineyard Sound), and then being sucked through the Hole an hour or so after the beginning of flood in Buzzards Bay, and a couple of hours before the current turns eastward (let's call it flooding) in Vineyard Sound. Whether the post-Woods-Hole part of the trip goes seaward *via* Vineyard Sound or *via* Nantucket Sound would depend on when the chelo-niphorus water came through the Hole. One might also think of the effect of cold Cape Cod water coming through the canal with the ebb in Buzzards Bay. How do you feel now, pilot?

The main way I felt was, how did the ridleys get to Massachusetts to start with? Schevill being after all predominantly a cetacean man, went happily on to say:

> I am inclined to reverse my irreverent hypothesis that ridleys breed on Cuttyhunk. Seems more likely that it's further up—maybe Scraggy Neck or Buzzards Bay. . . .

By then I wasn't sure whether Bill was advancing a facetious hypothesis or a serious one. But in any case, I was an old hand at deflating such specious ridley theories as that. However phlegmatic you might conceive the inhabitants of the Buzzards Bay shores to be, it was not thinkable that they would have let ridleys dig their beaches for centuries and never have said a word about it. There is no published record of a sea turtle of any kind nesting on the coast of the United States anywhere north of Virginia. So to me the importance of Bill Schevill's information was not its direct bearing on the problem of the unknown ridley nesting grounds. It was the implication that sometimes, at least, Atlantic ridleys travel in aggregations. That fact alone, if spread about, might help take people's minds off abiogenesis as a theory of ridley reproduction, and lend spirit to the hunt for unrecorded migration lanes that might lead to a hidden breeding ground. But the Martha's Vineyard ridley school still stands as the only aggregation of surely identified Atlantic ridleys ever seen by anyone, at least by anyone who told of it. How that flotilla of yearlings got to Buzzards Bay is as unaccountable now that the Rancho Nuevo nesting colony has come to light as it was before, or maybe more so.

Trying to trace down the origins of the *arribada* by tracing schools of ridleys is not a profitable undertaking. There simply are no schools of ridleys. In all the years since Bill Schevill told me of the Martha's Vineyard episode, the most Atlantic ridleys I ever heard of traveling together was three yearlings caught by a Marineland boat thirty miles off the east coast of Florida. The only known groups of any older age-class are the loose bands on the Florida Gulf coast feeding grounds, which evidently are drawn into a given area just because the crabbing is good.

I mentioned in another chapter that a standard migratory procedure, followed by various kinds of marine animals, is to travel upstream to nesting or spawning grounds—up rivers, or upstream in ocean currents. That pattern lessens the problem of the small, weak young in finding and traveling to the residence area. Only the adults have to breast the current and solve the problem of locating the breeding ground. This is by no means a universal pattern, but it is one adhered to by animals as diverse as eels, salmon, and sharks. Unfortunately, little is known of the life cycles of many marine animals. As more is learned it may turn out that upcurrent breeding migration is even more prevalent than it is now known to be. In trying to make sense out of the ridley *arribadas* it is interesting to theorize that they have arranged their migratory cycle in that way, and to look about the map to see how such a pattern might fill out.

In the case of the ridley, tracing out the pattern furnishes no understandable evidence as to where the *arribadas* form, but it reveals a curious zoogeographic situation. Tracing the Gulf Stream upstream from Rancho Nuevo leads straight through the Yucatán Channel and into the Caribbean. There the trail abruptly dead ends, because there are no ridleys there. No ridley of any state of development has ever been found in the Caribbean Sea. This Caribbean gap is a striking anomaly that no amount of searching or of figuring will fill.

To see how odd the lack of ridleys in the Caribbean really is, you have to know the distribution of *Lepidochelys*, the ridley genus, in the whole Atlantic system. Going back to Rancho Nuevo and following the south-trending branch of the Gulf Stream also leads to a dead end. The southernmost part of the Gulf is also apparently devoid of ridleys.

Going down the current of the main stem of the Gulf Stream current leads over to Florida, out between the tip of the peninsula and Cuba, and then up along the Atlantic coast of the United States. Along that way there is more to see—at least there are ridleys there. But there are problems in that direction too. First of all, a lot of the spirit gets taken out of the search when it becomes clear that the ridley consigns its first-year young to the same never-never land that baby sea turtles of all kinds go to. It seems reasonable that the first clue in the downstream search ought to be finding first-year young, either a migratory train of them or an accumulation somewhere down the line. But just as is the case with all other sea turtles, very small ridleys are never seen at all. Except for hatchlings taken off the nesting shore at hatching time, the youngest ridley that anybody ever told of finding was the one found in the Azores thousands of miles away from Rancho Nuevo where it was almost surely hatched.

There is really no known place that can be said to be the home ground of the Atlantic ridley, a definite range in the ordinary zoological sense, where sexually mature turtles regularly occupy a recognizable habitat. If you get a map and plot the distribution of records of the Atlantic ridley, including all known specimens of all ages, you might wind up stating the range as the western Gulf of Mexico eastward to Florida, northward to New England, and across the Atlantic to the Azores, the British Isles, the coast of France and the Netherlands, and straggling finally into the Mediterranean. That is the range of the ridley, providing "range" be defined as the territory in which people have caught the species. But if the definition is refined by excluding all records of turtles that seem lost from the reproductive body of the race—that is, if you throw out all the current-waifs that seem unlikely ever to get back to the place where they were born, then the ridley range should be pruned back to the Atlantic coast of the United States; perhaps clear back to the southern states. It is important to know how far toward Florida from

England one ought to prune, to set meaningful limits to the range.

Only when that question is answered can the migratory pattern really be understood. Answering it is not easy. Certainly, the Mediterranean is not nowadays ridley territory. I mentioned it as occurring there only because I believe that a turtle found at Malta in the 1920s was a ridley. Some people have quarreled with me about this judgment; but I am probably right. Any reader who might want to decide for himself ought to look up an article by a zoologist named Despotte, and carefully examine the photograph he published. The article was called *"Cottura di due essemplari di Chelone mydas Scw. nei mari de Malta."* It came out in volume seven (1930) of the journal *Naturalista Siciliana,* where it occupies pages 73 to 75. As the title says, Despotte believed that he had a couple of green turtles. This is incorrect. Both the *due essemplari* are illustrated in the article. One is a green turtle, as Despotte said, but the other is certainly not. To my eye it is a ridley. European zoologists disagree. They prefer to call the Despotte turtle a loggerhead. I am not asking any reader to take sides in the matter. I will say though that I have seen a whole lot more ridleys than my European colleagues have. On the other hand, it just occurs to me that they live closer to the Mediterranean, and that maybe that lends weight to their view. Nevertheless, I am pretty sure that that turtle is a ridley anyway. I tried to settle the question by writing Professor Despotte and asking to borrow the specimen, but he said it was lost when the Malta museum was destroyed by bombing during World War II.

If I seem to make too much of this Malta ridley, it is just that it represents the farthest flung record—that is, farthest from Rancho Nuevo—of any Atlantic ridley ever found, and thus a great curiosity of sea turtle zoogeography. All the other kinds of sea turtles once occurred regularly on the Mediterranean, where they have been overexploited to the point of extirpation by Mediterranean man, beginning with the Phoenicians, Egyptians, and Romans, and winding up with practically everybody. There is no evidence that the ridley was ever a regular Mediterranean species, but it could have been.

Tracing ridleys back upstream toward America, the next record is that of the ridley from the Azores. It was found years ago, by the Prince of Monaco. It is only four inches long, as I believe I said. How it got so far away from home is hard to see. Perhaps it lodged in a good sargasso raft that drifted straight to the Azores by the shortest current route. But however it made the crossing, being so little and so alone in the wild Azorean sea, it surely ought to be thought of as just a waif, cut off forever from the life of its race.

Maybe not. Maybe it was bound on some regular developmental migration that ridleys make, and would ultimately have got back to Mexico. I doubt this; but then I once would have doubted that there could be such a thing as an *arribada*.

Back northward of the Azores, ridleys, only immature ones, are found sporadically but with some frequency on the coasts of the British Isles, France, and the Netherlands. These are always small, and they often drift ashore, numb from cold. So they, too, would seem unlikely to have been destined to rejoin the breeding stock of their kind. And if they never go back to Rancho Nuevo, they obviously furnish no clue as to where the *arribadas* come from.

It may be that the *arribada* will be understood only when the whole life cycle and zoogeography of the ridley in the Atlantic are known. Just as the lack of a known breeding place was not the whole ridley mystery, so, finding that breeding place has not cleared the mystery up. Ridley natural history is still full of anomalies and unknowns. One that I have mentioned is the lack of ridleys in the Caribbean. Another is that the population in the Atlantic is not one species but two. One of these is the *cotorra;* the other is the *batali.* The *batali* is a freakishly far-flung outpost colony of the Pacific ridley. Besides having an extensive nesting range in the Indo-Pacific, it nests along a great extent of the coast of West Africa from Dakar southward at least as far as Guinea. Although it and the *cotorra* live in the same ocean, the two never breed in the same place. Their nesting ranges are separated by the width of the Caribbean Sea. There are only two known differences between the two species. One is a disparity in the number of big scales or laminae on each side of the shell. West-Atlantic ridleys have five of these on either side; Indo-Pacific ridleys have six or more. The other feature that distinguishes the two is the shape of the shell of the mature turtle. As seen from front or rear, the outline of the carapace of the west-Atlantic ridley is a low, slightly peaked arch; that of the Pacific ridley has steeper sides and is flattened on top. With respect to both these features the ridleys of the coastal waters of the bulge of West Africa are like those of the Pacific and Indian oceans. They thus seem to be a discontinuously distributed enclave of a Pacific stock that got left in or transported to West Africa at some past time when oceanic highways and barriers were different from those of today.

Ridley distribution makes no sense at all under modern conditions of climate and geography. There is evidently no traffic of ridleys between West Africa and the Pacific, either around the Cape of Good Hope or from South America in the frigid West Wind Drift. For the years that he was Director of the Cape Town Museum, Dr. Frank Talbott used to watch for sea turtles in the waters off the tip of Africa, and periodically used to write me of his observations. During a whole decade there, the only sea turtles he saw were a hatchling leatherback and four young green turtles. So the cape water is not always too cold for sea turtles. But even in the odd years when shifting water masses bring higher temperatures to cape waters, ridleys apparently never came by from the Indian Ocean. One reason for this is that another of the several odd gaps in ridley range occurs along the whole East African coast. After reconnoitering the coasts of Kenya, Tanganyika, and Natal and searching museum collections in the United States, Europe, and Africa, I had to conclude that the ridley is absent from that side of the Indian Ocean. There is an old record from the island of Socotra. To the south, a single ridley shell was recently found on the beach near Durban. Mr. George Hughes, who with Messrs. A. J. Bass and M. T. Mentic has been engaged in a study of the colony of leatherbacks and loggerheads in the Zululand coast, sent me photographs and measurements of the shell. It is quite clearly that of a ridley. That one shell was the only trace of the ridley they ever saw.

In other words, the ridleys that ought to be on the Pacific side of

Africa are not there; and this reinforces the anomaly of the Pacific ridleys breeding on the West African coast.

You can imagine how shaking it was to learn about that, to a man already at his wits' end trying to find the nesting place of the west-Atlantic ridley. It was so demoralizing that it set me to toying with the desperate notion that West Africa might be the breeding ground of both the Pacific and the American ridley. Maybe, I figured, little African ridleys born with only five shell-scales are regarded as misfits and kicked out of the African colony, picked up by the Equatorial Current and Gulf Stream and carried eventually to the Gulf of Mexico, where they grow into Florida ridleys. That way it would be only natural for them to have no breeding habits or nesting ground. That was several years before I saw the film of the *arribada* out at Austin, and you can see what bad condition I was in.

Next to learning of the *arribada*, the most exciting advance in the ridley story was the materialization of the *batalí*. At first the *batalí* was only fishermen's talk that I heard in Trinidad. I don't know what language the name *batalí* is; Carib probably. During a sea turtle reconnaissance on the north coast of Trinidad I found that people knew of five kinds of sea turtles. After sifting out four species that corresponded with the hawksbill, loggerhead, leatherback, and green turtle, I was able to concentrate on the fifth. The descriptions of the shape, color, and disposition of this, and its alleged infrequency of occurrence made it seem clearly a *Lepidochelys*, a ridley of some sort, and several facts suggested that it was the African ridley. For one thing, I had seen a six-scaled ridley from the northeast coast of Cuba, where the Gulf Stream moves past the island and washes land for the first time after leaving the African bulge. The *batalí* was said never to nest on Trinidad, but to show up occasionally in coastal waters, where it was caught with nets or harpoon. Because the northern coast of Trinidad bears the same relation to the Gulf Stream that north coast Cuba does, it seemed reasonable to predict that the *batalí*, if it should ever come to the hand of a zoologist, would turn out to be the six-scaled Pacific species.

I had to wait a long time to see whether this was so. If it had not been for Felix Assam, an energetic Trinidadian fisheries official with a lively interest in sea turtle problems, I might not yet have seen a *batalí*. On two trips to Trinidad I was unable to find a single one, whole or in pieces, and nobody could even produce a photograph of one. I eventually gave up the search for more rewarding work with green turtles. Mr. Assam promised to send me the first *batalí* he got his hands on.

Years passed; then one day a box came by air-express. It was a cubical box only about eight inches on a side. It was from Felix Assam, and therefore bound to be a ridley. I was puzzled over the small size of the box, because the Trinidad fishermen all had told us that only big *batalís* show up in Trinidad. But I opened the box in a sweat to see the *batalí* at last. Inside I found the severed head of a turtle.

It was a big head, freshly cut off and well pickled. It was obviously the head of a ridley, but it was a very frustrating object. Clues in the ridley mystery were still turning up in bits. The trouble now was that my *batalí* theory had said two separate things: that the *batalí* was a *Lepidochelys*, a ridley; and that the ridley involved was the African kind, the so-called Pacific ridley, and not the *cotorra* at all. It will be remembered that the Atlantic and Pacific ridleys are told apart by the features of the shell. The ridley in the box had no shell. The head was enough to clinch the identification as far as genus; that is, to distinguish the bearer from all other kinds of sea turtles, and to prove it to be a ridley. But there is nothing about the head of the Atlantic and Pacific species of *Lepidochelys* that differentiates between the two—at least nothing that I know of. To have got that far and still not to have been allowed to see to the end of the darkness was demoralizing. Nevertheless, I wrote Felix and thanked him warmly for the head, and urged him to move more mountains to get a complete turtle. Then I went back to work with green turtles some more.

A year later a carapace came. Eight years after I had decided what the *batalís* ought to be, I was able to look at a whole shell of one, and along with it a clear photograph that Assam had taken of the animal the shell had belonged to. It was a ridley, and this time there was no doubt at all, it was the Pacific kind. With the coming of that carapace the legend of the *batali* was fact at last.

At that time I figured that the *batalís* probably came to the Antilles straight from West Africa on the Equatorial Current. The distances were no greater than those that little Atlantic ridleys regularly travel, in going to Europe in another section of the same great swirl. An African origin seemed substantiated by a catch made by the research vessel *Oregon*, and reported to me in a letter from Mr. Harvey Bullis, Chief of Gulf Fisheries and Gear Research for the United States Fish and Wildlife Service. While making an exploratory trawling run fifty miles off the coast of Surinam, the *Oregon* caught a full-grown female ridley with eight laminae on either side of her shell. She was taken at a depth of a little over a hundred feet inside the Equatorial Current, which there is fresh in from Africa and is moving down on Trinidad. I took this as further evidence that *batalís* were waifs from Senegal. And so some of them may be; but it now seems likely that they come mainly from outpost nesting colonies in the Guianas.

The Guianas were a place I had been vaguely uneasy about for quite a while. In a couple of articles I called attention to the gap in exploration that remained in northern South America and in a notebook of the time I wrote myself this memo:

> An area that remains to be searched for ridleys is the shore of Northern South America, especially the coasts of the Guianas. Current-charts show the North Equatorial Current striking land first in the Guianas. This is a place where flotsam from upper West Africa should come in . . .

That much of the note was prophetic. But then I finished the sentence this way.

> and one from which ridleys just possibly might be carried on to Florida.

So the insight was marred by wishful thinking, by my hope that the Florida ridley might be coming from the Guianas. The nesting ground being searched for was not that of the African species. In those days the groping was all after the home ground of *Lepidochelys kempi,* the American five-scaled ridley. Ridleys have now been found nesting in both British and Dutch Guiana, but as I said, they are the six-scaled "Pacific" species.

At the time I wrote that note, the Department of Forestry in Paramaribo, Surinam, was studying a mixed colony of sea turtles that nested on the remote and almost inaccessible coast of Surinam, at a place called Bigi Santi. The colony included the green turtle, the leatherback and another species, first identified as the loggerhead, that turned out to be *Lepidochelys.* The Bigi Santi shore on which these turtles nested was also the abode of scarlet ibis, egrets, flamingos, and the "sea deer" that comes out on the beach to feed and to flee the inland mosquitoes. In 1961 a strip of shore thirty miles long and five miles deep was designated the Wia Wia Wildlife Preserve. Today the turtles there get as good protection as any sea turtles anywhere.

In 1964 Director J. P. Schulz of the Surinam Forest Service published an extensive account of his studies of the Bigi Santi sea turtle colony. This showed that an enclave of the Pacific–West Africa ridley stock had established, or had retained from days when it spread through the south Atlantic, a beachhead in Surinam, and that it nests there regularly every year.

A comparable nesting association, including a good admixture of hawksbills, was found in British Guiana by Peter Pritchard of Oxford, now a graduate student at the University of Florida. In 1964 Mr. Pritchard found remains of sea turtles including ridleys that had been killed by Indians on a wild stretch of shore in British Guiana. In 1965 he went back with camping equipment and tagging tools, marooned himself on the beach for two weeks and tagged ten female ridleys on their nests, besides a number of hawksbills and green turtles.

The ridley of the Surinam colony is locally known as *warana.* In British Guiana the name is *terracai.* Both these ridleys are clearly the West African species, and they round out a curious pattern of distribution in the Gulf Stream system. At three widely separated nesting places the great eddy picks up ridleys. One is the Tamaulipas rookery, where five-scaled *cotorras* move into Florida waters on the Gulf Stream. The *"cotorras"* become "ridleys" there, and then on hidden routes and for unknown reasons ride on with the current to New England and even to the other side of the Atlantic. Over there they seem never to go on south with the current. South of the Azores no *cotorra* has ever been seen. No ridley of any kind is known from Morocco, Spanish Sahara, and the Canary and Cape Verde Islands, or from anywhere in the open ocean from Mauretania up to the Azores.

On the shores of the bulge of Africa, as I have said, you come upon ridleys again. Here incomprehensibly, they are of another kind —the species that inhabits the Pacific and Indian oceans. In West Africa this turtle nests along hundreds of miles of the coast. It, too, evidently gets picked up by the current—the Canaries Current north of Dakar and the Benguela Current coming up from the south—and is carried across to the New World. Whether the ridleys that nest in the Guianas have become wholly cut off as a separate colony from those of Africa is not known. It seems likely that the Guiana enclave may be joined by occasional current-waifs from the African populations. Neither, however, apparently ever gets inside the outer shores of the Antillean screen and enters the Caribbean.

The two ridley species in the Atlantic Ocean—the *cotorra* and the *batali*—thus never come in contact with each other, and I would give a lot to know why. Usually in such cases of separation of closely related species, some sort of active mutual exclusion can be suspected, some severe competition that makes life easier for both, outside one another's territory. But there is obviously no competition between these two species. They never get within hundreds of miles of each other. The Caribbean is a big ridley no man's land in the western section of the great world river they live in, which keeps them wide apart. And, over along the coast between France and Mauretania, something else keeps them apart. If ridleys ever meet at all in both those great gaps in their range, it is only as waifs lost in seas strange to them both. If by remote chance they

ever do breed together anywhere, it cannot be often enough to affect the genetic makeup of either species.

So ridleys are remarkable beasts in a number of ways. But the
great ridley wonder is the Mexican *arribada*, and for finding that
before it disappeared, the world is indebted to Andrés Herrera and
to Henry Hildebrand.

While I was scratching for clues in other sectors of the mystery,
Henry was making a fisheries survey of Laguna Madre on the
Tamaulipas coast. Down there he repeatedly heard an irresponsible-
sounding rumor. The rumor was that an Arab trader had come into
Tampico driving a long train of burros. The trader had come from
Punta Juarez, some forty miles to the north. There were forty or
fifty burros in the train, the rumor said, and they were loaded down
with turtle eggs.

It was the sort of wild, ridiculous tale you are bound to hear if
you keep asking around about sea turtles. Most people would have
paid no attention to it. But Henry Hildebrand did. He patiently
tracked it down, and it finally led him to Andrés Herrera. And that
was how I came to see the greatest moving picture of the age.

Since I wrote the foregoing chapter, there have been two important developments in the ridley story. One is exciting, one is
melancholy.

The exciting thing is this. Peter Pritchard decided to do his Ph.D.
research on the ridley problem. To start it off he went to Surinam
and set up a tagging project out at Bigi Santi beach in the Wia
Wia Preserve. The Dutch officials gave the project their generous
co-operation, and Peter and his camp mates, Tom Stubbs and Tom
Lesure, learned a lot of new things about sea turtles. I went down to
make movies of the nesting of the leatherback and to see the *warana*,
the legendary *batali*, come ashore. While I was there I heard talk
of a beach to the south near the French Guiana border called
Eilanti, where the *warana* came out to nest in masses that in the
telling sounded like the *arribada*. When I left, Peter was planning
to go to Eilanti to get the straight of the story. Now he has gone
there. This is what the letter he wrote me about it said:

By chance we went to Eilanti a few days early, on June 7th, and met up with the *arribada* that night. The beach is about 700 yards long, and dense nesting occurs on a 200-yard section. The first few came out by daylight, but the big mob came a few hours later. The whole thing lasted about six hours. At one point I counted 97 ridleys on the 200-yard shore simultaneously, and probably about 500 nested during the whole period. They crawled over each other and would have dug up each other's eggs, only the Indians had removed them. At least 90 percent of the eggs got taken away. I used my remaining 130 tags in about 2½ hours. The next night about 80 turtles nested, and the third night about 300. An old Indian who had seen the *arribada* every year for 50 years said they always occur in that one place. You start looking out for it on May 20. If that fails, watch for it on May 29th. They say there may be another group on June 15th, but that the biggest group of all, about 700 turtles, usually nests within a day of the 24th of June.

So there is another *arribada* in the world. It is not the equal of Andrés Herrera's hosts, but it is a wonder all the same. And it came just in time too, because the Mexican *arribada* may be gone. I have told a little about its going in the last chapter of the book. Some years ago people began lying in wait for it all along the coast, and once in a while they chanced to be there when the *cotorras* swarmed ashore. They killed turtles, distributed the meat in the interior, dried calipee for sale, and mined the eggs in masses. Three years ago I realized that I had heard no definite report of an *arribada* since some time in the latter part of the 1950s. Now I have just finished canvassing every possible source of information, and it adds up to the dismal certainty that no *arribada* has been seen for at least seven years. Two or three skipped years might be attributed to chance, because ninety miles is a long beach and there are not really very many people there. Now, however, there is no escaping the snowballed evidence that the great arrivals have failed. *Cotorras* still straggle ashore along the Tamaulipas coast, but they are few and scattered. The fabulous conclaves of former years have gone the way of a thousand other sea turtle colonies before them.

6

THE WAY TO *ISLA META*

There is really no such place as *Isla Meta*. I thought it up to illustrate some points I want to make. Partly, it is any lonely little ocean island where animals congregate at predictable times. Partly, it is the special island of Ascension, a crumb of land out in the sea between Africa and South America. Ascension is so small and far from other shores that human navigators even have trouble finding it. During the Second World War it used to be a way-stop for airplanes of the Air Transport Command flying from Miami to the Burma Road. Airplanes that left Recife on the coast of Brazil had to make the Ascension landfall or go on almost a thousand miles to Dakar. If they lacked the fuel for that, it meant ditching in the wild south Atlantic. The possibility of not finding Ascension Island was one of the hazards of the job, and one the pilots thought about a lot.

"You miss Ascension," they used to sing over their beer, "and your wife gets a pension."

Those pilots were well equipped with all sorts of aids to navigation. Their having felt that way about locating the island makes you want to know how any animal can possibly do it.

Meta means goal in Spanish. In a way that is a bad name for my island. One important difference between the navigation of man and that of animals is that animals probably don't purposefully travel toward distant goals. All we have any right to assume is that they are simply stirred to travel, and then respond correctly to the guideposts along the way. *Isla Meta,* then, is just the far end of any scheduled high-seas journey made by an animal out of sight of land.

TURTLE TALES AND TAG RETURNS

When I first went to Turtle Bogue I took along a lot of folklore that seemed to indicate that the green turtle was a long-range traveler. Almost from the start, results of the Tortuguero tagging project seemed to support the folk belief. Now, eleven years later, it would take a fairly cranky outlook to doubt the snowballed evidence that supports the stories the turtle captains told me. The circle of proof is still not closed, but room for doubt is very limited. The green turtle is a periodic, long-distance migrant; and few green turtles live where they are hatched or where they go to breed. The hawksbill travels long distances too, at least on occasion, and so do the loggerhead and the ridley. The leatherback may be the greatest traveler of all. Whether, and to what degree, and on what schedules, the journeys of these others is a seasonal commuting between different habitats appropriate to different stages of the life cycle, as it is with *Chelonia,* is not yet known. Almost nothing, in fact, is known about the migrations of any of the other sea turtles. They turn up in queer far-off places; but what plans, whims, or misadventures take them there is not known. Ridleys and leatherbacks may aggregate to nest—the ridley to a spectacular degree—and this happens in places in which they are not seen between nesting seasons. This fact alone indicates that migration probably occurs. The young of all five of the sea turtles disappear for at least a year after hatching. This too suggests that a migration of some hidden sort must be involved in getting the turtles back to the ancestral nesting ground when they reach breeding age. Here again, however, there is only logic to build with. There is no observed evidence of any kind.

Of all sea turtles the green turtle is the best known, and the only one whose travels can be shown to take comprehensible seasonal shape. Its grazing territories and breeding sites are usually well separated and clearly delineated. It masses at predictable seasons both to nest and to feed, and can thus be sampled regularly both at tagging time and at tag-recovery time. This not only is convenient for the green turtle project but is in itself more evidence of a regular migratory schedule. So despite the fact that nobody has watched a green turtle go through its complete cycle of travel, to doubt now that it is a periodic long-range migrant is to strain at gnats.

Another fisherman's belief that I carried to Tortuguero was that the green turtle is an able navigator. From many Caribbean people I had heard that the Tortuguero migrants were able to guide their journeys straight across open ocean to Turtle Bogue, on courses accurate enough to let them pick up Turtle Mountain as a landmark. The turtle captains I talked to all agreed that the green turtle had "senses beyond the sense of man." As the map on which our tag returns are kept began to fill out, it seemed to support that folk belief, too. Just looking at the map it seemed almost sure that the turtles coming to Tortuguero to nest, from the distant pasture grounds that the map showed they lived on, would be bound to navigate long stretches of open water without the help of any fixed landmarks.

Here again, however, the proof was circumstantial, and was much less solid than that which supported the fact of migratory travel. It was at least conceivable that green turtles going to the Bogue, from any of the places pinned on the chart, could get there by just swimming till they found the nearest mainland shore, then turning appropriately left or right and groping along the coast until an old, ingrained smell or taste—or the sight of Turtle Mountain—told them that the journey was done. Tortuguero was in most ways a good place to study turtle migration; but because of this nagging possibility that the migrants reached it by simple landmark piloting, the Bogue would not be a good place to investigate open-ocean navigation, or even to prove conclusively that *Chelonia* is capable of such navigation.

For that kind of proof tagging would have to be done on an island nesting ground. In many parts of the world green turtles nest on islands. In fact, they seem to prefer island beaches to those of mainland coasts, as many sea birds also do. If it could be shown that the habit of nesting on islands actually involved island-finding —that is, that the turtles converged upon the nesting island from far off, and were not just the resident population derived from pastures lying close about the island iself—it could be assumed that they navigated with the use of guideposts more subtle than the solid signs on shorelines or on shallow bottom.

A suitable island seemed at hand. It was Ascension Island, in the south Atlantic between Africa and Brazil. Turtles nested in abundance at Ascension. Nobody knew where they came from, but they arrived and disappeared seasonally, and between seasons there were no green turtles anywhere near the island. As the Tortuguero tag returns began to show definitely that *Chelonia* was a migratory animal, I started traveling about to see what could be learned of routes and seasons of green turtle migration, and particularly to get clues bearing on the origin of the Ascension nesting colony. Among other places, the search took me to various sections of the African coast, and to the shores of South America from Fortaleza down to Argentina. I learned that in Africa green turtles were fairly abundant in places along the coast of the western bulge, and that nesting also goes on there. In the coastal waters of Brazil there were extensive feeding grounds, and there were turtles grazing on some of these, but I was not able to find any sign or rumor of nesting anywhere on the mainland. A few green turtles nested on Trinidad Island off the coast but the colony there seemed much too small to produce the aggregations on the Brazilian feeding grounds.

These observations gave me a working theory to start with. It was that the Ascension nesting colony was recruited from distant mainland shores, probably Brazilian, possibly also African. If the theory proved to be true, then automatically the green turtle would stand out as a spectacular navigator. And Ascension Island would suddenly seem to be an extraordinarily good place for field experiments in animal navigation.

ASCENSION ISLAND, AND THE ENIGMA OF ISLAND-FINDING NAVIGATION

The most clear-cut and imposing problem in the study of animal navigation is to explain how a small island can be found. The importance of finding islands is that all the familiar forms of piloting—that is, guidance by reference to landmarks—are ruled out automatically. There can never be any doubt that animals that make scheduled convergences on small oceanic islands are doing some pretty far-out navigating. Unless, perhaps, you can believe that they do it with no guidance at all, merely shotgunning the tiny, distant target with their numbers, trusting that enough of them will blindly barge into the island to keep the race alive. This alternative theory seems altogether unreasonable. To provide the hundreds of turtles that reach the island of Ascension, for example, and that arrive there at more or less the same time, the Brazilian recruiting ground would have to send turtles spreading across the sea in tight ranks along a front so broad that ships would be bound to see them. Ships' logs would say, "Sighted long rows of traveling turtles, thousands and thousands of them, in close order for miles and miles." Ships' logs don't say that.

In the Ascension migration the problem is to account for the periodic arrival of Brazilian turtles that almost surely have traveled against the Equatorial Current for at least 1200 miles through the open sea. It is possible that as they leave the mainland waters, landmarks put them on the right course and that these help them hold the course for a short way out to sea. That is, the turtles may keep looking back over their shoulders and holding their original compass bearing by keeping the same line of retreat from some high point on shore. At the other end of the journey, too, there will be landmarks by which to correct any small navigation errors in the crossing. There is a 5000-foot mountain on Ascension Island, and clouds often pile up high above it. Such a feature may be visible from a long way out to sea, to a race adapted to seeing it. A turtle has to look at the horizon from pretty low over the water, but I suppose that on the wave crests the Ascension clouds might possibly be made out from 50 miles at sea. If so, then twice that distance would be the error allowable in the navigation of the turtles coming across from Brazil. When they lose the mainland landmark astern they have got to start navigating. If they hold a course to within 50 miles on either side of the island they will get there safely. If they pass more than 50 miles to either side, they will have some excruciatingly exacting navigation to do to correct their heading, or else swim on west to Africa, or to limbo. The open-sea guidance process, then—whatever it may be—has got to keep the eastward-swimming turtle within a tall isosceles triangle over 1000 miles in altitude and with a base 100 miles wide.

The penalty of bad navigation to Ascension is increased by the current, which flows westward past Ascension toward the easternmost bulge of the South American mainland at a rate of something over one knot. If this current were breasted squarely the whole way, which is obviously impossible, it would only hinder the speed of the voyage. But any navigation error would be greatly magnified by the set of the current. Even if a journey such as that out to Ascension should be made across a calm, currentless sea it would be an amazing feat of pathfinding. In the steady current and high seas of the south Atlantic the trip seems fabulous indeed.

In meditating on possible guidance processes in the Ascension migration it is necessary to decide whether you think that it is bound to involve more than a compass sense. If there were no current, say, and no waves—at least no angling waves—and if the turtle left Recife on the correct course to Ascension, how long would she be able to keep heading toward the island by compass sense alone? That is, if the right initial heading was due east, how long would that remain the right heading, and how wrong would it have become by the time the turtle reached the longitude of Ascension? Said still another way: for an animal swimming in open sea, a bilaterally symmetrical animal who pushes just as hard with her right flipper as with her left, and who has no barnacles off-center on her shell, how close would she come to hitting a five-mile target after a thousand-mile swim, if she guided herself by compass sense alone?

That is important, because there is no trouble postulating the compass sense. The ability to use moving celestial bodies for finding directions, first discovered in ants sixty years ago, is now being demonstrated in a growing number of kinds of animals both vertebrate and invertebrate. As might be expected, the green turtle appears to have this sense. In some preliminary tests with hatchling *Chelonia* from Tortuguero made at Duke University, Dr. Klaus Fischer found that they could locate a reward when it was repeatedly offered at the same place in an enclosure in which a moving artificial sun was the only landmark. Curiously, the turtles were able to retain the instilled direction sense for only three days. In other experiments made under the natural sun, Tortuguero hatchlings showed a consistent tendency to take a southwesterly heading. What the preference means is completely unknown. These experiments ought to be followed up by more extensive tests with great numbers of hatchlings. Far more badly needed, however, are investigations of the compass sense of the mature female, preferably using turtles physiologically ready to set out on their migratory journey from the residence area to the nesting beach. The experimental turtles should be taken from a population that nests on an island, because it seems possible that different stocks may have hereditary differences in the character and keenness of their travel guidance senses. Such experiments would be relatively simple to arrange. It is only the problem of finding recognizably motivated turtles and transporting them in an undisturbed state that has held up the work. When properly designed tests are made it will be very surprising indeed if no light-compass sense is found.

But after that there would remain the question whether compass sense alone can take a race of turtles reliably from Brazil to Ascension Island. To me this seems impossible. There has got to be something more to the navigation process than that. The great enigma that one day has got to be solved and explained is how animals—birds of a number of kinds, seals, and turtles—find all the islands that they regularly visit. How, that is to say, is the high-seas part of any animal travel guided?

Of the 547 turtles that now have been tagged on Ascension Island, there have been 15 recoveries—long-term recoveries, that is, not tagged turtles coming back to nest again the same season. Ten of these were made on the coast of Brazil, at various places between Vitoria down below the hump and Fortaleza above it. Five of the recoveries were made out at Ascension Island itself, three of them after three years' absence, and two after a four-year interval. The turtles that returned three years after being tagged had without much doubt passed the interim in Brazil. The two that turned up four years later almost surely had made two round trips to Brazil, and had simply not been found by any observer on their first return to the island two years earlier.

Although these tag recoveries are exciting, they are not direct, absolute proof that round-trip journeys to Brazil had been made. Other contributory evidence strengthens the case, however. Ascension Island is a high point on the Mid-Atlantic Ridge. This rises abruptly from great depths. Although green turtles are confirmed bottom feeders, they are not often seen foraging at depths of over one hundred feet. Thus, a short way out from the island the bottom is out of reach for green turtles. There is no food available for a resident green turtle colony, and there is, in fact, no colony there. When the nesting is over the turtles go away, and the nearest feeding grounds are along the African and Brazilian coasts. Africa is a little closer, but it lies upstream in the Equatorial Current. To get there the young would have to swim against the current. None of the Ascension tags have been sent back from Africa, even though the turtles are heavily fished there, and although I know people there who would collect and send in any tags that fishermen found. The more probable migratory exchange, and that postulated at the beginning of the Ascension project, is one between the island and Brazil. And Brazil is the place that tag returns come from.

It therefore seems likely that the Ascension nesting colony of *Chelonia* comes from Brazil, and that the three-year returns there represented round trips by turtles nesting on the three-year cycle that is most prevalent in the genus, while the four-year recoveries were made on second returns by turtles on the two-year cycle. In any case, the turtles that reach the island quite obviously do so by a very advanced navigation process of some kind, and this makes Ascension an extraordinarily favorable natural stage for experiments in animal orientation. For purely logistic reasons, however, the right kind of experiments are frustratingly hard to arrange.

The first thing that needs to be learned is whether the journey is guided by celestial guideposts, by inertial guidance, or by some combination of cleverly detected landmarks unknown to, or undetectable by, man. These landmarks could be either signs we have not yet thought of, or features of the environment that turtles detect by especially keen refinements of one or more of the regular senses that all vertebrate animals have.

LANDMARKS IN THE SEA

One kind of sophisticated landmark that people often suggest as a possibility in the Ascension-finding process is an odor gradient of some kind. Maybe the turtles smell their way out there. The idea is attractive, because the shortest route from the mainland out to the island is all upstream. It is engaging to make a dot on a page and say it is Ascension, and then scratch lines out toward the west in a radiating patch that spreads as it gets farther away and then spreads much faster as it approaches the hump of Brazil and the current splits into north-flowing and south-flowing branches.

I have thought a lot about that patch of Ascension smell, or Ascension taste if you prefer, spreading over to Brazil. I have no doubt it is out there, constantly and clearly, a beacon for anybody able to follow it in. Not just *smell* it, you understand. That won't do any good. What you have to do is smell it, then move on, then smell it again; and then meditate and decide which time it smelled stronger and take off the way of the growing strength of smell. I have discussed the Ascension smell with physiologists qualified to comment on the stature of the olfactory feat required. After figuring about possible kinds of smells an island might have, and about diffusion rates downstream in a current in the deep ocean—and then figuring how many molecules of the smell there might be per cubic meter five hundred miles out from the island—almost everybody I have talked with has begun to look doubtful. And then it occurs to them that to follow the growing smell the turtle would have to compare two adjacent patches of water and then judge which way the smell seemed to be growing stronger. That is, she would have to remember the exact strength of the smell in one place, and then compare that with the strength in another. Then after that there is a fatigue-effect to be considered, a tendency for any given smell to weaken when it is smelled for a long time, and this might make following a smell gradient impossible anyway.

I could go on from there, making it sound more hopeless for the turtle. For instance, just detecting an increase in the strength of the smell would never take the turtle to the island, because any south-easterly or northeasterly heading would bring some increase in the strength of it. So the problem would not be just detecting the strong-est of two separate smells, but making repeated back-and-forth comparisons so as to be sure you are moving in the direction of the most rapidly strengthening of many strengthening gradients. One way olfaction might be used, downstream from an odorifer-ous island, would be for the traveler to move over to the edge of the triangle of odor (the half-of-a-cone, actually) and then keep swim-ming zigzag into and out of it, to keep the smell-sense from getting fatigued. Maybe that would work. I can't really see how, though.

But there is no comfort in sneering at the idea, because there is no way of escaping the certainty that turtles do some such astonishing thing when they find an island. Other kinds of landmarks that come to mind seem just as tenuous as smells. Bottom contours are land-marks, and can be used as crude guideposts in some parts of the sea. I don't really know whether a mariner who had a perfect chart of the bottom of the south Atlantic, and was able to measure great depths accurately and thus scan the bottom topography, could use features of that topography to pilot out to Ascension Island. I doubt it. In any case turtles have no known means of keeping contact with the bottom. They have no equipment for echolocation or even for making any sounds that anyone ever heard.

Nevertheless it would probably be a good thing if somebody could think up a series of experiments to test the ability of loggerheads, ridleys, and hawksbills to find isolated rock patches by the racket made by snapping shrimp. Some waters could probably be navigated pretty well by using snapping shrimp guideposts, by detecting the presumably different sonographic patterns the different species and combinations of species make and then plotting the depths and configuration of the patches of snapping shrimp country and comparing these with snapping shrimp charts you somehow had got hold of. You could probably grope your way about some places that way, although I doubt that you could ever get to Ascension Island.

I mention snapping shrimp and thousand-mile-long smell gradients mainly just to show how hard it is going to be to find any landmark that might guide animals precisely in the open ocean. And anyway, if turtles do smell their way to Ascension Island one still has to explain how the sooty and noddy terns get there. Their feats of navigation are even more imposing than the known feats of any aquatic animal, and the smell theory is no good for them. To a bird an olfaction gradient would be even more tenuous a thread than I have described—more quickly diffused, more hopelessly disrupted by currents of the air.

One way you look at the island-finding phenomenon, it seems best to search for a theory applicable to all the great island-finding navigators whether in the air or in the water. Before deciding to do that however, I ought to call attention to features and conditions of the planet that vary regularly with geography and that might be involved in the navigation of water animals. For instance, the edges of masses or patches of water that have different origin and characteristics, might, like the edge of smell emanating from Ascension, be strikingly evident and meaningful to a turtle. Even without any special, or especially keen, sense to detect them, the lines of contact between different kinds of water sometimes remain narrow and clear-cut for long periods of time. Where the Gulf Stream moves past milky coastal water from Florida Bay, for instance, the zone of contact is not a broad region of gradual replacement of one kind of water by another. Instead, each kind keeps its identity right up to within a few feet, or even to within a few inches, of the other. Any animal to whom that zone of contact meant something as a geographic signpost could easily travel along the line, or could correct his course each time he came to the sudden change from one kind of water to the other.

A place where this sort of thing probably actually does guide turtles is out around the mouths of the rivers of Caribbean Costa Rica. In the rainy season the water from successive floodings back in the interior mountains spreads in series of concentric semicircular zones, each separated from the next by a thin line where one shade is replaced by another. If the Río Reventazón, say, has a particular smell or taste, an aquatic animal traveling far out at sea would suddenly come upon a guidepost to tell him where he was. Those are coastal waters, however. I know little about the possibility that different kinds of water exist at predictable times and places in the open ocean; or if so, whether the transition zones between these are defined sharply enough for them to serve as landmarks.

As I said, I brought up the possibility of piloting by smell and taste, not as my favorite theory of island finding, but only to suggest the keenness of the detection process that must be involved if landmarks are used in the island-finding process. Not very long ago it would have been preposterous to say that bats catch insects in flight by bouncing sound off them, or that electric fish sense the presence of prey and enemies by feeling disruptions of electric fields that the fish throw out around themselves; or to tell how far away one kind of moth can detect the dilute scent of the female. Those once would all have been called outrageous hypotheses, before the proof of them came in. And it is going to seem outrageous again, I forecast, when someone finally tells how animals find the islands they go to at breeding time.

MAGNETIC LANDMARKS AND THE CORIOLIS FORCE

Another theory of landmark piloting that keeps sticking its head up is navigation by reference to the magnetic field of the earth. Certainly the earth has a magnetic field; and there is no doubt that the field has features that offer travel information to anyone able to use them. Almost since biologists first became interested in the guidance feats of migrating animals, the possibility that magnetic guideposts might be used has been a subject for controversy. It still is. There is evidence that various animals are able to align themselves with the magnetic field of the earth. The sensory structures involved are not known, and in no case has it been clearly shown that the sense is or could be important in long-distance guidance. But the magnetic field theory is by no means completely dead.

Another landmark, or system of landmarks, that seems even farther out of reach of animals is the Coriolis Force, which reflects the zoned speed at which points on the surface of the earth are traveling through space at different latitudes. If you move to the north of where you are, you will be spinning in space a little slower. If you suddenly step from the center of a spinning platform, you are likely to fall on your face, just as you would if a truck should move off quickly with you standing on the bed; and for the same reason. It is the same way on the globe of the world. In the Northern Hemisphere each little move toward the south accelerates your eastward speed and each shift northward decelerates you. If you only had the right sort of very sensitive accelerometer you would be able to say how far north or south you had moved, and in that way calculate your new latitude.

Thus, the varying speeds of the successive parallels of latitude are landmarks, too, just as the lines of force of the magnetic field are. Used together, the two could furnish data for a grid that would tell a traveler where he was anywhere in the world. But until physiologists find the anatomical instruments that might be used in such detection, to explain animal navigation by magnetic fields and the Coriolis Force, though stimulating to think about, is not very helpful. I should say, however, that it is even less helpful to rule them out altogether.

DEAD RECKONING BY AN ACCELERATION SENSE

Anyway, an animal able to detect and keep track of the accelerations of the Coriolis Force would, it seems to me, not need to know its latitude. To feel the Coriolis Force, the requirements are an ac-

celerometer and a recording system sensitive enough to keep the
traveler aware of the net extent of his north-south displacement at
all times, by feeling, recording, and summarizing all the changing
velocities of spin of all the points he has moved to ever since he
was born or since he started any given journey. An animal able to
do that would almost surely find it natural and easy to perceive
and record not just the Coriolis accelerations, but every other change
in velocity his body experienced too, whether produced by his own
locomotor activity or by outside forces such as wind or currents.
If that is conceivable, then the course-holding sense could be simply
an "inertial sense," a fantastically keen ability to perceive and record all changes in speed, and direction, throughout any journey
or movement, however long and tortuous, or however slow and insignificant it might be. That is the inertial-guidance theory of animal
navigation. It is one of the theories that has got to be considered
in the effort to explain the island-finding ability. To test it you put
an animal with a strong homing sense into a box and carry the box
about through a long and tortuous course. Then you let the animal
out and see what he does. If the theory works, the animal just thinks
back through all the twists and times of continuous velocity that
there were during the crazy journey, and then starts following them
out in reverse. Or maybe he will average them all up into a straight
line, reverse the direction of the line, and travel back along it to
the place he started from. In that case the experimenter will have
to start all over again trying to distinguish among several possible
systems of navigation the animals may be using.

So the current theories of animal navigation are these: (1) inertial
guidance, with or without the Coriolis Force; (2) latitude finding by
the Coriolis Force; (3) a magnetic sense that recognizes qualities
and local aberrations of the earth's magnetic field; (4) celestial
guidance. I think it is fair to say that the last is the prevalent theory.
It is not on very solid ground, however, as the explanation of the
island-finding feats of animals; and it will not be, until more is known
of what animals are really able to see, and until the courses they
follow on their navigated travel are precisely plotted.

With all the theories seeming so preposterous, it may tempt some people to stick their heads in the sand and say that there probably is really no such thing as island finding, and that the homing of displaced animals is always just the result of random wandering. This, without any doubt whatsoever, is the most preposterous theory of all.

CELESTIAL NAVIGATION AND THE PROBLEM OF ISLAND FINDING

A few years ago it seemed that the explanation of animal navigation would soon be found. The light-compass sense had been shown to be standard orientation equipment for a great many kinds of animals. There were snowballing volumes of data on initial headings taken by caged birds anxious to be off on homing flights or on seasonal migration. Various theories as to how the sun might be used in position finding were being discussed in the journals. After their experiments revealed that warblers have a star-compass sense, E. G. Franz and Elinor Sauer went on to show that warblers ready to migrate, when shown the starry sky of a planetarium, were able to take migratory headings that would be appropriate for the localities represented by different arrangements of stars and constellations. This indicated that birds not only see stars but get from them information necessary for bico-ordinate guidance; that is, for determining their position and taking correct headings after being forced off course.

During a period of seven or eight years of the 1950s, interest in these problems held steady, and a considerable number of able students, mostly European, seemed just on the verge of providing a solid celestial navigation theory that would eventually explain how animals find islands. Recently, however, the field has lost momentum. Few younger biologists seem to be taking up such studies. It is hard to see exactly what has happened, but there is no doubt that research in animal navigation is languishing. This is a great shame, because the navigatory adaptations of long-distance, overwater migrants are among the most spectacular of all the products of natural selection.

THE TALENTS OF LITTLE SALMON

Some seemingly complex feats of migratory guidance can probably be explained on a basis of sun-compass sense alone, or of that
in combination with landmark piloting. One astonishing piece of
recent orientation research was that of the Dutch zoologist C. Groot,
who investigated the direction sense of young Pacific salmon in
British Columbia. A very keen compass sense has been found in
Pacific salmon. Dr. Groot recently published the results of his studies
of the movements of salmon yearlings, called smolts, in going across
a lake from the shores where they hatch to the outlet stream down
which they go to begin their long developmental migration in the
Pacific Ocean. All around the shores of the lake Dr. Groot found that
the smolts began moving toward the outlet at about the same time.
Their trip was an accurately oriented movement that followed the
most direct route to the mouth of the outlet stream, and in holding
the heading the schools of the little fish were neither hindered nor
helped by currents in the lake.

Samples from different migratory schools were taken to the laboratory and tested in orientation tanks in which only blank circular
walls, and the sky above, were visible. The young salmon were
found to fall into three groups, with respect to direction preference.
In each case the direction chosen was that appropriate for reaching
the outlet from the place at which the smolts had been taken.
Since the salmon were fresh out of the nest and had never been
anywhere at all, it was clear that the ability to choose the right
way to the outlet was an inherited virtue of the strain of salmon
involved, and that the ability to use the sun as a compass for finding that direction was also inherited.

In similar tank experiments with smolts from another lake, Groot
found that as time passed the fish changed their minds about the
direction they thought they ought to go in. This lake was a long,
narrow, crooked one. Groot was able to show that the changes in
chosen direction corresponded to changes made necessary by the
configuration of the crooked lake, and that the shifts in direction

came at times that might be right for the places where migrating smolts might be in the lake at the time the changes occurred.

That seems to me a very fancy capacity that the smolts had in-herited. Their direction sense turned out to be even more versatile. Dr. Groot's experiments convinced him that the migration of the smolts from the nursery area to the outlet could be guided by more than one system. On clear days they were able to use the sun and perhaps also the pattern of polarized light in the sky. Guiding by polarization is in a way just a form of sun-compass orientation. The distribution of differently polarized patches of light in the sky indicates where the sun is at the time. Polarization patterns would probably be especially important to the smolts, because Groot says that most of their migratory travel is done around dusk, when the sun cannot be seen, and the patterns are the most strongly marked.

Groot found no evidence of bico-ordinate navigation, and actually smolts have no need for this. He did, however, find a mysterious ability in the smolts to assume a constant preferred direction, inside the blank circular tank, even when the top was covered with an opaque sheet. This unsettling skill he called X-orientation. What it was is an exciting mystery. Dr. Groot was pretty self-possessed about it, but I am not. In other experiments like Dr. Groot's, people have been tricked by the fish finding tiny imperfections in sup-posedly perfectly blank walls of the test chamber. Having nothing else to do in their featureless environment, the fish just stare fixedly at the imperfection in the wall as a man in solitary might stare at a crack. This might seem like a preferred direction tendency. But Dr. Groot surely knew about such pitfalls and avoided them. If so, then the fish being able to align themselves in the particular direction—not just in any direction but in that appropriate for the migration they ought to have been carrying out—must have been some kind of inertial sense. Dr. Groot saw this clearly, and his com-ments about it were as follows:

> Orientations in the expected direction during high cloud cover conditions, especially during the dusk period, and some results of the sheet-tests, suggested that sockeye smolts have a non-celestial

compass orientation (type X-orientation). Experiments performed under completely enclosed conditions, using diffused light, showed that smolts do not need a view of the sky to orient in directions appropriate to the migration route. This may, however, not mean that an unknown set of reference cues is used by the smolts for orientation under these enclosed conditions. It is possible that all the twists and turns made during transportation to the enclosed experimental tank are memorized (inertial-guidance orientation) and thus can still result in preferences in directions related to the migration route. The original directions could have been acquired previously in relation to celestial phenomena.

Experiments using deep general anesthesia during transportation to the test setup, however, revealed no differences in orientation as compared with untreated controls or with those tests in which a view of the sky was available. The possibility that angular accelerations can still be perceived in their proper relation to an original direction during general anesthesia seems remote; nevertheless, other techniques of interfering with the perception of the vestibular apparatus will have to be performed before the possibility of an inertial-guidance orientation can be definitely excluded.

Those experiments show how hard it is to be sure what it is that is being tested. I hope Dr. Groot gets on with his research as fast as he can.

THE SEARCH FOR AN ISLAND-FINDING THEORY

In a field as unexplored, and for the time as unexplorable, as the open-sea orientation of animals is, one has to scratch together every bit of available circumstantial evidence. While this is going on it seems helpful to make two fundamental initial assumptions. First, long-range open-ocean guidance should be assumed to be a composite process, one in which the animal takes advantage of every kind of existing signpost that his senses can detect. This keeps you from getting too doggedly single-tracked in the pursuit of one of the several possible explanations of the phenomenon. After that is understood, I think it may be useful to clear the field by grouping together all known island-finding animals, and saying that it is the phenomenon of island finding that both needs explanation most badly, and is the most elusive to study. The people working on the problem may work with albatrosses or seals or something else, and these animals may have private ways of navigating that are not shared by others. Still, I believe that, as diffuse as the campaign to understand animal navigation is, it will be a good idea to keep insisting that the thing to find out is what the *island-finding* process is.

Of the island-finding animals some travel under water, some at the surface, and some in the air. These probably take advantage of different landmarks to piece out their guidance, simply because different landmarks are available in their particular sections of the environment. A high-flying bird can see a mountain perhaps ten or twenty times as far as a turtle can, for example; a tuna may not be able to see it at all. The turtle and the tuna, however, if they have the olfactory mechanism for it, might follow the shearline at the edge of a patch of dissolved material, or of current-carried particles in the water. There are no stable gradients or shearlines for birds to follow in the air, because the winds quickly disrupt or reverse them. So there are bound to be differences in the ways each different navigating animal navigates, just as each is bound to do different kinds of navigating at different stages of his journey. But in the longest island-finding journeys of high-seas migrants, great stretches of the travel goes across abyssal ocean devoid of any known landmark either in the water or outside of it. It is in these central sections of the island-finding journeys that it may pay to assume that birds and turtles use a common navigation system. It is hard enough to figure what that system could be. It may be even harder if the theorist doggedly excludes possibly helpful clues from observations of species other than the one he is specially concerned with.

SAILORS, TERNS, AND TURTLES

Let me suppose that I have been able to locate and enlist the help of a sailor, a sooty tern, and a gravid green turtle, all three

with a burning urge to get out to *Isla Meta*. *Meta* is, as I said at
the start, a tiny oceanic island that sits all by itself in a lonely sea.
From the place where I found the sailor, the turtle, and the tern, the
island lay out to the east. Why the three wanted to get there is not
important. Anyway, I thought them up, and I can think up for them
any whim I choose.

Well, I took the three of them, and put them in a box or in a
sort of capsule, say, and loaded the capsule aboard an airplane,
and flew it through an irregular course of zigs and zags to some
place far out in a strange part of the ocean.

When they were put aboard, the bird and the turtle took along
only the anatomy and ways of thinking they inherited from their
parents and race. They had no traveling bags. The sailor on the
other hand did have a little bag and in it there was a compass, a
good clock, a sextant, *The Nautical Almanac, The American Practical Navigator*, and a set of charts of the seas of the earth. He also
had a parallel rule, a pair of dividers, and a lot of pencils. He had
plenty of food and water, too, and a small rubber boat. The bird
and turtle had none of these, only what inheritance and experience
had stowed away within them.

The capsule was put down and the hatch opened. The bird flew
out and began to circle. The sailor helped the turtle over the rim
of the hatch, and it splashed happily into the sea. The man put out
his boat, inflated it, and got in, taking along the victuals and bag
of instruments.

Now you have got to keep in mind that none of these three creatures had any idea where he was; and I am telling you that, in
spite of their strange experience, each retained his strong urge to
get to *Isla Meta*. Each of the three started out knowing in what
direction the island lay. It was due east, as I said. The sailor knew
that from his chart; the animals in a way didn't really *know* it, but
they would have been guided to go due east by appropriate east-
pushing reactions that they inherited from their *Meta*-finding ancestors. So in a way, all three knew the direction to the island from
the place at which their blind trip in the capsule started.

When the three left the capsule, each started off east, happy to

be out in the open, anxious to get to the island. The man was the
first to stop. He shipped his paddle and thought a moment, and
suddenly realized he really hadn't the foggiest idea where he was
—how far away he was from where he had started, or in what direction. So east, he figured, might no longer be the right course to
Meta at all. Probably wasn't. Maybe one hell of a long way off, he
thought; and he was right.

The sailor sighed. He hated to do navigation. He wasn't even
sure he could make a sighting without falling out of his little round
boat, bobbing about on the big waves the way it was. But he got
out his things anyway, and started to navigate. His first problem,
of course, was to find out where he was, to calculate his position,
as one says nautically. There are various ways to go about this, but
they all depend on the principle that heavenly bodies have predictably shifting positions over particular spots on earth. So if you
know what season it is and what time of day or night, and have
a way of measuring angles, especially the angle the stars or sun
make with the horizon, you can figure what point on earth it is at
which the heavenly body seems to have that place in the skies. You
can figure this because somebody has done a great deal of spherical
trigonometry and has made tables that relate spots on earth with
the regularly changing positions of objects on the celestial sphere
—that is, in the sky.

The sailor got out his clock and sextant. He found a star he knew,
and by skillful balancing managed to measure the angle of the star
above the horizon. After the altitude had been corrected for the
refraction of the atmosphere and for the height of the sextant above
the water, he looked at the clock and wrote down the exact Greenwich time. The altitude of the star, expressed in minutes of arc,
gave him what is known as the co-altitude. It told him the number
of nautical miles to the place where the star was directly overhead.
Then by looking in the *Nautical Almanac* and *American Practical
Navigator,* and by filling a big sheet full of calculations, the sailor
figured the latitude and longitude of the place on earth over there
underneath the star. He put that point on his chart and inscribed a
circle around it, using the co-altitude as the radius. He then knew

that he was somewhere on that circle. To find out just where he was on the circle, he had to go through the same process again, using another star, or using the same star a little later on. His position then was the point where the circles crossed, or the most reasonable looking of the two places at which they cross.

That process required quite a lot of calculations. It would have been better if the sailor had taken along *Hydrographic Office Publication No. 214*, a many-volume set of tables that give computed altitude and azimuth, within ten-degree strips, all around the earth. If you use these tables there is less arithmetic to do. But the sailor wasn't able to take *Publication No. 214* with him in the rubber boat; it was too heavy.

The bird and the turtle didn't have it either. In fact, they didn't have the *Practical Navigator*, or even the *Nautical Almanac*. There was no shortcut for them. All the astronomic data had to be hoarded away in their heads, and all the mathematics had to be worked out there. The spherical trigonometry those animals had to do would have filled a great many big sheets of paper. They didn't even have any paper, however. Everything had to be done inside them. They did it though. They must have, because they eventually got to *Meta* too. They reached the island, in fact, a long time before the sailor did.

But to get back to the sailor's navigation, when he found the point where the circles crossed and knew where he was, he laid his ruler on the chart with an edge running from his calculated position out to *Isla Meta*. He walked the parallel rule across to the compass rose, and read the heading he had to take. Then he picked up the aluminum paddle and began to paddle the boat away toward the island.

In evaluating any of the theories of animal navigation there are two questions that at once come to mind: is the necessary information available? and: can the animal possibly have the genetic and sensory equipment necessary to use the information to find his position and correct his course after being displaced? That animals have a light-compass sense has, as I have said, been solidly proved. It follows that they must have a clock sense, too, because the two are inseparable. To get direction from a moving celestial body, its movements have to be compensated for time. So when you say an animal can take direction from the sun or stars you are saying also that the animal has an internal clock.

The clocks of animals are physiological rhythms. The exact nature of the timing mechanisms involved is not understood, but a number of things are known about them. One of these is that some of the clocks—those that are tuned to the cycle of the solar day—can be reset, if the animal is exposed to an artificial cycle of light and dark out of phase with the natural cycle of the region the animal lives in. If you expose an animal to such a change and reset his internal clock, his compass orientation ought to make him orient in predictable ways. It does. After a few days under the new light-dark cycle the animal gets in phase with it, and uses the new cycle in making his compensations for the sun's position. Experiments of this kind have been done with birds, reptiles, fishes, crustaceans and spiders, and with various kinds of insects. In each case the animal has taken the predicted orientation when its light-dark cycle was manipulated in the laboratory.

It used to be thought that these internal clocks were a sort of hourglass mechanism that was set in motion by some event like sunrise or sunset and then took a predictable time to run down. That this cannot be the way they work is shown by orientation experiments with animals kept under constant environmental conditions. Under conditions of unchanging light and temperature the daily rhythms may continue to run on their original cycles. With all outside time-cues excluded, the free-running clock may vary slightly from the frequency of the rotation of the earth, and if the animal is kept confined long enough the period may slowly shift away from its original frequency. This can be shown by the gradual shifts of direction they make in orienting by the sun.

Demonstration of the sun-compass sense furnished one explanation of direction finding by animals that migrate during the daytime; but many birds, and probably other animals too, migrate by night. The experiments of the Sauers showed that warblers were able to find direction from the stars of the night sky. There is some evidence that the moon can also be used as a compass, although it has not yet been shown whether in this case the timing is done by another clock attuned to the lunar cycle, or by some application of the solar time-rhythm.

All in all there seems no reason to doubt that both biological clocks and a light-compass sense are widely distributed among animals. This might seem to open the gates for acceptance of a theory of bico-ordinate navigation by animals. But this does not necessarily follow. Finding your position is a far more complicated operation than just finding which way north is. To get to *Isla Meta* by celestial guide signs the bird and the green turtle had to go through the process the sailor went through, or one very like it. They had to measure and compare angles made by the sun and stars with the horizon and, having no sextant, they had to do it with the naked eye.

That is the first place where a legitimate doubt of the celestial navigation theory may appear. Can the eye of a vertebrate animal—bird, turtle, fish, or seal—measure angles with the necessary accuracy? To say a bird might, but the turtle probably could not, may possibly turn out to be true; but it leaves the aquatic animals out of our general theory of open-sea navigation. For the time being it seems to me that the most promising way to reason is to assume that the finders of islands share an open-sea navigation mechanism. So the question remains: are eyes good enough to be used as sextants? There is some evidence that in the case of birds they may be. The tests were not made on the wing, however, and whether that would help, or would make accurate measuring of angles wholly impossible, I can't say. In any case it is impossible for me to visualize the process being carried out by a turtle, whose horizon bobs about incessantly in front of wet eyes in air an inch or two above the surface of the crest or trough or sloping side of a wave.

Nevertheless, to keep working toward the general theory let's say that all the animals can somehow measure altitude: the man in the little tub of a rubber boat, the turtle a little boat of his own, and the bird in the air above. But measuring a single altitude is probably not enough. To get a line of position the animal will need to measure, to remember, and to compare at least two altitudes. In the daytime the two altitudes will, of course, be those of the sun, because that is the only body in the sky. Since not much information can be got from the height of the morning or afternoon sun alone, what has to be done is to take two sightings and extend the arc they make so as to see what the noon altitude of the sun would be. The main trouble here is that, out in the ocean, the sun could not possibly seem to an animal to describe any arc at all, but only to bob up and down. There would be no reference point from which to gauge its sideways movement. So that way of using the noon position of the sun seems out of the question. And as for the possibility that the animal waits until high noon to measure the altitude of the sun, that is hard to believe too. I doubt that a bird or a turtle could tell when the sun had reached its noon position. It is difficult enough for a sailor to do it. Some information can be got from the sun at rising and setting time, but it is not known that a cruising animal could tell a rising sun from a setting sun. A great deal of experimental work is needed to reveal what animals may be able to see in the sky. One fundamental flaw in the whole celestial theory of animal navigation is the lack of experimental data on the ability of animals to see celestial bodies, and to measure and compare angles they make.

The night sky is much more filled with information than the day sky is; although, as I say, how much of it can be seen by any animal is not known. At night, compass direction of varying degrees of accuracy can be found from many marks instead of from only one, and some stars tell you direction without using a clock. Besides the angles they make on the azimuth circle and with the horizon, stars and planets spread in clusters that change in shape, and wheel and sweep about the sky in ways that are wholly foretellable, if you only have your almanac along. It is therefore going to be necessary to do a lot more work just testing what the gifted animal navigators are really able to see, what intensities and colors of light, what faintnesses of stars and palenesses of planets. How accurately are they able to measure celestial angles, how well do they remember angles for later comparison with other angles? It has been said that birds may even see stars by day. This is probably not so, but if

it were, it would markedly change the kinds of inquiries to be made
to explain their navigation. The kinds of work the Sauers began in
the Bremen planetarium ought to be done exhaustively, beginning
where the Sauers left off with warblers and going on to test all the
important migrants—especially the island finders—the animals that
cruise the open sea.

Another celestial position-finding requisite is a clock that accurately holds on to home time. The time the sailor carries is probably
Greenwich time. To the bird and to the turtle, Greenwich means
little. The time they carry is probably that of the region they started
from. The clock that carries this inflexible time cannot be the clock
used in the compass sense. The compass-sense clock has to keep
getting reset, to be useful in the various regions it is to be used in.
The navigation clock has got to stick religiously to home time. The
reason for this is that to find position, you need longitude. Longitude
can only be found by knowing the time back home at Greenwich
or Recife or wherever you started your journey. The only way to tell
how far east or west you have gone is to note the difference in the
time where you are, and the time back where you started. If your
clock has got itself reset to the time of the place you're lost in, it
will serve as a compass clock all right, but it is no good as a longitude
clock. For finding longitude a traveler needs a stubbornly inflexible
clock that brings along the time he started with. So for bico-ordinate
navigation an animal apparently has got to have two clocks.

I suppose that is no obstacle. Animals probably have a great many
more clocks than that.

Another of the many questions to be asked before embracing the
celestial-navigation theory is whether biological clocks are really
accurate enough to be used as chronometers in the navigation that
animals are known to do. The most accurate biological clock so far
found experimentally was one that times the onset of activity in
flying squirrels. It deviated by only two minutes after periods of
about ten days. Navigating with a clock like that, a flying squirrel,
after being blown about in a storm for ten days, could recalculate
his longitude to within thirty minutes of arc. At the equator this
would be thirty nautical miles; at latitude forty-five degrees it would

be twenty-one nautical miles. Anywhere it would be pretty good; and there may be still better clocks. There almost surely are.

A chronometer, a sextant, and a compass were the tools the sailor used to locate himself and *Isla Meta*. The turtle and the bird had to do the same thing using only eyes and the reliably oscillating events in their innards to tell time with. What the biologist has to do is make up his mind whether he believes that an eye and internal rhythms are really accurate and flexible enough to take the place of the sailor's instruments.

Other equipment the sailor used, you recall, was his almanac and tables. It is in looking for the natural equivalent of these that most people get restless over the celestial theory of animal navigation. It is necessary to assume that all the star-map and earth-map sense that it has taken man so long to accumulate is stored up in the nervous systems of the navigating animals. It is held there in the shape of tendencies to respond in appropriate ways to positions or arrangements of celestial bodies or to the angles they make with the horizon at specific times. From any point on earth, to get to some other point on earth you only have to look at celestial bodies, know what they are, know what angles they make with the horizon and perhaps also with north or with each other; and then, being also aware what season it is and what exact time, just start moving. If you know all that you will move off the right way. Call that finding latitude and longitude if you want to. In a way it is, but in a way it is very different. The most important difference between the celestial navigation of the sailor and that of the turtle and the tern is not in their instruments. It is in their state of mind.

The mariner is guiding himself toward a place he needs or longs to be in. The tern and the turtle are not doing that. They are just reacting to stimuli. They simply behave appropriately on signal. The signals come from the clocks inside them and from the sun and stars outside. Animals never get out a chart and draw a line from their own position to their goal, as a sailor does. They only move away and follow signals. If they do this vastly complicated thing it is because it is bred into them to do it, because racial trial-and-error through ages of time made it reproductively profitable to follow signals that were correct for a given season, time and place. Doing so let an ancestor leave a heavier stamp on the race; not doing so weeded out erroneous ancestors.

That is the real marvel of the thing—if it really exists—the inherited familiarity with the dynamics of the celestial sphere and the relation of points in the heavens with points on earth. Actually there is frustratingly little known about the character and extent of this inherent map of the earth and the sky that some animals seem to have. Is the whole Pacific a grid in the genes and brain of the golden plover, do you think? Are the skies of the whole earth mapped by season and time of day in the mind of the arctic tern? That is what the celestial-navigation theory suggests, and what students have not even begun to explain.

THE NEED FOR HOMING AND TRACKING TESTS

Although much careful experimentation to test the visual skill and acuity of animal navigators is needed, the problem will never be solved until a lot more field work is done. Two general kinds of field experiments are needed: homing tests and tracking. The two can be combined with great profit, once the tracking techniques have been worked out; but meanwhile they ought to be undertaken separately.

Homing is the name given the ability of some animals to go back to familiar territory after being carried away from it. Homing is bound to involve navigation, because it requires two very exacting operations: determining position, and finding the course to a distant destination. If a Florida cat is put into a box, taken to Oregon, and let go there, and then walks straight back to Florida the cat will have navigated, most interestingly. She should be made to do it over and over again. There are many stories of cats doing such things, and of dogs, horses, and a lot of other domestic animals that did them too. Some of the tales are obviously false; others seem puzzlingly plausible. All are pretty inadequate as scientific evidence; and even if true, they only suggest the existence of a homing ability—they do little or nothing to help explain it. To explain homing, the feats of the animals must not be heard from one's grandparents. They have got to be carefully arranged. Accurately designed homing tests could take us a long way toward clearing up mysteries of animal navigation. The dearth of such tests is a curious thing and a serious obstacle.

The most needed homing experiments are island-finding tests. Conditions are under best control in island finding, because fewer possible alternative kinds of guidance are available to the traveler. The species of island-finding birds include most of the best known navigators, and these would logically be expected to be also the most expert homers. The known island finders include a number of kinds of birds—various oceanic terns, the albatrosses, the golden plover, the penguins—seals, and the green turtle. There probably are many other kinds of migratory animals that navigate as well as the island finders, and that could find islands if they racially wanted to. But part of being a good subject for a homing experiment is being motivated in a way that lets you produce clean-cut and unambiguous results.

The main disadvantage of homing tests is that, no matter how massive they are or how cleverly the sites of release are arranged, the only contact with the experimental animal—the tern let go a thousand miles from its home island, say—is at the points of release and recovery. Anything else you must get by deduction. Point-to-point homing data may fortify one's faith in the reality of the homing capacity, and may tell a little about speeds of travel, but they never reveal much about the detailed route taken by the traveling animal. It is unreasonable to hope to understand a complex and probably composite process like long-distance navigation without knowing the route that the navigator follows.

I have spent a great deal of time the last five years trying to figure out ways to keep accurate track of the courses and schedules of traveling green turtles. Brazilian green turtles, for instance, ought to be tracked all the way out to Ascension Island. If this could be done a number of questions could automatically be answered. It would be learned, for instance, whether the course of the Ascension migration, as seems most likely goes directly from Brazil to the island, and thus against the Equatorial Current. By stretching one's imagination, two other routes by which Ascension could be reached by a passive, partly unguided sort of travel can be conjured up. One of these is via the Gulf Stream. By swimming a short distance northward, Pernambuco turtles could get into the part of the global Gulf Stream swirl that heads northeastward. Part of this sweeps through the Caribbean, and part stays outside along the fringes of the West Indian islands. Then the two branches rejoin and the stream turns eastward into the northern Atlantic, swings down to the African coast, and opposite the bulge, heads out toward Ascension as the North Equatorial Current. The other way to get to Ascension from Brazil would require of the traveler even less initiative, but would present more problems. This would be to swim offshore a few miles and catch the south-trending current there. When the Equatorial Current strikes the coast of Brazil and the part I just spoke of goes northward, another part is shunted southward as the Brazil Current. A turtle that got into this might be carried across with the West Wind Drift to South Africa, and there be dumped into the Benguela Current, which flows northward along the African coast. Just south of the equator this turns westward as part of the Equatorial Current which, as we saw, goes on out past Ascension and back to South America. But this latter route, besides being terribly long and hungry like the Gulf Stream way, would carry tropical turtles into the dismal Antarctic cold of the West Wind Drift, where the water ranges between five and fifteen degrees Centigrade. This would be very rough on a green turtle. This route seems the least likely of all. All three routes are at least possible, however, and the possibility distracts theorizing about possible navigation techniques. Well-designed homing tests might clear up the uncertainty. Successful tracking would quickly clear it up.

In doing homing experiments the advantage lies with the bird men, and it is a mystery why they have not done more of them. Birds nest on islands in tremendous numbers. Being small, they can be caught, banded, hauled away to distant places, and released there in groups big enough to give the recovery data statistical stature. Why bird men don't carry more tagged birds around the world is beyond me to understand.

In tracking tests, the advantage would seem to be with the turtle man. A full-grown green turtle is as big as a tabletop. She swims at sedate speeds near the surface, and sticks her head out every now and then to breathe. When her head comes out the top of her shell is usually exposed too, or at least awash. Her shell is made of bone and hornlike stuff. Its edges are practically lifeless and can be perforated for bolt attachments with no pain to the turtle and no loss of blood. I cite these virtues to contrast the green turtle with a plover, say, which flies like the wind and would despair if any object were hung about her neck. Or with a whale, who resents perforations and dives or jumps out of harnesses and halters. So the green turtle seemed an almost ideal subject for tracking tests, and several years ago I happily set out trying to track them.

A turtle will tow a float without complaint. If the float is on a twenty-foot line fastened with a swivel to a hole in the back margin of the turtle's shell, it runs easily along the surface without being dragged under and seems not to irk or sadden the turtle at all. If the float is painted a good, blaring orange you can see it a long way off when it rises on the crests of the waves. You can see it farther than the turtle's head can be seen; and, moreover, the float stays on the surface all the time, without constantly disappearing between breaths, as the head of the turtle does. You can track a turtle, therefore, simply by tying a float to the hind overhang of her shell.

Because the earth is a spheroid, however, the float quickly moves out behind the curve of the sea. For a while it is in your line of sight only on the wave crests and after that, not at all. The distance the float can be seen varies with conditions, of course, but reliable track of it can never be kept from more than a mile away. In other words, using a towed float, the tracker has to follow the turtle from a distance of a mile or less. From that distance a green turtle can probably see the tracker. This gives you the uneasy feeling that the turtle is running from the boat and not orienting normally. She might be guiding herself somehow, but her motivation to be off to some special place might be interfered with. The results of the test would thus be hard to interpret, if there were any results at all. If you tie a big air-filled balloon to the turtle by a twenty-foot line, the balloon skitters along on the surface with almost no drag and is visible from much farther away than the chunks of styrofoam we use as floats. Using a balloon as a float might be expected to introduce some psychological hazards for the turtle. The balloon looks very big and unnatural, and no matter which way the turtle turns, it is always back there, round, red, and inescapable. A tin can tied to the tail of a dog sends him tearing about the neighborhood in a panic, thinking of nothing but outrunning the can.

But turtles can stand quite a lot of such interference without evident concern. At Tortuguero, as I said earlier, females have come ashore to nest dragging big chunks of wood tied to their front flippers. Even with such a cumbersome, off-center load in tow the nesting drive is not dimmed. That a light float on a long line, tied centrally behind, would interfere with the urge to migrate or with orientation ability seems unlikely. One season at Tortuguero we tied floats to a lot of turtles to see what directions they took in leaving the nesting ground. All that could be learned that way was the initial heading, the course of the first mile or so. It quickly became evident that the tracking radius was less than a mile, and that this was not going to be enough for tracking in the open sea. Even if it could be assumed that the sight of the tracker so near was no distraction to the turtle, to keep a float in view from a following boat was difficult, and contact could not be counted on for more than a few hours at a time, even in the best weather. Short-run tracking is useful only if done with great precision. The plot of the course of the turtle can only be as accurate as that of the tracking boat. Boats I have been on rarely know their own position within limits that would give any significance to short-distance tracking plots. A boat might take bearings on landmarks on shore, but if it could do that, the turtle might too. So tracking with towed floats proved to be not very useful.

As they apply to problems of animal navigation, tracking tests can try to answer three separate questions. The simplest of these is merely whether a turtle is able to keep a constant heading in the open sea, with no landmarks in view. To answer this you only need to observe the travel of the turtle long enough and accurately enough to be able to furnish a statistician with the data he needs to figure whether the turtle is orienting or is swimming at random. It is not easy to decide how long a turtle could continue to swim in a straight line simply because she is a bilaterally symmetrical animal that paddles equally hard with both her big front swimming flippers. But the question can be answered, and if the answer turns out to be that the animal is guiding herself, then you immediately know that her orientation is of some very fancy kind, and you can begin to test the various theories of open-sea orientation by studying conditions along the course the animal took, and looking for possible guideposts there.

The next question to be asked is whether the direction of open-sea travel is a consistent direction preference—a course that is clung to when the turtle is released repeatedly in different places or when several turtles of the same population and stage of development are tracked.

Then finally it should be asked whether the constant direction, held to without landmarks, seems to show any relation to a goal, to a locality that the experimenter thinks might be an appropriate one for the turtle to go to. To get a reliable answer to this requires a number of trials. Direction holding can be shown by tracking one subject, but "goal" sense, that is, *appropriate* direction holding, requires a number of different subjects. The problem in this case is to determine whether the headings are just individual foibles, or are a racial tendency that corresponds statistically with the proper heading to reach the assumed destination. There is an obvious pitfall in these experiments. It is the possibility of assuming that the tracked animal is going to a place it is not really heading for at all. The first problem is to get a subject that is motivated to travel. The next problem is to know where the subject "thinks" he is heading.

The uncertainties are illustrated by the results of some trials we made with six big loggerhead turtles that we tracked for a few hours in the Gulf of Mexico off Cedar Key, Florida. The tests were made several years ago, but they are still the only accurate plots we have of the movements of turtles traveling without fixed landmarks

in sight. One trouble with those trials was that they were too few
and too short. The other was the difficulty of deciding where, if
anywhere, the turtles figured they were going.

The loggerheads used in the tests were caught, just as they
came out to nest, at Fort Pierce on the east coast of Florida, and
then were hauled across the peninsula to Cedar Key. It was clear
from the start that it would not be easy to interpret the performance
of the subjects, simply because we had no way of knowing what they
would conceive their positions to be when they were released. How
would a female turtle, interrupted in her nesting emergence on the
east coast of Florida and hauled belly-up in a covered truck at night
to the other side of the peninsula, interpret the homing problem
that faced her? Would she look around and see water everywhere
and just figure she was out at sea somewhere—anywhere—and head
for the nearest shore? If so, how would she detect the direction of
the nearest shore, which was out of sight? Or, reacting in a different
way to the same assumption, would she head due west, which would
be the way to go if she had indeed been displaced seaward from
her nesting place on the Atlantic shore? Or, assuming that she somehow knew her position but had no built-in sense of the details of
earth geography, would she head for home by the airline route—in
this case straight across the peninsula of Florida? Or, could the turtle possibly be expected to show that most advanced of all orientation capacities: map sense—combined with position sense—and
either head south to circumnavigate the peninsula without seeing
it, or move in and follow the shoreline around to her home on the
opposite coast. Obviously there is no knowing any of this in advance, nor any sure way of reasoning from short sample segments
of the courses plotted. Uncertainties such as these are bound to
complicate most heading tests with aquatic animals in shore waters.

These turtles were rigged with weather balloons filled with helium. Each turtle towed a float tied to the back-edge of her shell,
and the balloon was anchored to the float on a twenty-five-foot line.
So long as the balloon stayed at the full height of its line it was
visible for several miles, and with a telescope on an elevated station
it could be made out at least eight miles away. The tracking was

done with transits located on two channel-markers and the positions of the turtles were determined at two-minute intervals. The plots were very accurate.

Six turtles were tracked. Of these, four wandered or foraged for crabs. Two, however, made off due south on what seemed obviously well-oriented courses. Throughout the experiment the turtles remained well out of sight of the mainland, and from their depressed angle of observation no fixed landmarks were visible to them after the first short period of their travel. A contour chart of the area shows no way in which depth might have been used for guidance reference. The routes taken cut across a mosaic of water types and through tidal currents that varied in direction and strength along the way. The detailed similarity of the courses of the two turtles is striking. There were long periods when they could not possibly have seen each other. They remained in sight of each other's balloons, but this cannot have been a bond between them. One conceivable landmark was a rank of cumulus clouds over the hinterland, fifteen or twenty miles away. That a navigating animal should fail to use such a guidepost appears unlikely. I doubt, however, that the clouds could have kept the turtles on the precisely co-ordinated southerly headings that they held to. The same thing can be said of any possible form of sun navigation.

The results of these trials proved little. They did show the usefulness of balloons for short-range tracking with optical instruments, however, and they made me even more anxious to find a way to maintain contact with traveling turtles through long distances in the open sea.

Radio tracking seemed the only way. A big green turtle would think nothing of carrying a little transmitter on her back, and, with the advent of transistors, little transmitters were becoming available. In fact, the Office of Naval Research already had some that seemed just right for tracking turtles. They were all properly miniaturized and encased to withstand the pressure of deep water. They had been made for my friend Bill Schevill, who was trying to use them for tracking whales. Whales move a lot faster than turtles, though, and they resent holes being put in them. They have brains, too, far more than turtles have.

Even with the solid support of the Office of Naval Research, Woods Hole Oceanographic Institution, and the American Electronics Laboratory behind him, Bill was not tracking any whales. I won't try to tell the things the whales did to keep from being tracked—Bill ought to write about that. But I will say he had never tracked one, the last I heard, and that I have never tracked a turtle by radio, either.

I don't believe Bill Schevill will ever get anywhere in his tracking project until he gives up force and trickery and enlists the cooperation of the whales. The way cetaceans learn things, it ought to be no trouble explaining to them the aims of the experiment and awakening their intellectual curiosity. They are evidently as amenable as they are bright, and once their interest got aroused they would probably collaborate as ably as astronauts do in a satellite flight. It might even turn out that all Bill's questions could be answered by interviews with whales.

Anyway, I inherited Bill's transmitters, and the receivers and Yagi directional antennas to go with them, and started trying to track turtles. The simplest thing to do seemed to be just to set a transmitter on a rubber cushion on a turtle's back, and fasten it firmly down with wires running out to four holes in the thick, horny, overhang of the shell. A turtle so equipped probably doesn't even know she is carrying anything extraneous at all. Each time she rises to blow, the whip antenna comes out of the water, and for whatever time it stays out a signal is sent. If you manage to hear the brief signal, you start madly scanning with your Yagi antenna in an effort to locate it. The Yagi is a vast array of mast, rods, and wires that looks like a television antenna. You start sweeping this back and forth toward where you think the turtle is, and there is time for perhaps one swing and then the signal disappears, because the turtle submerges—if not for some more esoteric electronic reason.

Our first efforts to maintain radio contact with a turtle in the water failed completely. So did all later efforts. Attributing the fault to my own ignorance, I decided to make a sounder, simpler beginning. We got some boats, boards, and students, carried them out to various bodies of water, and tried to track the boards. We fastened radios to the boards, set them afloat, then tried to find them with the antennas. That way the transmitter stayed out in the air all the time and emitted a continuous signal. This removed the distraction of the turtles carrying the signal down under the water; but still, the results were disappointing. We could never pick up the signal more than three miles away, and its direction could not be judged in more than a uselessly general sort of way.

Various things were wrong, authorities told me. One was the polarization that radio waves undergo over water. The other was the curvature of the earth. The polarization might be circumvented somehow, but nothing could be done about the curvature of the earth. You simply had to rise above it. With the wave lengths we were allowed to use, transmission is restricted to the line-of-sight. The signal won't go anywhere beyond the horizon. For tracking anything on the near-side of the horizon, there is of course no point in using radio unless you simply want to appear technically advanced. A far more accurate bearing can be taken with an alidade or a transit than with any directional antenna.

To get more range we tried putting the little radios on balloons. For a time the only balloons we could find were spherical weather balloons, made of rubber. Helium leaks out of rubber; and what is worse, being round the balloons blow down onto the water in any slight wind. Finally, however, we found some magnificent little blimp-shaped balloons that stayed aloft in a pretty strong breeze. They were made of plastic, or of a rubber encased in plastic. They lift a pound, easily stay up in winds up to eighteen knots, and are a great blessing. They cost too much, but they are worth it. With the new balloons we could raise the little radios above the curvature of the earth, or at least above part of it. By tying the radio to the balloon and mooring the balloon to a float towed by the turtle to be tracked, it was easy to get fifty or sixty feet of elevation for the transmitter, even when the trade wind was blowing.

The balloons are four feet long and bright yellow. They can be seen at sea a long way off, up to nine or ten miles on a good day.

You can see them, in fact, just about as far as you can hear the signal the radios transmit. And as I said, sight bearings are far more accurate than the bearing that any directional antenna will provide.

That is about where the radio tracking of sea turtles stands. The best thing that has come out of it so far was finding the balloons to increase range for tracking visually. Besides its application to the problem of sampling short sections of long-distance journeys, balloon tracking will be useful as a way to find out what sea turtles do during the month or more they stay at the nesting beach, on their biennial or triennial visits there.

Down at Turtle Bogue, *Cerro Tortuguero* rises five hundred feet high just north of the Green Turtle Station. From the summit of the *cerro* there is an open view of a great sweep of the coast and ocean. On the beach in front of our old camp house three miles south of the mountain we have built a forty-foot tower. By putting one man with a transit on the tower and another on Turtle Mountain, very accurate plots can be made of the movements of marked turtles along the shore. By spacing the tests carefully—arranging some before nesting has been completed, and some afterward, some at the beginning of the season and some at the end—much can be learned about the habits and local travel of green turtles during their stay at the nesting ground. By installing a little light on the balloon so that contact can be kept at night as well as by day, it will be possible to learn what a female turtle does during the twelve-day interval between the times she comes out on the beach to lay her eggs. Tracking during October may also yield good data on the initial headings of turtles that have finished their series of nestings and are leaving on their homeward migration.

But that is getting nowhere with the procedure and equipment that will be required if island-finding navigation is ever to be understood. For that, animals have got to be followed all the way to their island, or for a good part of the journey. Such a tracking operation cannot be carried out by simply staying in sight of any balloons. It will almost surely have to be done by radio. And since it seems next to impossible to arrange a system by which two surface stations can keep in touch with a turtle in mid-ocean, the tracking will have to be done from some high elevation. A turtle cruises slowly, probably only thirty to fifty miles a day. To track her through long distances an airplane will have to make daily sallies out to find her and record her position, and then fly back to land again. I don't know how many turtles would have to be simultaneously tracked to make the experiment statistically reliable. It is clear, however, that there will have to be a lot of flying; and that it will have to be by airplanes able to keep exact account of their own positions.

The ideal way to maintain contact with island-seeking turtles cruising in the open sea would be by satellite. This thought occurred to me a long time ago, when Telstar was put into orbit; but I dismissed it as grandiose daydreaming, bound to lead only to discontent. Then, lo, a letter came asking me to submit a plan to use tracking facilities of one of the experimental satellites of the Apollo program. My brother, Tom, who is a physicist and radio astronomer, and David Ehrenfeld and I quickly put together a proposal to be submitted to NASA for tracking turtles by earth-orbiting satellites. More recently I was invited to a conference in which we learned that the facilities of the IRLS (Interrogation, Recording and Location System), to be flown with the Nimbus satellite, might also be available for animal navigation studies, including tracking green turtles. There is no telling whether or when these prospects will materialize. The phenomenon of island finding is surely worthy of the attention, however, and satellite tracking appears to be the only procedure that can plot the open-ocean courses with the necessary precision.

SPECIAL FEATURES OF THE ASCENSION MIGRATORY ROUTE

Some pages back I suggested that, in trying to explain island-finding orientation, it might be advantageous to glean clues from the feats and behavior of all the different kinds of animals that regularly migrate to oceanic islands. While this search for a general theory goes on, however, one ought to keep one's mind open to the possibility that very different guidance systems may be used by different species or in different geographic situations. It is possible that the

Ascension-finding feat is a special case, with its own peculiar set of problems and advantages. Perhaps the turtles migrate to the tiny island because the guidance problems involved are actually much less severe than they look. One of these special conditions is the location of Ascension on the same parallel of latitude as the nearest jut of the mainland South America. This arrangement could simplify the navigation problem in a number of ways.

For instance, when migration time comes for the Brazilian turtles, let's say that those north of Recife start swimming south, and those south of Recife swim north. Both stay in coastal waters until they realize they are in the latitude of the Ascension Island. They are instinctively notified of this, say, by shoreline topography, by a particular smell or taste of the water, or perhaps even by some such specialized signal as the sound of a patch of snapping shrimp on the bottom. At that point, if they all headed due east it is at least remotely possible that compass sense alone could guide some of the migrants out to the island. In any case, they would be starting the journey at the place where the distance between the mainland and the island is shortest, and by staying in that latitude there would be no need to find longitude at all.

Another special feature of the Brazil–Ascension route is that it runs directly up the Equatorial Current and not slantwise across it. For the hatchlings that enter the sea out at Ascension Island, the advantage of this is obvious. The advantage for the grown-up turtles migrating eastward is that it might minimize their position-finding problem, as compared with the problem of trying to maintain a heading across a current. Any turtle able to keep heading due east will be moving directly upstream the whole way out. This not only reduces the error of current-set, but it causes telltale emanations from the island, such as smells, tastes, or floating debris to stream out in a fan of island-sign that leads back to where the emanations come from. Of course none of these advantages may actually be exploited by the migrating green turtles; but at least they are there, and they have to be carefully considered if the navigation of turtles is to be explained separately from that of other island finders elsewhere.

THE EVOLUTION OF ISLAND FINDING

It is as hard to account for the evolution of the Ascension migration as it is to explain the navigation mechanisms involved in it. If you get out a map, or look at map inside the back cover, and ponder the Ascension migration, it seems almost impossible that the ancient green turtles that evolved it could really have found it a feasible biological venture. It seems impossible that natural selection could ever have produced the pattern, with the lay of the land and water as it is today. Some different arrangement of land and sea must have prevailed, one that would kill off fewer turtles during the early stages of evolution of the habit. There is bound to have been some slow evolution of geography that would allow more time for natural selection to refine the guidance system, that would provide more survivors to take home more Ascension-seeking genes during the early stages of evolution of the Ascension-finding ability. The same seems true of island-migration patterns of *Chelonia* in other parts of the world.

It appears likely that the Ascension migration is partly vestigial behavior, a trait that once had strong survival value that now is waning. A case that may reinforce this idea is that of the nesting colony at Aves Island, in the eastern part of the Caribbean Sea, the tiny bit of exposed sand that I spoke of earlier as the only site of mass nesting by green turtles in the eastern half of the Caribbean. Nesting is injuriously heavy there. The problem is not just to explain the scheduled seasonal arrival of turtles at such a tiny speck of land, but also to account for their coming there in such intemperate and seemingly disadvantageous numbers. The cause of the crowding seems to be an extraordinarily rapid rate of subsidence of the bank on which Aves is the highest point.

It is not known where the Aves nesting colony is recruited from. The turtles are certainly not wholly derived from surrounding waters or from about the nearby islands—Monserrat, Martinique, Guadalupe and Dominica. They probably converge on the islet from all along the Leeward and Windward archipelagos. Like other colonies of green turtles, thus, they appear to go far beyond practical necessity in their reproductive travel, making breeding journeys that take them past great extents of beach which, to a human judge, meet all requirements as nesting ground. While a green turtle is admittedly a better judge of nesting beaches than a man, it nevertheless seems fairly evident that some of the present-day migratory patterns of *Chelonia* are to a degree left-over behavior, once of prime survival value, but now adhered to simply because adverse selection has not had time to choke them off.

In explaining any migratory pattern it is easy to say that the species involved travels in order to get to a more favorable environment. A safer thing to say would be, merely, that the animal travels because it inherits the tendency and ability to do so. The tendency and ability were not built into the strain yesterday, but at some earlier date. In many cases, as in the Ascension and Aves green turtle migrations, it seems evident that the territory traversed at the time of origin of the trait, or through its time of maximum utility, must have been different from that of today.

As I see it, you might generalize upon the evolutionary development of a typical green turtle migratory pattern like this. The original stimulus for the migratory habit, in ancestors of the herbivorous green turtle, was no doubt the separation of habitats that the grazing habit imposed. Good grazing grounds occur in shallow, protected places, and these are usually located far away from the high, surf-built beaches that *Chelonia* requires for nesting. In the beginning, say, a population of turtles begins moving a short distance from its pasture along a mainland shore out to a nearby island to nest. The tendency to do this might favor the survival of strains that do it because the island has better beaches where there is less predation or where the sand is better for incubating eggs than that of the mainland. That is to say, the trip out to the island is made because more turtles survive that way. Each generation, mainland nests are flooded, or the eggs and young are extensively dug out and eaten. Any female born with the drive and capacity to go to the island will send back more of her kind of genes, and reinforce the island-breeding pattern in the race. The migration is thus a successful evolutionary venture, and it becomes established in the population.

But sea turtles are older than present configurations of land and seas. At some time in the history of some populations, a nesting island slowly sinks, or is otherwise reduced in size. This brings two disadvantages to be weighed against the original advantages of the habit. The island gets harder to find, which kills off growing numbers of the migrants; and the growing distance lengthens the journey of the hatchlings back to the resident ground. Even though this trip is probably made downstream in a steady current, the young would face longer exposure to the hazards of the open sea. This might be no disadvantage—perhaps the open sea is where all hatchlings are when we are unable to find them. But in any case, as the island gets smaller, more distant, or both, the ratio of advantage to disadvantage would grow less. Eventually the pattern, though still for a while carried out, will have become actually disadvantageous. This is the only way I can explain the existence of the Aves turtle colony; and I suggest that it may in some way explain the nesting of Brazilian *Chelonia* on Ascension Island.

It is interesting to try to think through the process of natural selection that would be required to instill the Ascension-finding urge and capacity in south Atlantic green turtles under the conditions of today, with the island as small and distant as it is, and the current flowing the way it does. What one would have to suppose is that a female West African green turtle in a mood to nest was somehow carried out to sea from her home waters around Dakar by the Equatorial Current. After long, aimless paddling about, she by chance was washed ashore on Ascension Island. Grateful for any sand, the turtle hauled herself up the beach, dug a nest, and left a hundred eggs in it. Then she went back into the ocean and swam away. Lord only knows what ever happened to her.

After sixty-odd days the eggs hatched. The baby turtles came out with the typical infantile urge to swim away somewhere. They quickly found the sea, then swam and swam for days. Perhaps they guided themselves in some direction they instinctively deemed appropriate, perhaps not. In any case they were carried inexorably westward by the current, toward the nearest curve of the South

American mainland. After a crossing of maybe three weeks' time they reached the coastal waters of the mainland, where they strung out both to the north and to the south of where Recife is today.

Obviously, I am planning to try to make these little turtles the ancestral stock from which, ever so slowly, the Ascension-finding habit developed. I don't really see how it can be done, but I don't see any better way of getting the necessary ancestors, the way the map is today. To get the evolution started, I have got to propose that the first little Ascension green turtles were very impressionable, as baby animals usually are, and that the Ascension seas, skies, and landscape, and later their first contact with Brazil, made terrific impressions on them. Ascension impressed them with both its odor and with its look from out at sea; and being green turtles, which were already a migratory breed, and prone to view geography in the context of precise time and conditions of the sky, they automatically recorded the hour, the season, and the arrangement of celestial bodies at the instant their impressions were received.

Then the current carried them steadily away westward, and all along the way each turtle kept somehow being impressed—*imprinted* is the proper ethologic term, but impressed sounds better to most people, probably—with celestial changes that took place as the westward distance from the island grew, and with the precise time at which all changes were noted. In other words, though they were being carried passively away, the hatchlings were a breed attuned by ages of previous evolution to storing travel signs for use on later nesting migrations. So the whole drifting journey westward was recorded as a chain of travel signs changing with time. Because the turtles were drifting along one parallel of latitude the whole way to Brazil, the changes they had to keep track of were not great. They were mainly just a tendency for meridian transits, risings, and settings of celestial bodies to be a little later each day, and for certain smells to stay in their noses. The only impression the turtles could have got with respect to latitude was that it always stayed the same. It was natural for them to do all this, say, because they were green turtles.

It might be added that from the start the little turtles were impressed also, deeply and indelibly, by the fact that during the whole drifting journey from the island to Brazil they were moving in a westerly direction, although they might feel this only if they actually swam continuously. If they just drifted passively with the current the only feel of change would be the feel of passing time and that of the slowly differing looks of the sky.

Anyway, the little turtles kept going west and then, suddenly, Brazil rose blue in the distance. Instantly, the look, taste and smell of that part of the land imbedded itself into the nervous systems of the hatchlings, in ways and in detail unknowable to a man.

The sequence of travel signs that the little turtles recorded was, of course, arranged from east to west. To be of any use for a later return trip to the island, the signs would have to be followed in reverse. It may be reasonable to suggest that sea turtles are born with proficiency at reversing lines of travel, at remembering guideposts, and then running the return route by them. Salmon are probably born this way, too. There are probably a lot of other animals in which the young, in going out from the breeding ground, record the signs leading away from there, then read these signs in a reverse direction to get back when they are ready to breed. An ability to do something like this would have to appear before any elaborate pattern of migratory navigation could ever evolve at all.

But even with the nervous equipment to time and record a schedule of signals, and then five or six years later to follow these in reverse—even granting that these capacities may have been a part of the heritage of ancestral green turtles—it is impossible for me to see how the Ascension-finding pattern could have been built into the race. The island is just too little. For a colony ever to establish itself, enough of those first young left by the original African waif would have had to be so thoroughly and precisely imprinted that from the start they would be both anxious and able to leave the places on the Brazilian coast that they had drifted to, and to go back a thousand miles to a mid-ocean island five miles long. Out at that speck of rock they would have to rendezvous in numbers sufficient to let them mate, nest, and send back new growing generations of imprinted waifs to Brazil, with improved ability to return to Ascension when they in turn grew up.

To think that through once again: a lost African turtle drifts to Ascension and nests; her young crawl into the sea and are carried to Brazil in the current. Automatically they record guideposts, all the way out to wherever it is the current is taking them, which turns out to be Brazil. To simplify things, say that the little turtles grow up there. Then one day six years later, they are stirred by migratory hormones and start swimming. They instinctively trace back along the chain of travel signs, through the serially arranged smells or tastes or position of sun or stars, or shifting configurations of clusters of stars and planets—or through whatever other signs they recorded on their westward trip as hatchlings. Reversing the series precisely will take them to Ascension.

To me the weakest point in this hypothesis is the assumption that all that information is gathered and stored with sufficient accuracy to let some of the turtles swim back twelve hundred miles, against the current, find the speck of an island, and in their turn produce young to reinforce the tendency in more Brazilian turtles to be able to do the same thing the next go around. If it were just a question of their having to hold a constant heading on the trip to the island it might work out from the start. But a thousand-mile voyage against a current in the open sea is bound to require more navigation than just knowing which way east is. From the very beginning of the first return trip out to the island, the turtles would have to have the flexibility to correct their headings properly each time any small veering off course made the original heading a wrong one. To make these corrections by celestial navigation would require among other things a sky almanac for all the region the travel goes through. But the first generations that struck out toward Ascension must have been repeatedly carried off course into regions where the look of the skies had never been known to their race before. It is how this original off-course star map could ever get into the strain that is hardest to understand.

It is at that point that the evolution of a celestial guidance system for the Ascension migration seems obviously impossible. Too much equipment had to evolve too quickly. If any other theory seemed less wild I would quickly clutch it; but none does. All the other conceivable means of high-seas travel orientation—by detection of features of the earth's magnetic field or by responding to accelerations of the Coriolis Force, by inertial-sense dead-reckoning, by piloting with hidden landmarks—all these at present seem to me even less plausible than the celestial-navigation theory. So it really appears impossible that turtles or terns could ever gather at Ascension—and yet they do.

It is a shame that there is no evidence of any diminution of exposed land area in the Ascension region of the Mid-Atlantic Ridge during the last fifty million years, through either sinkings of land or changes in sea level. With shrinking of the island as a possibility ruled out, you have to look for other paleogeographic changes that might have allowed a slow refinement of the Ascension-finding capacity under conditions that combined gradual improvement of navigation ability with the gradually increasing difficulty and the gradually diminishing advantage. One possibly relevant event is the growth of the Atlantic Ocean through continental drift. It would help if one could think of Africa as once having been much closer to South America, and of the two moving ever so slowly apart and leaving Ascension Island behind in the middle of the ocean that grew between them. If in the times when this was happening there were green turtles living in Brazil and nesting on the nearby African coast, then the eastward migration could have been built in ever so slowly, as natural selection likes to work, with the evolving migrants gradually adjusting the sophistication of their navigation system to the demands of the growing distance. A few years ago this would have been an outrageous proposal, because continental drift was in virtual eclipse as a theory. Today, however, among geologists and geophysicists at least, the drift theory is no longer dead. There now seems no reason to doubt that the Atlantic is a relatively new ocean.

A possible relation between drift and bird migration was suggested by Albert Wolfson in 1948, as a means of accounting for some of the more elaborate bird migrations. His theory was weakened by the weakness of the drift theory itself, and by the apparent anachronism in relating the evolution of modern birds with major fragmentation of the ancient world. If birds made migratory flights about Gondwanaland, the critics pointed out, they must have been little more birdlike than archaeopteryx.

The recent evidence for drift was brought together in *A Symposium on Continental Drift,* published in 1965 in the Philosophic Transactions of the Royal Society of London. The new information comes mainly from paleomagnetic studies of rocks, which show that the ancient positions of land masses were different from their positions today. Assuming that the earth's magnetic field has remained an axial dipole, when you find that the directions of magnetization of rocks of the same age on different land masses do not agree, you are bound to conclude that the continents have moved, relative to each other. Unfortunately the measurements give only latitude and orientation—not longitude—for the continents on which they are made. They nevertheless have brought a reawakening of confidence in the theory of continental drift. The "drift" process is now thought most probably not to have been a floating apart of land masses, as used to be suggested, but convection in the material of the whole mantle.

In the case of the Ascension green turtles, a reasonable background for the evolution of its navigation equipment would have been provided either by the moving apart of Africa and Brazil, or by a growing separation of Brazil and Ascension Island. That the latter has not happened seems indicated by current opinion that the Atlantic Ridge, of which Ascension is a high point, was formed by uprise caused by the same convectional movements that created the Atlantic Ocean. The exposed island is a volcanic structure on the ridge. It therefore seems bound to have appeared above the sea long after the ocean started growing between the continents.

If you accept the new views on continental drift, there is still the question whether the separation of the lands occurred too long ago to be reflected in the natural selection of migratory patterns of modern animals. If the later stages of this occurred during times when the genus *Chelonia,* or a responsible ancestor, was evolving travel habits that lasted into present times, then it is easy to suppose that the original commuting was done between Brazil and Africa, and that the slow growth of the distance between the two was accompanied by gradual selection of the navigatory capacity to hold an accurate east-west course along the eighth parallel of south latitude. The Ascension rendezvous could have been an old way-stop along this route, with the island later becoming the main target of the eastward migration.

The trouble with this idea is that the spread of the Atlantic Ocean is supposed to have been nearly completed some sixty million years ago—before the beginning of the Tertiary—while the genus *Chelonia* is known to paleontology from no earlier than ten to twenty million years ago. The anachronism makes it necessary to assume either that *Chelonia* has just been missed as a fossil in earlier rocks, or that the Ascension-finding trait comes down from an ancestor older than the genus. Both are troublesome thoughts, but either seems more acceptable than to suppose that Brazilian green turtles evolved their Ascension-finding ability under the present geographic conditions.

So finding islands presents two unsolved problems. One is to understand how a race of animals could learn to do it—how evolution could ever instill the complex instinctive equipment required to find the tiny target. The only logical answer to that seems to be that in the beginning the target was either less distant or less tiny. The other problem is to explain how the finding is done, what the navigation mechanism is. In thinking about that it will almost certainly be helpful to assume that finding islands is a composite process in which every kind of available information is used by the traveling animal; and that each species solves some of the guidance problems in its own peculiar way. But another thought that ought to be kept in mind is this: every long-range oceanic migrant is bound to be swept off its course into unknown regions of the sea. Out there in those unfamiliar places, the signposts to *Isla Meta* are few, and are very likely shared by turtles, terns, and navigating men.

7

SEA TURTLES
AND THE FUTURE

A light made a thin arc through the dark of the beach ahead. The talking stopped, and there was only the swish of feet in the backwash and the slow chuck of surf coming in with a beat instead of the usual clamor.

"Who's down there?" somebody said, and I said I didn't know, although I was pretty sure I did.

The light winked off and on in the distance, in hurried streaks like a click-beetle dodging trees in a dark forest. It skittered about for a while, like a light that was up to something secret, then it went out and stayed out and we all walked quietly in the dark except for the feet splashing and the rhythm of the surf.

We were walking near the topmost reach of the waves, some of us barefooted in the wave ends, some barely dry-footed just above their reach. The night was cool in spite of the calm; and the slow, small surf broke white in the dark with thin phosphorescence, less like fire than like just white foam somehow seen in darkness. There was a crowd of us there. There were the regular denizens of the place—David Ehrenfeld from the University of Florida, Billy Cruz from San José, my wife Margie, my son David, and I; and Shelton Martinez, who takes care of the Green Turtle Station, was walking with us. Besides these there were visitors of a special kind. They were José and Karen Figueres. Don José is a former President of Costa Rica, and a man of humanity and wisdom who speaks his mind plainly in explaining things the United States does wrong in Latin America. It would be hard to overestimate the good sense in his plain talk, or the good it has done us down there.

Don José was out there on the beach with us that night and we were all anxious for him to get a good impression of it, or some kind of impression of it, so he would go away sure that sea turtles were in bad shape and ought to be saved. With him on the side of turtles, their outlook was bound to be better.

We had already seen several turtles nesting peacefully, and were walking on mainly because it was a pleasant night. We had passed the station, and only a wild half-mile lay ahead to the pass where the river turns and goes into the sea. The only light that could be seen on that last bit of the shore was a poacher's light. I swayed for a moment between saying we ought to go back, because calipee poachers leave bad signs; and saying see, the *cabrones* come right up to the station to kill them.

The light winked on again and instantly out, and this time Don Pépe said, as if he wanted an answer:

"Who do you think it is?"

"A poacher, sure," Billy said.

"How do you poach a sea turtle?" Karen asked. "They must weigh three hundred pounds. He must be a strong poacher."

Billy told them about calipee, the cartilage that you cut out from among the bones of the bottom shell. You get half-a-dozen pieces that weigh in all maybe five pounds wet, and less when dried. The days are gone when turtle poachers had to carry whole turtles to the market. The makers of green turtle soup pay more for the calipee alone than a whole turtle brought ten years ago.

"What happens to the turtle?" Karen asked.

"*Esa es la cosa*," Billy said. "The buzzards get her."

The whole troupe went along quietly again in the dark for a while. The light did not come on any more, and I could picture the poacher in my mind threading his way back through the scrub to his dugout hidden somewhere along the shore of the lagoon. I thought of the mess he would have left, and again was about to say maybe there was no use going any farther, when I saw the backwash curling white fringe around a dark body on the sand ahead, and then it was too late.

It was a calipeed turtle. I ran up and pulled at one of her limp flippers, and there was no life in it and the head was washing loosely with the surf. So at least the turtle was dead. They are not always dead when you come on them that way. You can find them lying there back-down with the belly shell gone, the flippers waving, the many-colored viscera glistening, and the heart beating staunchly on in the ruin.

Everybody crowded around the corpse. Flashlights played over the open insides and the people all made sounds appropriate to the sight. Then after a while they turned and walked away by twos or threes, talking about the complicated, melancholy matter of the calipee trade.

I turned the other way and trotted on up to the point alone. I found two more turtles, both dead. It was a humane poacher, this time; but the point is, for the sake of half-a-peck of hard gelatin to be sent off to make soup for a few people thousands of miles away, three full-grown, nesting female turtles that weighed, say, three hundred pounds had been killed and left for the next morning's buzzards to fight about. And this had taken place on the only remaining breeding beach of the green turtle in the western Caribbean, on a shore that is better protected from poaching than almost any other sea turtle beach anywhere. Dried on a rack in a secret place and taken out to Limón or Barra del Colorado, where nobody can tell illegal calipee from that of turtles lawfully harpooned or netted, those scraps of cartilage would bring more money than the poacher could make in any week of other work he would be likely to find.

The Problem of Saving Sea Turtles

So now, to the other troubles that sea turtles face there is the bad trouble of the calipee trade. Dried calipee is light, portable, and indestructible. Drying it is not much work, the market for it is insatiable, the price is high, the calipee of all the shelled sea turtles is salable, and nobody can tell the lawful product from the contraband. The coming of this trade is a bonanza to poor people, and nobody can blame them for their hunger. But the new stimulus to turtle-hunting is sure to hasten the decline of sea turtles, and to make the hard job of saving them almost impossible.

Not long ago I had a letter from Peter Scott asking for some data that I had promised to send him on the survival status of sea turtles. Commander Scott is head of the Survival Service Commission of the International Union for the Conservation of Nature and Natural Resources. A few years ago he invited me to join the commission, and to be chairman of a special group charged with keeping track of the predicament of sea turtles. The information he was asking about was to go into IUCN's *Red Data Book of Animals and Plants Threatened with Extinction.*

All I had to do was decide which kinds of sea turtles were endangered species, and to send in as many details of their status as I could gather. It seemed like an easy assignment, but I soon found that a fair, steady-handed appraisal of the outlook for sea turtle survival is hard to make. One trouble is that, if it is the long run you think of, *all* sea turtles are endangered. The aim of the *Red Book* is not just to bemoan the sad state of animate nature but to choose among many depleted species the ones that seem most in need of attention. Only with a certain basic amount of natural history at hand can this choice be made intelligently. To do intelligent saving of either species or landscapes, you usually have got to know a great deal about the biology of the species involved. Some localized troubles can be remedied by laws and regulations. Some species can be husbanded in enclosures, bred there, and in a sense be saved for posterity. But to plan a strategic campaign to save for the distant future any species in its natural habitat, you have to have a working knowledge of the life cycle of the species.

Even before that there is the problem of deciding what separate kinds of the animal you are interested in exist, and how they are distributed about the world. The two questions are closely interrelated, both bear heavily on any protection scheme, and in the case of sea turtles, neither can be answered in more than an elementary way. Nobody knows exactly how many species there are; it is even difficult to give concise definitions of the ranges of the five genera of sea turtles. Published statements of animal distributions in handbooks and texts are generalizations that somebody has made after a more or less careful search of museum collections and the literature, pieced out by his own observations and data, if he has any. In some cases definitions of ranges based on such a process have a good deal of meaning; in the case of the sea turtles they have little.

For instance, there is a Scottish record of the hawksbill turtle, yet no sane Scot would list the hawksbill as a member of the fauna of Scotland. One lost turtle drifting about the world on an ocean current is not of any zoogeographic significance. On the other hand, there are Nova Scotian records of the leatherback and these do seem to have meaning. The leatherback is of seasonal and fairly frequent occurrence in Nova Scotia. Those caught there have had food in their stomachs. The ones that don't get caught probably go back to their distant tropical nesting ground for the breeding season. So Nova Scotia probably ought to be included in the regular, natural range of the trunkback, while the hawksbill is certainly not in any sense native to Scotland.

That is my own private judgment of the Scottish hawksbill record. I could be mistaken. The uncertainty illustrates the difficulty that plagues any effort to make clear definitions of breeding and foraging ranges of the various kinds of sea turtles and to distinguish these from waif-and-stray distribution.

To distinguish between cases of normal wandering that will be followed by eventual homing return, and permanent expatriation by currents, is one problem. Another is to know when to trust a pub-

lished record. The interest of zoologists in sea turtles has been desultory. Most reliable classification of animals is done by studying
museum specimens. Museum collections of sea turtles are inadequate and only raggedly represent the existing populations and species. Even the genera have been repeatedly confused in print. Only
a couple of decades ago few zoologists believed there really was an
Atlantic ridley, and even fewer could tell it from the loggerhead.
The Pacific ridley has often been mistaken for the loggerhead, for
the hawksbill, or even for the green turtle. The dramatically distinctive leatherback ought to be easily recognized, if any animal
could, but even it has been confused with the loggerhead. So one
trouble in figuring out the distribution of marine turtles is to know
how far to trust a record that somebody has published somewhere.

Worse than that, no matter how much energy and judgment may
be put into the effort to define the natural ranges of sea turtles, this
can never be finally accomplished because of the gaps that man
has made. All sea turtles show some tendency to aggregate to nest,
some heavily, some only in feeble concentrations. Except for the
Atlantic ridley, all to some extent nest separately, too, emerging
one by one over enormous extents of coast. Many of the original
mass-nesting sites have disappeared completely, and all the marine
turtles are today missing from great stretches of shore on which individual nesting once took place.

Thus, to summarize what is known of the natural distribution of
sea turtles and to put their ranges on clear-cut distribution maps is
a frustrating undertaking. Some generalizations are possible however; and some, however faulty, are necessary if the effort to forestall
the eventual extinction of sea turtles is to succeed.

Another fundamental problem is to decide precisely how the
terms "survival" and "extinction" are to be defined. The aim of
survival programs can be stated in a general way as to prevent any
kind of animal from becoming extinct. For this aim to have meaning
it is necessary to say what category of living thing it is that must not
be allowed to disappear. In the case of the sea turtles the five main
kinds are genera: the green turtles, *Chelonia*; the loggerheads,
Caretta; the hawksbills, *Eretmochelys*; the ridleys, *Lepidochelys*;

and the leatherbacks, *Dermochelys*. If all these genera were kept alive, no basic stem of the modern sea turtles would be lost. Some people might be satisfied with that.

Most survival work, however, aspires to saving at the species level; and a fundamental trouble here is, as I have said, that the species of many groups of animals have not yet been adequately defined. The science of classification is one of the oldest branches of biology, but its work is still far from finished; and the sea turtles clearly show how unfinished it is. Only the most irresponsible informant would claim to be able to tell anybody how many species of sea turtles there are in the world.

The reason for this is partly just neglect, but another part of the trouble is inherent in the animals. It is that the differences among widely separated breeding populations of sea turtles are mostly slight and seem not to conform to expected geographic patterns. Sea turtle breeding is very parochial, and this might be expected to produce differentiation of the separated populations. This is not often the case. From one nesting colony to the next there may be slight detectable differences, but they are mostly trivial. Even from one ocean to another differentiation of marine turtles is astonishingly slight. In fact, there is more divergence within a single ocean than between stocks in separate oceans, by far. The sea turtles are an ancient group. The existing genera, and probably even the lesser categories, have been around for millions of years, in many cases for longer than the lands have had their present shapes and positions and the seas their present currents and temperature zones. The turtles have outlasted old highways and barriers and their modern distribution reflects conditions of long ago. Much of it makes no sense in terms of existing geography.

THE GREEN TURTLES

If one made a comparative statistical analysis of features of every important nesting population of the green turtle the world over— there seem to be about eight of them—differences could probably be found to distinguish each of them. They all will probably one day be described as species by zoologists inclined to taxonomic splitting. Of clearly recognizable green turtles, however—kinds that anybody could distinguish after a brief examination—there seem to be only three. These are the very wide-ranging *Chelonia mydas;* the black turtle, *Chelonia agassizi* of the eastern and Central Pacific; and the very different *Chelonia depressa* of northern Australian waters.

As in the case of the ridleys, none of these "kinds" of green turtles separate along the expected lines. The *mydas* stock appears to spread through parts of all the oceans. Nobody has yet shown any regular genetic difference among green turtles of, say, Ascension Island, Heron Island on the Great Barrier Reef, and the Turtle Islands of the China Sea. The three kinds of Chelonias now recognized by zoologists do not fall into three separate oceans. The Atlantic system has only the big, flattish, light-colored *mydas* stock. The Pacific has that too, and also the black turtle, and the aberrant *Chelonia depressa.* The black turtle, which appears to be pre-eminently an inhabitant of the eastern shores of the Pacific, was first described from the Pacific coast of Guatemala by the French zoologist, Bocourt. David Caldwell, of Los Angeles, has recently described as a separate subspecies the form of this black turtle in Baja California. The green turtles of the western Pacific and Indian Ocean are often called by the old name *Chelonia japonica,* but no grounds other than their occurrence in a different ocean are ever given for recognizing them as a separate species.

The black turtle has a high, steep-sided shell and extensive black pigmentation of the carapace, plastron, and skin of the neck and legs. Little is known of its nesting and migrations. It apparently nests in the Galapagos Islands, although the specimens I have seen from there seem slightly different from those of Guatemala. The big nesting colony that James Peters found at Maruata Bay in Michoacan, Mexico, is almost surely this turtle, although this has not yet been proved. In the enormous extent of shore between Michoacan and the Galapagos, green turtle nesting colonies are unknown. Females emerge separately or in small groups to nest in Nicaragua, and very probably elsewhere, but no aggregations have been reported.

The black turtle, thus, is a good example of a species that can be protected only when a great deal more study has shown where the protection should be applied. Meanwhile it is heavily exploited almost everywhere.

One problem in the zoogeography of *Chelonia* is the difficulty of determining whether all the green turtles in a given year-round foraging territory are derived from the same breeding ground. In some cases there is evidence that different stocks may converge for part of their life cycles and then go away to widely separated places to nest. While the black turtles and *mydas*-like stocks generally segregate in the Pacific, in some places they seem to mix. At several points along the American coast and in the islands of the Central Pacific I have seen individuals of what I took to be one kind in places inhabited mostly by the other. Mostly the mixing seemed desultory, however, and it was never clear whether the aberrant turtles were anything other than variants in the local population.

Recently, however, more convincing evidence of two kinds of *Chelonia* living in one locality has come to light. The place is the Galapagos Islands. The observations are those of a remarkable woman named Carmen Angermeyer, who lives with her husband and children on the island of Santa Cruz. Three years ago Mrs. Angermeyer read an article of mine about sea turtles and wrote me a very exciting letter. She said that there seemed to her to be two kinds of *Chelonia* in the Galapagos Islands: a dark kind that nested locally, and a light-colored one, known in the islands as the yellow turtle, which never nested there and never had shelled eggs when it was butchered. That was a stirring thing to hear, and something else that Mrs. Angermeyer said reinforced the impact. She said that when the fat of these two kinds of turtles is tried out for oil, the yellow turtle yields six to eight times more oil than the black turtle does.

According to Mrs. Angermeyer the two kinds of turtles are found regularly in the islands, and during part of the year both are there in some abundance. The black turtle nests on several of the islands, and it shares with the Chelonias of the Central Pacific the habit of hauling out to bask on shore by day. Because the yellow turtle is never seen nesting locally, it presumably is a long-range migrant. If its oil represents fat stored as a travel ration, then it seems logical to suppose that the black turtles produce little fat because they go no great distance to nest. The yellow turtle, like birds that make long, foodless migratory journeys, is the one you would expect to find laying up fat to support its travel; and according to Mrs. Angermeyer, it is the one that does. Some specimens and pictures that Mrs. Angermeyer sent me suggest that the yellow turtle may be different, not just from the local black turtle stock, but from *Chelonia mydas* as well.

If the situation is as it seems, then it is urgent to know where the yellow turtles go for their breeding. Tagging them in the Galapagos is not practicable, simply because it is too laborious and costly to tag green turtles in sufficient numbers in a feeding ground. Unless you have great logistic resources, tagging has to be done where the turtles converge to nest. In the case of the yellow turtle, it is the nesting ground that is being searched for.

Besides being interesting zoogeography, the Galapagos sea turtle situation illustrates one kind of obstacle that gets in the way of any effort to protect sea turtles. The black turtle can be protected in the Galapagos by laws prohibiting the molesting of the nesting colony. This obviously ought to be done. To give the yellow turtle more than token protection, however, its unknown nesting place will have to be found.

The Leatherbacks

Until recently the only prevalent unrest over sea turtle survival involved the green turtle. Now, the concern cannot be so restricted. All five of the genera are threatened with extirpation through large areas.

At the moment it seems to me that the leatherback may have the least dreary outlook. The leatherback has the great advantage of being almost everywhere considered inedible. It has no shell and it yields no calipee. Fishermen sometimes catch leatherbacks in nets, and each year a few are speared or noosed for sport. Otherwise, about the only depredations man makes on the leatherbacks of the world are made at the nesting beaches.

There are four known localities at which *Dermochelys* assembles to nest: Trengganu on the eastern coast of Malaya; the Tongaland coast of Zululand in Africa; the coast of Surinam; and the Caribbean shore near the mouth of the Matina River in Costa Rica. Little quantitative information on these colonies is available. That at Trengganu is apparently the biggest. The nesting turtles are not molested there, but controlled taking of eggs is legal. In Surinam, very effective protection is given the leatherbacks that nest on Bigi Santi, in the Wia Wia Preserve; but a far bigger colony that comes ashore south of there is, according to Peter Pritchard, heavily raided by Indian egg hunters. At both the Tongaland and Matina beaches both eggs and turtles on shore are protected by law, but enforcement is not wholly effective in either place.

In all these places the eggs are an important windfall of protein and are avidly harvested during the season. The mild optimism I expressed over the survival outlook of the leatherback is based on the belief that cutting off the egg traffic could be done without great effort or expense. At the big Malayan rookery, for example, the whole operation could probably be bought out for a few thousand dollars. At the African and Surinam colonies the problem appears to be arranging effective patrol of the beaches. In Costa Rica the situation is somewhere between those of Malaya and Tongaland. Taking any turtle eggs is against the law in Costa Rica; but the Matina beach remains wholly unguarded and the *veladores*—the egg hunters—do as they please. Eggs are bootlegged out on mule cars and in canoes and sold with only moderate surreption in the coastal towns, or clandestinely, even in the capital. The leatherback in the Caribbean nests mainly in March and April. The other turtles nest mostly between June and October. It is then that the Costa Rican green turtle industry operates, and then that whatever law enforcement there may be, goes on. There is no supervision of the leatherback colony at all. And since most of the eggs harvested are used only locally along the coast, the poaching is easy to sweep under the rug.

The eggs of sea turtles are in most places wanted for one or both of two reasons: as a source of protein, and as an aphrodisiac. The former is a valid motivation. You can't blame any poor man for digging turtle eggs if his family is hungry, as usually it is. The aphrodisiac idea is, of course, a baseless folk belief. It is a deeply rooted one, nevertheless. In some places it will probably turn out to be a greater obstacle to enforcement than the demand for the eggs as food. Tampering with a man's sex life will make a poacher of an upright citizen.

Besides the breeding it does in assemblages, the leatherback nests separately over a great extent of tropical shore. The northern limits of nesting lie well below the 30th parallel. In the Western Hemisphere the northernmost record of nesting is St. Augustine, Florida. In the Pacific it is Amami Oshima Island, south of the Japanese island of Kyushu. The known sites of colonial breeding also lie well within the tropics.

Of all of the sea turtles the leatherback is probably the greatest traveler. Green turtles may be more highly specialized for scheduled long-range group migration, but certainly some leatherbacks cover more of the globe in their normal travel. If one looks over the accumulated records of the sightings or capture of mature leatherbacks they turn out to have been made chiefly in the temperate zone. The regions in which the most leatherbacks have been found are not contiguous to any nesting grounds, but are far to the north: Canada, Maine, Scotland, Norway, the coast of Vancouver, the northern island of Japan, and the Maritime coast of Russia.

The Japanese biologist Sabura Nishimura gathered a great deal of data on the occurrence of the leatherback in Japan. He found two peaks of arrivals there. One occurs during the summer, from June to September, on the Pacific coast of Honshu Island and on the coasts of the northern island, Hokkaido. The other comes during midwinter, in January and February, on the Japan Sea coast of Honshu. There is no way of knowing where these Japanese leatherbacks come from. The single nesting record for Amami Oshima is surely not indicative of a center of dissemination there. The nesting ground must lie far to the south. Perhaps it may even be Trangganu on the eastern coast of Malaya.

Nishimura was not able to decide whether the Japanese leatherbacks complete their invasion of Japanese waters during one season away from the nesting ground, or whether the split seasonal peaks represent two separate arrivals, one made on fast-moving warm currents in the summer of the turtles' departure from their nesting ground, the other involving turtles that have overwintered in the Japan Sea. These possibilities are, of course, not mutually exclusive; and others suggest themselves. There appears no reason to believe that all mature leatherbacks go back to the nesting ground during a given breeding season. In fact, it seems sure that they do not. Each nesting ground is used each year, but different females probably make up the assemblage there in successive seasons. If the leatherback breeds on a two-year cycle or longer, as other sea turtles do, it would seem pointless for the non-ready fraction of the population to go away on a long migration just to watch their colleagues reproduce. Moreover, nothing is known about where the young go or on what schedules they travel. They are, of course, the most abundant leatherbacks of all, and they certainly never gather about any nesting ground. This is a fundamental uncertainty, and the work that Nashimura has already done tracing routes and seasonality makes Japan seem a good place in which to work out part of the puzzle.

Another good place to learn new things about *Dermochelys* seems to be Maine and Nova Scotia. James Moulton found that leatherbacks occur regularly in Casco Bay, Maine. He concluded that those that go there stay in the vicinity for at least several weeks. Sherman Bleakney gathered leatherback records for New England and Nova Scotian waters and concluded that the turtles that turn up there could not reasonably be dismissed as strays out of the Gulf Stream, benumbed by cold and lost to the breeding race, as others have suggested. He believed they were regular seasonal migrants to Nova Scotia from tropical breeding grounds. He wondered whether when September comes the leatherbacks in Nova Scotia and New England head back south directly, go on around with the Gulf Stream, or perhaps return to the tropics by both routes. The same uncertainty is a part of the ridley puzzle that I have told of in the chapter "*Arribada.*" There is an important difference in the two cases, however. The leatherbacks that turn up in northern waters are mostly big ones and are probably mature. The ridleys of New England and the British Isles are always young.

In the stomachs of five Nova Scotian leatherbacks, Bleakney found only pieces of the big, cold-water jellyfish, *Cyanaea capillata arctica.* This brought him to the conclusion that the curious array of flexible, backward-projecting spines that line a leatherback's esophagus might be a device to aid in the swallowing of soft, slippery prey, such as jellyfish. Dr. Bleakney suggested that *Dermochelys* may rely heavily upon pelagic jellyfish as a source of food, as the ocean sunfish, *Mola mola,* does. If so, this might help explain the ability of the leatherback to make global cruises in the open sea.

The suggestions of Moulton, Bleakney, and Nishimura that the leatherback ought to be thought of as a regular migrant to the temperate zone is important. Certainly *Dermochelys* is seen more often in northern waters than anywhere in the south except at its nesting grounds. Partly, this may be a result of heavier human populations along temperate coasts, and of the greater fishing activity there; but it seems unlikely that this is the only reason so many leatherbacks are found so far north. *Dermochelys* probably is a periodic summer visitor in cool waters, which travels back to tropical breeding grounds by unknown routes to mate and nest. To what degree the same applies to other kinds of sea turtles would be good to know.

THE LOGGERHEADS

The loggerhead has the most northerly breeding territory of any of the Atlantic sea turtles. It has been so consistently persecuted at the nesting ground, however, that the original pattern of nesting can no longer be discerned. In America, loggerheads still nest in numbers as far north as the coast of North Carolina, and once they came ashore on the beaches of Virginia. There is apparently no such temperate extension of the nesting range in the Pacific loggerhead, although the records are so confused by misidentification that no clear picture of loggerhead geography can be pieced together there.

The loggerheads of the world seem to separate into two feebly distinct races, an Indo-Pacific one, *Caretta caretta gigas,* and another, *Caretta c. caretta,* in the western Atlantic. There is a little evidence that the loggerhead of the West African coast, like the ridley there, may be the "Pacific" form and not that of the other side of the Atlantic. This has not been proved, however.

Until recently the loggerhead appeared to be in no serious immediate danger. Much of the nesting of the Atlantic race takes place on beaches and coastal islands of the United States. On these the turtles are protected by law, and varyingly effective patrols keep down poaching. Lately, however, two factors seem increasingly to threaten the future of *Caretta.* These are the rapid development of coastlines as real estate and recreational areas, and the marked expansion of raccoon populations. Because the raccoon is able to live well with man the two factors often operate together against the loggerhead, and in spite of the laws on the books, the hold of *Caretta* on shores of the United States is slipping fast. Many of the best of the old loggerhead beaches have become cluttered with people and the constant traffic of cars. Even where the beach itself is not invaded, lights along coastal highways confuse the turtles when they come ashore to nest, or draw the emerging hatchlings away from the sea to be mashed by the thousands on the highways. Even in places in which good will toward sea turtles is highest, the nesting females are interfered with by well-wishing posses who walk the shores at night, and arrange themselves in rings around every turtle that comes out.

The main hope for the Atlantic loggerhead in the future appears to lie in state and national parks and reserves where human interference, at least to some extent, can be controlled. Such reserves already exist in Florida, on several of the coastal islands of Georgia, the Carolinas and the Gulf States, and in the Bahamas. The best of the Bahamian nesting beaches are not in the reserves, however.

At most of the loggerhead beaches in the United States the raccoon has become an important obstacle to protective measures. In primitive times raccoons were no doubt kept in check by natural predators. Certainly, for instance, they are a favored game of the few remaining pumas today. Then man moved in and thrived, and from pioneer times until thirty years ago, coon hunting was everywhere a rural sport, and coons became scarce and wary in most of the southeastern states. Now times have changed again. Farmers buy television sets instead of hound dogs. Only a few old diehard coon hunters still follow their dogs at night, and raccoons are more abundant than anybody ever heard of in the old days.

To raccoons, turtle eggs are manna from heaven. Being bright animals, they harvest them with deadly efficiency. On one stretch of Hutchinson's Island in St. Lucie County, Florida, that I traveled not long ago, eight loggerheads nested before midnight and every nest was destroyed by raccoons before daylight. The same situation prevails in all the less-settled shore between Palm Beach and Melbourne, once the heart of the nesting range of the Atlantic loggerhead. The magnificent Cape Sable beaches lie within the Everglades National Park. The cape is almost completely free of human interference of all sorts. In a recent study, however, Ranger Max Holden found that of 199 loggerhead nests on a five-mile extent of the east cape beach, 140 were destroyed by raccoons.

In the case of Cape Sable a remedy seems at hand. The beaches there are backed by miles of low, flat prairies inhospitable to raccoons. Removal of raccoons from the beach zone would probably result in lowered predation for several years—for whatever time it would take new pioneer coons to accumulate from inland habitats. The removal has begun. Displaced raccoons are being marked, to determine to what degree and from how far away they make their way back to the cape turtle grounds.

Other predators of loggerhead nests are feral hogs and ghost crabs. Neither of these is a limiting factor in most protective efforts, but in some places they team up with raccoons in raiding the turtle nests. On Little Cumberland Island, Georgia, this triumvirate was so effective in destroying nests that the owners set up a hatchery where eggs could be incubated in a safe place and the hatchlings released into the sea. Dogs, vultures, wildcats, and house-cats-gone-wild all eat eggs and young loggerheads, but the damage they do throughout the nesting range of the species is negligible, compared to the ruin brought by men and coons. As with all the sea turtles, the main controlling influence is invasion of the nesting habitat. This is going on everywhere. In the southeastern United States the loss of nesting beach to human progress is so rapid that if loggerhead preserves are to be set up they will have to be acquired soon or not at all.

Besides its nesting on the coast of the United States, the logger-head of the Atlantic system nests occasionally on Bermuda, on the Mexican coast of the Gulf of Mexico, throughout the West Indies, and on the coasts of Colombia and Venezuela. Except for Bermuda and a few of the West Indian islands, all this territory is heavily poached, and nesting becomes more desultory each decade.

In the Indo-Pacific, nesting colonies of *Caretta* are being protected on the islands of the Great Barrier Reef of Australia, and on the Tongaland coast of Zululand in southeastern Africa, where the loggerhead and leatherback share a section of the shore.

The Pacific loggerhead appears to have a dilute but very extensive nesting range, and so may be in less immediate danger than its Atlantic counterpart. On the other hand, little reliable information on the race is available. Like *Lepidochelys*, it has unexplained gaps in its distribution. On the whole eastern coast of the Pacific for instance, the loggerhead is so seldom seen that the few that arrive there seem probably to be casual current-waifs. Surveys to determine the location and extent of loggerhead breeding shores in the Indo-Pacific are badly needed, both for the sake of the loggerhead itself and for that of the ridley with which it is confused. Meantime, all encouragement ought to be given the agencies in Natal and Australia that have extensive loggerhead nesting grounds under surveillance.

The Ridleys

The most precarious survival outlook of any sea turtle appears to be that of the Atlantic ridley, *Lepidochelys kempi*. I have told its curious story in another chapter. There are two species of *Lepidochelys*. The Pacific species breeds along a great extent of the borders of the tropical Pacific and Indian oceans, with peculiar gaps in both the breeding and the foraging ranges. Two of the most conspicuous of these gaps are the coast of East Africa and the Atlantic coast of South America, south of the Guianas. Another is the Caribbean, where there is no record of a ridley of any kind. Still another zoogeographic anomaly is the occurrence of the "Pacific" ridley on the coast of West Africa, and in an outlying enclave far down the Equatorial Current on the coast of the Guianas.

With respect to its survival outlook, there can be no doubt that the Atlantic ridley is in a critical position. It has always been obviously vulnerable. It now has evidently been decimated and is still on the downgrade. Unless immediate protection is provided for the scattered *cotorras* that still come ashore in Tamaulipas the species seems destined to be lost.

The same tendency to concentrate reproductive activity that made the *cotorra* a vulnerable species makes it, of all the sea turtles, the most susceptible to protective supervision. All that would be required would be systematic patrols of some sixty miles of shore during the months from March through June. The failing colony now gets no protection at all. The situation is not one that obtrudes itself upon the attention of officials in Mexico City. They have a great many other conservation problems that seem far more important. The *cotorra* never contributed much as a marine resource. It is rarely even seen by anybody except a few poor fishermen and a handful of gringo sportsmen. Only a consistent, careful vigil along the shore will save the species; and obviously, only Mexico can patrol a Mexican shore. It is very seldom that the fate of a species has so clearly depended upon the prompt and wholehearted application of a simple enforcement operation.

The status of *Lepidochelys olivacea* is less grave, but there is no comfort in it either. Its broad distribution in the Indo-Pacific, in West Africa, and on the northern Atlantic coast of South America brings it into contact with diverse conditions. In Surinam it is well protected at Bigi Santi, but not on even more important nesting beaches farther south. In West Africa, in Burma, and on the coasts of India there are protective regulations, but there is also legal harvesting, and a great deal of uncontrolled exploitation goes on too. On the whole eastern shore of the Pacific from Baja California to Ecuador, people do whatever they please with the nesting ridleys. Some kill the turtles, some only take the eggs, some do both. Nowhere is the ridley left in peace, and nowhere is its future safe.

THE HAWKSBILLS

When I first began traveling about the Caribbean in search of nesting grounds of sea turtles one species seemed to me to be in no immediate need of special protection. That was the hawksbill, or carey, *Eretmochelys imbricata.* From colonial times up to the 1930s the Caribbean hawksbill was hunted avidly for its shell. By the time I got to the Caribbean, however, plastics were being made to look like, or almost like, anything one desired, and the market for genuine tortoise-shell had declined to the point that nobody was hunting hawksbills. Although their eggs have always been more highly esteemed on American shores than any other, the diffuse and extensive nesting range and long nesting season of the hawksbill made catastrophic exploitation seem impossible. Much of the nesting took place on small beaches in remote places never searched for turtles' eggs. The carey was being eaten in the few localities in which it is favored as food, and young ones were still being stuffed and polished for sale in curio shops. But those inroads alone appeared to be no real threat to the survival of the species.

Now times have changed. The hawksbill is heavily persecuted. Its predicament in American waters can be clearly shown in dollars and cents. In 1934, hawksbill had no value; now, a big one is worth a week's wages in many places in the Caribbean. Under optimum conditions—when the shell of the turtle is prime, and when buyers for the by-products are available—a hawksbill will bring as much as fourteen dollars.

The most important change was the return of the market for genuine tortoise-shell. Tortoise-shell is attractive, and the imitation carey shell produced by the plastics industry is dismal stuff. It lacks both the beauty and the mechanical properties of the kind the turtle makes. The Japanese knew this all the while, and after the war they got prosperous and greatly extended their exploitation of the products of the sea. Among many other projects, they started ransacking the world for sources of tortoise-shell. Other people gradually saw the light, tourism boomed throughout much of the tropics, and tortoise-shell articles became a thing one takes home from a cruise or from an island-hopping trip.

In Costa Rica today the turtle laws protect the hawksbill, along with all other sea turtles, on the nesting beaches. There is extensive poaching, however; and whenever hawksbills gather at feeding reefs and rocks, the boats also gather in increasing numbers to harpoon them. There is a small rocky bank off the mouth of the Tortuguero River, just north of the Green Turtle Station. In good weather there may be a dozen dugouts there, spending the day waiting for hawksbills to rise and blow. Some of the boats come by outboard-motor power from Puerto Limón, fifty miles away. Some go out from a seasonal carey camp located on the shore opposite the bank.

A more important hawksbill ground is Greytown Banks in Nicaragua. Here, a group of eleven rocks lie under ten to fifteen fathoms of water some twelve miles off the coast near the old port of Greytown, or San Juan del Norte. In the former days of good markets for tortoise-shell as many as sixty boats, most of them from Bluefields, congregated at Greytown Banks. Then twenty-five years ago the price of shell began to decline, and soon no boats at all were to be seen on the banks. Now they are back again in force and it is hard to see how any hawksbill escapes the harpooners in this most important of its Caribbean feeding grounds.

When I visited the carey camp at Tortuguero in 1965 an enterprising buyer in Barra del Colorado had taught the *careyeros*—the hawksbill fishermen—to skin out the forequarters and roll and salt the skin in a special way. If the skins were properly prepared he paid a good price for them, and sent them away, along with green turtle skins, to be used for making leather. Several years before that, the same man had started buying hawksbill calipee and exporting it to makers of "green turtle" soup.

So now the hawksbill has three prices on its head: one for its shell, one for its hide, and one for its calipee. With people everywhere hunting carey eggs, with a few preferring it to green turtle for eating, and with most of the novelty shops of the seaside tropics displaying stuffed, polished yearling hawksbills for sale, the pressure seems greater than the species is likely to bear for long.

SEA TURTLES AND THE SPREAD OF MAN

The preservation and wise exploitation of marine turtles is an international problem. All the species cross boundaries and some of them commute over a quarter of the world. In different parts of the world they are put to different human uses, and local conservation agencies disagree as to both the survival status of sea turtles and the steps needed to protect them. In one place only eggs are harvested; in another only the mature turtles, away from the nesting beach, are hunted; in still other places both eggs and nesting females are ruthlessly taken. In southeastern Asia, there are important nesting grounds of *Chelonia, Dermochelys* and *Lepidochelys*. Because the people are mainly Moslem, their chief interest in the turtles is the egg harvest. In some places this is an important part of the yearly food ration. To cut it off would bring real hardship and even, perhaps, political unrest. Thus, people who appraise the sea turtle situation in southeastern Asia tend to oppose the killing of the females and to lean toward plans of controlled exploitation of the eggs. The policy recommended by the sea turtle students, Tom Harrisson and John Hendrickson, for managed egg harvest in the Sarawak Turtle Islands was of this kind, and it probably was sound procedure for its time and place. But even then it was a compromise, and now two factors are rapidly eroding the value of that and all similar plans of exploitation. One is the rising rate of increase in seaside populations of man, with the attendant rise in local demand for turtle products and in cultural intrusion at nesting grounds. The other trouble is that, in managing a migratory animal such as sea turtles, no matter how carefully controlled the harvesting of eggs may be, the balance is sure to be disrupted by factors operating in distant places.

Protection of sea turtles is not a parochial problem. They cannot be saved in any one place, or by controlling any one phase of the life cycle. Of the five genera, only one—the hawksbill—shows any tendency to stay in one locality for both its nesting and its year-round foraging, and even the hawksbill is to some degree migratory. No local closed season on size-limits or seasonal quotas set in one place can possibly maintain turtle populations if egg harvests are being levied at the various unknown places from which the turtles of a given foraging range are derived.

I used to believe that the green turtle would not be threatened by the fishermen who net and harpoon them. It seemed to me that effective protection of the nesting colony alone would save the species. I no longer believe this. It is now clear that people are so abundant, and the life cycle of a sea turtle is so complicated, that nobody really knows what he is doing to a population when he kills a turtle or takes the eggs from a nest. The capacity of people to consume and their ability to destroy are growing beyond the tolerance of the small populations in which sea turtles live. If a carefully planned, comprehensive strategy were worked out, sea turtles could no doubt be permanently saved; and the green turtle certainly could be made an important link with the vast production potential of the sea. Without such a strategy, however, we are likely to lose some of the species completely before much more time goes by.

It is possible that I have been oversensitized to sea turtle plights by what has happened to the ridley in Mexico. I recently talked again with Francis MacDonald, of Brownsville, Texas, who has a fishing camp at Rancho Nuevo where the *arribada* used to swarm ashore. Mr. MacDonald flies regularly between his camp and his home in Brownsville, and on each trip he can inspect the whole nesting beach. I telephoned him to see whether by some chance the lean years had passed after all, and an *arribada* had come in late this season. I got no encouragement. MacDonald's opinion is that unless something is done next year or the year after to guard the straggling remnants of the colony, the *cotorra* is finished. Where a few years ago tens of thousands of ridleys nested, this season he saw only about a dozen. The local people were killing those, and taking the eggs of the ones they missed.

This seems to me to be just the first of a series of losses to be expected unless some sort of co-operative program for protecting sea turtles is worked out. People tend to think of the productions of the sea as without limit, as fed by the limitless energy of the sun falling on the five-sevenths of the earth's surface that the oceans are. But this comforting thought does not apply to sea turtles. Huge nesting colonies of sea turtles have been wiped out before—in Florida, in the Bahamas and all about the Caribbean, in Bermuda, in the Cape Verde Islands, and in the Hawaiian Archipelago. The dependence on wild shore for nesting, combined with the heavy natural predation on eggs and hatchlings, deprives sea turtles of the resilience that such pelagic fishes as sardines and tuna have. Turtle food comes mainly from the bottom in the shallow fringes of the sea, and turtles require peace on the seashore to breed successfully. Sea turtle populations are small; and as man increases everywhere, they grow smaller.

One way to keep all the species for the distant future would be to work out international agreements that would provide immunity from molestation at every stage of the life cycle. But that will not be a popular campaign. The Japanese are not likely to agree to laws that cut off supplies of tortoise-shell. German soup makers will oppose any restriction of their sources of calipee. To stop turtle-hunting in the Miskito Cays of Nicaragua would change the lives of people in New York, Key West, and London, and in the Caribbean it would bring real suffering to some. To interfere with the turtle-hunting customs of Truk, Yap, Ponape, Palan, and the Marshall Islands would seem to folk there uncalled-for meddling, and would complicate the administration of Trust Territory affairs. Everybody acquainted with the turtle egg industries of southeastern Asia is sure that some solution other than complete prohibition of the taking of eggs has got to be found.

And yet I am sure that people are not going to eat the eggs of wild turtles for many decades more. The single most straightforward and promising measure that can be taken is protection of nesting grounds, and it is this that is surely going to have to be done. So long as people were few, controlled harvest seemed feasible, even to zoologists concerned with the welfare of species. Now, however, human populations are growing too fast for there to be any future in the harvesting of sea turtle eggs, and the wild turtle populations need every egg they can produce. Even when all human drain is prohibited, the eggs will still be harvested by wild and feral predators, and the young will be harried on the beach and in the sea.

RESTORATION PROJECTS

Theoretically, it ought to be possible to reduce natural predation on young sea turtles by artificially incubating eggs and rearing the hatchlings to a size too big for the enemies to eat. This seems a promising thing to try, but it will take a great deal of experimentation to show whether it really accomplishes the purpose. Young green turtles can easily be reared to weights of a half pound. All that is needed is a good supply of clean, warm, salt water and a cheap source of animal food. Within a few months, well-tended hatchlings grow to the size of a saucer, and most birds and many of the natural fish predators that attack the newly hatched young are supposedly no longer able to eat them.

But there remains the possibility that the young of a long-range migratory animal treated in that way—hand-fed on an abundant, easily eaten diet that requires no foraging, no finding and rending of food, no daily traveling between feeding and sleeping places—will not be able to fend for themselves when they are finally released in the natural ocean. Even if a respectable fraction is able to make shift to survive for a time, who knows whether it will fall into the series of habitat progressions that must be the regimen of the first four years of a green turtle's life? This is an important uncertainty. Releasing pen-reared sea turtles may possibly be just a laborious way to kill them. To go into any massive program of the sort before careful tests have been made seems irresponsible.

If little turtles are to be released as a way to circumvent predation, I believe they ought to be put into the sea as early as possible. The best time would seem logically to be the first ten days after emergence from the nest, when there is still yolk in the belly of the hatchling, and when the infantile swim-frenzy is still on him. Nobody knows for sure what the swim-frenzy is. What it *seems* to be is a frantic effort to travel fast, incessantly, and thus presumably, far. It probably has important bearing on the adjustment of the hatchling to its environment. I don't know how far to sea the swim-frenzy carries little turtles, but if it lasts as long in the ocean as it does in a tank it would take them a very long way. If so, it may be a key event in the early ecology.

It is for this reason that *Operation Green Turtle* releases hatchlings as quickly as they can be moved to the sites of introduction. Nothing is known of the mechanics and timing of imprinting in hatchlings, or of other vital processes that might be disrupted by not allowing them to emerge from a nest on the ancestral shore and enter the sea under their own steam. The most logical stage at which to transport sea turtles for introduction is in the egg. For young that hatch from eggs lodged in artificial nests on a strange shore, there is no curtailment of the series of events that lead up to their eventual ensconcement in the normal developmental cycle. It is not certain that these events are necessary to insure the imprinting of the little turtles with signs they need in adapting to the normal cycle and in guiding themselves back to the shore on which they hatched when they reach maturity. It seems safer, however, to assume that they are. The Caribbean Conservation Corporation, therefore, is testing methods of transporting eggs without undue mortality. To date it has seemed far more practicable to carry hatchlings about than to get the eggs to their destination in the first few days after they are laid, when they are most resistant to disturbance.

Some of the problems have been solved, however, and it appears possible that in the future it will be the eggs that are moved about. Within a few years it will be known whether hatchling introductions of the scale of ours can really produce new breeding colonies. Meantime, nothing is being done to find out whether releasing pen-reared young of any age is good turtle management or only mayhem.

Turtle Farms

The one move that appears most promising as a way to accomplish the dual aim of feeding people and saving natural turtle populations is to set up turtle farms. If the teeming people of the future are to have turtle products—tortoise-shell, calipee, meat, soup, hides—these should come from captive stock. They cannot possibly keep coming from the small, shrinking, natural populations of the world.

Farming green turtles seems practicable, and *Chelonia* has the qualifications of a meat animal of major importance. The feeding habits of the mature green turtle are unique. It is the only big, edible animal that fills the submarine grazing niche. When it disappears from turtle-grass flats the pasturage goes unharvested, or is only pecked at by small creatures uneaten by man. Much of the best turtle-grass pasture lies among reefs or archipelagos, and grows under only a few feet of water. Some of these tracts are almost surrounded by land, reefs, or mangrove swamp. Here installation of the necessary walls or fences across the passes would require only small investments. There is a big area of this kind on the island of Grand Cayman; and Union Creek on Great Inagua, in the southern Bahamas, is an extraordinarily suitable situation. A pilot green turtle-farming project has been undertaken co-operatively there by the Caribbean Conservation Corporation, the Bahamas National Trust, the Lerner Marine Laboratory, and the National Audubon Society. A thousand feet of rock walls installed with local hand labor bar the passes to four square miles of shallow embayment, much of it with turtle-grass bottom. *Operation Green Turtle* furnished the hatchlings that for three seasons have been taken to the Union Creek project. The Morton Salt Company, the only industry on the island, has helped the undertaking in a variety of ways. Even with such an able team of collaborators, and with the almost perfect natural situation that was there to begin with, the Union Creek farm would so far have yielded no profit as a commercial venture. Results indicate, however, that turtle farming will one day be practicable and they show what some of the attendant troubles are likely to be.

Finding an area of good *Thalassia* pasture and fencing it in as grazing ground for the big turtles is not the only problem in setting up a turtle farm. There also has to be suitable space and food for the hatchlings, which obviously can't be released into the pasture that they will occupy as mature herbivores. They have to be kept in small pens and fed on a well-balanced diet of whole animals ground to bite-size. Little is known of comparative growth of hatchlings fed on different kinds or combinations of food. It seems clear, however, both by logic and from results of small-scale feeding tests, that whole animals make a better diet than fish fillets or other forms of muscle meat. The tastes of little green turtles are catholic; they will eat nearly anything they can tear up or engulf. Bob and Jean Schroeder, who have had marked success growing green turtles on the Florida Keys, feed theirs table scraps, in addition to a staple diet of whole-ground fish. The Schroeders found that some kinds of vegetable scraps were taken almost as readily as fish, and that canned dog food is an attractive and effective ration. The Union Creek turtles grow to weights of up to eight pounds in two years on a diet almost entirely composed of conch.

In rearing little green turtles the kind of animal food provided is less important than the continuity of the supply. The turtle-culture projects that have so far been undertaken have been small and mainly designed to test feasibility and work out procedures. Turtle farming will be commercially profitable, however, only when it is done on a big scale, and in such an operation the first move, after finding pastures, should be to look for hatchling feed that will be available in abundance at all times of the year. If no single kind of food can be constantly counted on, the diet might be successfully pieced out by combining fish, mollusks, and crustaceans of various kinds, or by some kind of sorted garbage. In some places this problem of hatchling feed may be no obstacle, but in every case it is a fundamental requisite.

Another necessity is clean salt water of the right temperature. Again, there are no data available on growth rates at different temperatures. Hatchling activity visibly slows down, however, when the temperature of the water they are in goes below 70 degrees Fahrenheit. It is at that temperature, also, that green turtles leave the coastal waters of peninsular Florida in the fall. Temperatures ranging between 72 degrees and 80 degrees Fahrenheit would probably allow optimum feeding and growth to proceed.

Just as important as controlling the temperature of the water is keeping it clean. The best kind of hatchling feed is the most untidy. Whole-ground animals foul the water with their juices at every feeding. Unless there is a good flow through the tanks they quickly become polluted. If fixed pens are used they have to be placed where the action of tidal current or wave surge keeps the water changing.

The Schroeders keep their young turtles in live-cars. For various reasons this seems a promising system, even for a big-scale commercial operation. For one thing, hatchlings are able to feed well only at the surface or on bottom no more than two or three feet deep. In a live-car it is easy to control the depth at which the turtles have to pick up food that sinks. Little turtles kept in a pen that encloses shoreline tend to crawl foolishly ashore and dry up there. Live-cars foil them in this practice. Live-cars also make it easier to care for the hatchlings in stormy weather. Next to failure of the food supply and pollution of the water, hurricanes and high water are the main hazard of the sea turtle farmer. Floating pens can be towed to a protected place when bad weather threatens. At Union Creek the first-year turtles have been kept in fenced-off shallows within the walled-off pasture areas. Hurricanes and floods washed out the pens there in three successive seasons and released the little turtles into the main creek pasture. Rock walls keep them from escaping to the sea, but growth records have been badly confused, and many of the turtles have succumbed to predation. Since the walls were built three years ago the creek has never been completely freed of predaceous fishes. Groupers, sharks, snappers, and barracuda remain in the enclosure, and all of these are devoted to eating little turtles.

When we set up the green turtle project on Great Inagua, sixteen miles out across the flat scrub from Matthewtown, the limerock-and-tabby ruin of a building stood all alone on the shore of Union Creek. From the look of the old, gabled walls they might have been the ruin of a Spanish mission or an English trading post, but they were not. They were all that remained of an old turtle farm, a relic of another effort to exploit the virtues of the green turtle in the obviously propitious environment of Union Creek. We laid our walls on top of the walls of that old turtle farm, and the Lerner Marine Laboratory has made a field station of the old turtle farmhouse.

It was a good idea that that first Inagua turtle farmer had. He might have made a lot of money, and have changed the whole future of the island. Looking at the ruins of his hopes, you feel sympathy for him; but combined with the pity is irritation that he left no records. It is the same in the other places that turtle farming has been tried. There is not a recorded word to guide a new turtle project. Looking at the Union Creek ruin you can see plainly that there was great hope there and great industry, but there is no sign of what befell the place. The people who had the vision and failed just folded their tents, and nobody knows why.

It is not going to be easy to grow sea turtles in natural enclosures. To keep a few is no trouble, but to exploit the natural productivity of submarine spermatophyte pastures means stocking big tracts with big, healthy, pen-reared turtles, keeping them safe from the weather, and maintaining them in balance with the vegetation.

When the techniques have been finally worked out, and all about the tropics people begin raising green turtles for the market, another problem will arise. A source of little turtles will have to be found. So far, the demand for stock for the few small pilot projects has been easy to meet with an infinitesimal fraction of the production of one natural nesting ground—that at Tortuguero, Costa Rica. But when big commercial farms are in operation the need for little turtles will exceed the drain that can reasonably be imposed on the natural nesting colonies.

The obvious remedy for that is to keep breeding stock. Here again, nothing is known about possibilities or procedures. *Chelonia* is a strongly migratory animal. Its migrations are presumably a feature of an integrated reproductive pattern, and nobody knows whether it will reproduce in confinement. Turtle ranchers of the future will have to get their hatchlings from nests on artificial beaches. The nests will be made by female turtles that have mated with males living behind fences. No one knows for sure how big the enclosures will have to be, or what the specifications of a suitable artificial beach will be. These and many other questions will have to be answered. A technology of green turtle husbandry will have to be developed. Once that is worked out it will be a double blessing: people will be fed and species will be saved.

EPILOGUE

During the fifteen years since *So Excellent a Fishe* was written there have been great changes in the sea turtle world. Much has been learned that was unknown then, and the relationship between turtles and the human race has evolved, too, for better and for worse.

To get an idea of the nature and scope of the changes you should go to a big book, *Biology and Conservation of Sea Turtles*, that appeared in 1982. Published by the Smithsonian Institution and World Wildlife Fund, Inc., it was edited by Karen Bjorndal. The book and the symposium of which it records the proceedings represent the most dramatic advance in sea turtle affairs since turtles and mankind first came in contact with each other.

The symposium took place in the State Department Building in Washington, DC, in November 1979 and was attended by government representatives and private turtle people from forty different countries. More than three hundred names appeared in the conference register, and sixty-three papers were presented at the meetings. A world sea turtle conservation strategy was developed, turtle colonies deserving special attention were identified, and a set of recommendations for conservation action was composed.

People left the symposium with increased motivation to learn even more about sea turtles, or to do more to save them from destruction—or, in some cases, even to clear the way for commerce in turtles. So, since the symposium, the rate of change in the study and conservation of marine turtles has accelerated, and there is no way this epilogue could bring a reader fully up to date. But *So Excellent a Fishe* was partly a historical account to start with, so all I will do is record a few outcomes and afterthoughts most closely related to one or the other of the themes of the book, and otherwise hope that the changes that have occurred in sea turtle science and survival outlook may impart historic value that will compensate for any reduced timeliness.

Down at Tortuguero the Caribbean Conservation Corporation (CCC) has continued its program with no interruption of the twenty-six-year-old regimen of tagging and monitoring the green turtle nesting population. In 1981 the organization suffered a serious loss in the death of John H. Phipps. Ben, as he was everywhere known, was president and steadfast supporter of the CCC since its beginning. The presidency has passed along to his son, Colin Phipps, and headquarters of the organization remain in Tallahassee, Florida. The Tortuguero station has been named the John H. Phipps Green Turtle Research Station.

At Tortuguero, quarters for the tagging crew have moved from the Miskito Indian shack that housed Leonard Giovannoli in 1955 to the tiny thatched house where Larry Ogren put up for three seasons with Leo Martinez and his family; then on to our charming leaf-house on tall poles in the *cocal* between the lagoon and the sea at Mile 2⅜; and finally into a less picturesque but more comfortable structure, acquired when a tarpon-fishing camp went broke, down near the *boca*. The work on the beach is done by teams of five or six volunteers from the United States and from Caribbean countries, helped out by varying numbers of people hired in the village. Some of both sets of taggers have grown up with the work; some have even grown old and then retired.

The incomparable Sibella has moved to Limón to take care of grandchildren in school, but she passed on her genes and lore to her daughter Junie, who now brightens the victualing at the station. With the coming of Tortuguero National Park, and to set a righteous example for the villagers, the old succulent wild-meat dishes are no longer staples in our fare, and turtle has been totally eliminated. But despite the distressing deletions from her palette, Junie continues to work a daily magic that gladdens the hungry, weary, sandy turtle people, and haunts their dreams now in the same way Sibella's cooking did in the past.

The CCC has never wavered in its financial support for the Tortuguero operation. The main burden has been borne by the Phipps Florida Foundation. While the yearly budget is not large—as compared with the numbers of people, projects, and unbudgetable expenses that have been subsidized—the support has been generous and continuous. Everybody in the organization has subscribed to the original concept that its most important attributes are a single-minded resistance to any distraction from the central aim of keeping watch over the Tortuguero nesting colony and a determination to make it the most thoroughly studied sea turtle population in the world. This policy has not only increased knowledge of the green turtle; it has also reinforced the immunity of the colony to destruction by poachers. The continued CCC presence at Tortuguero has given heart to the Costa Rican government agencies responsible for wildlife conservation. Without any doubt whatever, the CCC program has saved the Tortuguero green turtle colony—by far the most important population in the Caribbean—from the total destruction that it faced in the 1950s. The continuity of the operation through more than a quarter of a century has produced unique insights into various aspects of the reproductive ecology of the turtle colony. Scientific results have been—and will continue to be—reported in a long list of published papers.

As of February 1983 about twenty thousand turtles have been

tagged at Tortuguero. There have been 1605 international recaptures, and many more subsequent returns to the beach by tagged females. One kind of insight that this contact with the population provides is suggested by the history of turtle No. 3438, an admirable old wind-turtle, as the local people call the ponderous, outsized females that often come ashore with strong winds. The record of her observed nestings is no doubt the longest ever compiled for a sea turtle. Her tag was first put on in 1965. When she came ashore the last time in the 1982 season, she had made twenty-six nesting emergences on Tortuguero Beach, in seven different seasons. Besides illustrating the reproductive periodicities of her kind—the characteristic remigration and renesting intervals—No. 3438 shows the remarkable green turtle ability to locate and go back to one particular short section of that beach, whether in returning after the two-week internesting interval, or after the two- or three-year absences between migrations from the home feeding ground. This nest site fidelity is not absolute, and it is easy to see why that is so, because too great rigidity would kill off a population when storms destroyed the nesting shores; and the trait is more strictly expressed in some females than others.

An even more impressive site fidelity record is that of turtle No. 5806, which also last appeared in 1982. She was first tagged in 1969. The record of her returns to the beach (which is 22 miles long, and is marked off in one-eighth-mile sections) is as follows:

YEAR	DATE	MILE MARKER	YEAR	DATE	MILE MARKER
1969	24 July	$4\frac{5}{8}$	1977	3 Aug	$4\frac{6}{8}$
	3 Aug	4		14 Aug	$4\frac{5}{8}$
				24 Aug	$4\frac{6}{8}$
1971	25 July	$3\frac{4}{8}$		3 Sept	$4\frac{4}{8}$
	6 Aug	$4\frac{7}{8}$		14 Sept	$4\frac{5}{8}$
	26 Aug	$4\frac{4}{8}$			
			1980	31 July	$4\frac{6}{8}$
1974	17 July	$4\frac{5}{8}$		9 Aug	$4\frac{3}{8}$
	18 July	$3\frac{5}{8}$			
	31 July	$4\frac{7}{8}$			
	21 Aug	$4\frac{5}{8}$			

How such homing-site tenacity could have been achieved on a shore such as Tortuguero, where the beach, the shore vegetation, and the underwater contours off the beach are constantly being remodeled by waves and wind, is wholly unknown.

Although the continuous monitoring of the nesting colony has been the main aim of the CCC program, many short-term projects have also been undertaken from time to time. Graduate students have done their research at Tortuguero; and other scientists have come down to take advantage of the resources of the tropical seaside locality, the roof over their heads, the turtles, and especially Junie Martinez's cooking; and they have carried out physiological, behavioral, and ecological studies of many different kinds.

Many of the tagging crew members have gone on to high places in sea turtle research, conservation, and management. Larry Ogren, who was the spirit of the place during several of the earliest lonely years, is now Sea Turtle Specialist for the U.S. National Marine Fisheries Service. René Marquez went home to Mexico and became the first government sea turtle official in the world. With astonishing consistency members of the Tortuguero tagging crews have gone away and done good deeds for turtles and the natural world. It is chilling to think what shape Caribbean green turtles would be in today if there had been no Caribbean Conservation Corporation.

The people in the CCC have begun to ponder how the organization should be guided in the increasingly complicated years to come. Times have changed at Tortuguero and in the world at large. There are new problems and new opportunities. A fundamental change was the coming of the canal that connects the natural coastal lagoons between Puerto Limón and Nicaragua, and provides easy water transportation from Limón to Tortuguero and on beyond to Barra del Colorado. This not only brings the villagers more of the emoluments of civilization—including the basic privilege of getting out to see a doctor if the need arises— but also is generating tourism. The tourists are not just Costa Ricans and wandering gringos, but people from as far away as Switzerland and West Germany.

The other big change has been the coming of the Tortuguero National Park. The park is a 19,000-hectare tract of beach, coastal forests, and streams. It extends for 15 miles along the coast from Jalova to a point just south of Tortuguero Village, and thus includes most of the nesting beach, and by far the most heavily used part of it. Even before the park was developed the turtle colony was protected by law, but now control of poaching is the responsibility of the park, and it is a heavy burden. The Limón *cayucas* still come up the coast and harpoon the cooting and courting turtles just off-shore. The new access to Tortuguero lagoon that is provided by the canal system has brought in egg-poachers from Limón, La Barra, and the railroad crossings up the coastal streams; and though access to the beach from the lagoon is difficult there are trails out to it, and people able to stomach the sight, or thought, of the *terciopelos* there are beginning to use them in their egg-poaching forays. The CCC has donated funds to support the effort of the National Park Service to scare off the egg-poachers, but systematic, continuous surveillance is needed on the beach. Off-shore, the only control imposed on the harpoon boats is bad weather, and nothing better can be expected until a fast, seaworthy patrol boat is available to the Park Service or the Coast Guard. So the new accessibility of once remote Tortuguero is a mixed blessing.

Although the place is no longer a sequestered outpost approachable at times only by a little airplane landing on the beach, it retains much of its original charm. The forests and woodland streams around Tortuguero are dramatic samples of tropical landscape— and every year the turtles keep coming ashore.

These things are what the tourists are coming for, and the job that Costa Rica and the Park Service and the people of the village face is to turn this new popularity to their collective advantage by meticulously preserving the values the visitors come to savor. For this to work, tourists will have to be screened in ways that will bring in only nature-loving folk. Water routes and woodland trails that display the diverse beauty of the lowland forests should be laid out; and a program of beach walks, carefully supervised by park rangers, will have to be organized if the nesting colony is to be perpetuated as a tourist resource. Personally, I would rather nobody ever went out on the beach among the quiet turtles except me and a few trusted colleagues. But, sadly, that is no longer the way the world is. The new people are bound to see the turtles, and the only thing to do is to turn this new popularity—and its economic promise for the village and the Republic—into ammunition with which to combat poaching and the perennial lobbying by turtle dealers for relaxation of protective legislation.

So despite the nostalgia for the tranquil magic of the days when there was no canal, when blowdowns blocked the Caño de Palmas route to La Barra, and the lagoon to Parismina would get choked up with continuous rafts of water hyacinths—despite the yearning for those halcyon years, when you waited a week on the beach up at Bertie's for the little worn-out airplane to pick you up, and there was no beer, and one cured the people the *terciopelos* bit by feeding them leaves and roots and kerosene and putting on snake brain poultices—despite the lost virtues of the old lonely, lovely Tortuguero, one has to accept the new times and make the best of the influx of outsiders. And a properly organized, edified clientele of visiting observers of the turtles and the wild woods will reinforce the motivation of the Costa Ricans and their government to save them both.

Recognizing the obligation to deal with the changes, we recently applied to the Tinker Foundation for funds to be used for a couple of modest ventures in public relations. One of these is a little information center at Tortuguero Village; the other is a small endowed fellowship to support participation in the Tortuguero beach work by qualified Central American students.

The aim of the information center is to orient the growing numbers of tourists, both Costa Rican and foreign, who are coming to Tortuguero over the new intracoastal waterway. When these people are put ashore at the village they find simple accommodations, but no means of satisfying their curiosity about sea turtles, the town, Tortuguero National Park, or the work of the Caribbean Conservation Corporation. The function of the information center will be to explain the history and interaction of all these. This not only will help visitors to feel less lost when they go ashore, but also will alleviate the embarrassment of the villagers over the sparse amenities of their community, and will prevent disturbance to nesting turtles by visitors untutored in turtle-watching. It will also relieve our overworked tagging teams of the obligation to double as tourist guides.

The proposed fellowship is a response to the spread of interest in sea turtle conservation and research during the last ten years. The CCC receives numerous requests for aid and advice in setting up programs elsewhere. To help meet this need, we decided to invite a qualified Central American student or conservation officer to Tortuguero from time to time to get experience in sea turtle work by collaborating in the tagging program. In 1981 the Nica-raguan chief of wildlife conservation and three young colleagues were brought in by bus from Managua and put up for three weeks as working visitors. The good that such people can do for sea turtles when they return to their home country with new experi-ence and understanding is obvious. Back in the early years, our first Latin American collaborator was, as I have said, René Mar-quez, who now, fifteen years later, is head of the sea turtle sec-tion of the Mexican Institute of Fisheries. Another visitor, Mario Hurtado of Ecuador, went home and became coordinator of ma-rine turtle and conservation research for the Galapagos Islands and mainland coast of Ecuador. An early Costa Rican collaborator was Alvaro Ugalde, who worked on the beach for one summer, and then went to the University of Michigan with a small CCC grant, received a master's degree in wildlife ecology, and became direc-tor of the renowned National Park Service of Costa Rica.

Both the center and the fellowship will bear the name of Joshua B. Powers, instigator of the CCC concept, whose verve and enthusiastic interest have for twenty-six years been an inspira-tion to its members and a major influence in its success.

Of the upshots of trends and events recorded in this book, none are as stirring as those involving the ridleys—not just Kemp's ridley (*Lepidochelys kempi*) of the Atlantic, but now the Pacific olive ridley (*Lepidochelys olivacea*) as well. It is strange how these turtles so consistently generate emotion and evoke superlatives. They do astonishing things, and astonishing things happen to them. Today, twenty-nine years after "The Riddle of the Ridley" saw the light as a chapter in my book *The Windward Road*, and sixteen years after *Arribada* appeared in the first edition of this volume, the superlatives are still in order, the stirring dramas continue. The old riddle of the ridley has dwindled before one ridley surprise and disaster after another.

The reverses have affected both species. The nesting colony of Kemp's ridley at Rancho Nuevo on the Gulf Coast of Mexico has diminished from the forty thousand nesting females that came ashore at the time the Andres Herrera film was made, in 1947, to no more than four hundred to six hundred nesters in the years from 1979 to 1982. The belated effort to save the species is probably without precedent as an example of international cooperation in a species preservation effort. The Mexican *Departamento de Pesca* has installed a permanent field station at Rancho Nuevo, and biologists and Marines are sent down to the beach each nesting season. Seven U.S. groups and agencies are collaborating with the Mexicans: Fish and Wildlife Service, National Marine Fisheries Service, National Park Service, Texas Park Service, U.S. Coast Guard, U.S. Navy, and Florida Audubon Society. During three seasons, Peter Pritchard of Florida Audubon supervised a group of students from the University of Central Florida who helped in tagging, egg collecting, and patrolling the beach. During the past two seasons Pat Birchfield, Director of the Gladys Porter Zoo in Brownsville, Texas, has been field director of the U.S. party. The work of this unprecedented posse is to reduce natural and human predation by constantly patrolling the beach, locating nests, and moving eggs to a central hatchery at Rancho Nuevo. During the 1982 season, 48,000 little turtles emerged at the hatchery and were released on the beach there.

In a supplementary transplantation effort, 2000 eggs were flown to Padre Island, Texas, where it is hoped that a new colony can be installed. Because it is possible that hatchlings are imprinted by specific tastes or smells of the natal shore or shorewater and later use these as reproductive homing cues, Padre Island sand is sent down to the Mexican hatchery, and the eggs are put into this sand and shipped to a hatchery on Padre Island. When they emerge there the young turtles are subjected to an eccentric-looking procedure that regrettably was not followed in our old *Operation Green Turtle*, and conceivably may have been the missing ingredient responsible for our lack of success in establishing new nesting colonies. The Padre Island hatchlings are allowed to crawl down to the sea, and once beyond the surf, they are netted and flown to Galveston, Texas. There, in the laboratory of the National Marine Fisheries Service, they are reared to the age of about a year and then released at various localities in the Gulf of Mexico.

The aim of this laborious and costly process—a procedure known as head-starting—is to circumvent predators. The idea is that yearlings fit fewer predaceous mouths than hatchlings do. As to whether the pen-reared young will one day rejoin the ancestral breeding population, there is some room for doubt; but in a case as dire as that of Kemp's ridley, the chance seems worth taking.

Our laboratory at the University of Florida has furnished tags, rewards, and coordinating correspondence for the yearling releases of the first two years. To people who return the tags we pay the rewards from a fund sent us by Mrs. Ila Loetscher, president of Sea Turtles, Inc., of South Padre Island, Texas. Results of this tagging experiment have not yet been published by the National Marine Fisheries Service, but the returns have been numerous and very interesting. Whether or not the operation ever establishes a nesting colony on Padre Island, the Galveston head-starting project has been productive as an experimental exercise. Besides the head-started yearlings, others have been sent to major aquaria to be kept as captive stock, against the possible eventual total loss of the natural species.

The big threat to *kempi* today is no longer the coyotes or egg hunters that brought about the original decline. The factor to reckon with now is incidental catch by shrimp trawlers. With the breeding population down to no more than twelve hundred mature females, each turtle caught by a net dragged for other species represents a significant loss. So despite the most powerful rescue effort that any sea turtle has ever received, Kemp's ridley is by all odds the most precariously ensconced marine turtle in the world.

The saga and plight of the olive ridley (*Lepidochelys olivacea*) of the Indo-Pacific and tropical West Atlantic are, although on a markedly different scale and without the loom of early extinction, no less melodramatic. Back during the years when I was obsessed with the puzzle of ridley reproduction, I had no inkling that *olivacea* was an *arribada* breeder. I lived in Honduras in the 1940s, and we used to go over to Isla Ratones on the Gulf of Fonseca to watch ridleys nest there. The density of that nesting colony was no greater than usual on any good sea turtle nesting beach anywhere. During the next fifteen years I walked many miles of beaches and talked ridleys with multitudes of coastal people from Costa Rica to Baja California. I learned that ridleys nested at scattered points all along the Pacific coast, but I heard no word of mass nestings anywhere. Seamen and airplane pilots told me or wrote me about sighting huge aggregations of turtles in the open sea off the coast between Mexico and Panama—such as the one Jim Oliver reported in 1945—but nobody had anything to say about *arribadas* on shore. I find this passing strange—incomprehensible, really. The most spectacular gap in the ridley story, as told in *So Excellent a Fishe*, is the total absence of any hint of the bewilderingly redundant assemblages of nesting *olivacea* that have since been revealed in Mexico and Costa Rica.

The first olive ridley *arribada* to come to light was over in the Atlantic range of the species, in Surinam, on the coast of northern South America. This was a relatively modest aggregation, of around five hundred females, at a place called Eilanti. It was first reported by Joop Schulz of the Surinam Forest Service. The turtles were later studied and tagged during two seasons by Peter Pritchard.

Then, one after another as if just invented, ridley *arribadas* began to turn up along the Pacific coast of Mexico. In 1967 Antonio Montoya of the Mexican Instituto Nacional de Investigaciones Biológica-Pesqueras reported great numbers of *olivacea* nesting on the Pacific coast of Mexico in northern Guerrero. Huge assemblages came to light in Jalisco, Guerrero, and Oaxaca. But then, at a meeting of the Marine Turtle Specialist Group in 1971, Gustavo Casas Andreu of the Mexican Sub-Secretaria de Pesca reported that 751,350 olive ridleys had been killed in one year. He said the number was compiled from official government figures and was thus probably much lower than the real number killed. He quoted as follows from the December 1970 issue of the Mexican journal *Técnica Pesquera* (trans.):

> The obstacles that the Mexican turtle program is encountering and the increased clandestine exploitation of eggs, meat, and turtle skin are causing Mexican and foreign biologists to worry over the fate of the Pacific ridley . . . which is intensively exploited. All along the Pacific coast exploitation during the closed season continues. The situation is particularly scandalous in the State of Guerrero. These adverse factors are nullifying the efforts of the Mexican turtle program, which was once pointed to as a world example of its kind.

So, just as in the case of Kemp's ridley, the existence of the Pacific *arribadas* was made known to the outside world only after their destruction was far along. Within a half dozen years, three of the original four Mexican aggregations had been destroyed to supply the leather trade. The fourth, at Escobilla near Puerto Angel in the state of Oaxaca, was still strong, but was being exploited at what most observers believed was an unsustainable level. The trade that was killing off *olivacea* met no utilitarian need. It supplied luxury items only—shoes for Italian pimps, as a friend of mine put it.

At Escobilla, the exploitation and the responsibility for enforcing regulations were taken over by a private operation known as PIOSA (Pesqueras Industriales de Oaxaca, S.A.), owned and operated under government license by an extraordinary Spaniard named Antonio Suarez. When attacked by critics in Mexico and outside for taking profit from the last of the phenomenal *arribadas*, Suarez pointed out that the old government-imposed harvest quotas and controls had not been enforced, that he was enforcing them, and that without the strong hand of his company the Escobilla *arribada* would quickly go the way of the other lost aggregations. He was no doubt right. In ways that were never clearly documented he had intimidated the tough Oaxaca *costeños* —fishermen and politicians alike—and had replaced their random slaughter of the ridleys with his own disciplined mayhem. The trouble was that that, too, clearly exceeded the breeding potential of the species.

Toward the end of his tenure at Escobilla, Antonio Suarez invited a group of nine turtle-oriented people from the United States to come down and hear his version of what PIOSA was doing. I was a member of the group. Don Antonio told us many things. When asked how it felt to be known as the man who had killed more sea turtles than any other, he replied that what really concerned him was his young daughter's worry that her father might one day be known as the man who caused the *golfina*—the olive ridley—to become extinct. He was an admirable host. He gave us a three-hour talk on his background and philosophy. He was obviously in control of everything that went on around Puerto Angel. The main flaw in his operation—humane considerations aside—was the fuzzy concept of population dynamics from which he worked. Like most people who exploit marine resources on a basis of "maximum sustained yield," he appeared to have no real idea what his inroads were doing to the population.

We were especially bemused by one thing Suarez said. He pointed out that his enterprise was an example of *industrialización completa*—that is, complete use of the turtles killed, as in slaughterhouses where hogs are totally turned to useful purposes. Thus, he explained, the inroads of PIOSA at Escobilla were far more justifiable than the unregulated killing that had wrecked the other Mexican *arribadas*. He said this with the clear conviction that a policy of complete use went far toward justifying the using up of a wild species.

During a break in our deliberations Don Antonio showed us around the slaughterhouse, hatchery, and laboratory, and then said it was time for us to go up to see how PIOSA captured the ridleys at Escobilla. He put us all—the nine gringo visitors, and assorted local *boteros* and turtle divers—into two boats. We cruised several miles up the coast from Puerto Angel to Escobilla, where the *arribada*—or *morriña*, as the Oaxacanos call it—occurs. In Castilian *morriña* means melancholy or homesick, so the Oaxaca people's application of the word to the homing frenzy of the ridleys seems a logical and not unpleasant anthropomorphism. Anyway, as we entered the edge of the *morriña*, a lot of sea snakes began to turn up; and these prompted me to an eccentric act that revealed unexpected strength in Suarez's character—and perhaps a weakness in mine. I relate this anecdote because it shows what an enigmatic man Suarez is, and because it illustrates the aura of strangeness that ridleys engender.

Sea snakes are a kind of cobra. They kill fish with a venom that is said to be exceedingly virulent. But *vis-à-vis* the human race, they are curiously docile even when handled. I knew that; Suarez did not. That makes his reaction to my behavior doubly admirable.

What I did was to indulge personal pride in a snake-snatching technique that I had developed in my youth. As we drew near one of the sea snakes, I leaned over the bow and with a single motion snatched it out of the water and threw it into the air. I meant for it to fall back amidships, but I must have misjudged the forces at work—the speed of the boat, perhaps the height of the snake's rise into the air, or the spin of the earth—because instead of falling back among Peter Pritchard, George Balazs, Carlos Nagel, Richard Felger, and a cluster of Indian divers and boatmen, the snake fell straight into Antonio Suarez's lap.

I don't cite this as a constructive move on my part—our aim, after all, was to conciliate Suarez and mold him into a better person; but

I did it, and Don Antonio's reaction revealed a single-minded aplomb that we found incredible. What he did was yell oops! or *¡queseso!* or something of that sort, draw his feet up from the floorboards where the snake was writhing in the inept way of sea snakes on solid substrates, hold that position while I scraped the snake back over the gunwale with a paddle, and then continue his discourse on *explotación completa*.

So now I have the probably totally unique distinction of having thrown a deadly snake into Antonio Suarez's lap; and he can lay claim to the most civilized reaction ever made to a similar affront.

The whole Escobilla story and its outcome, including the curious events that ended Antonio Suarez's reign at Escobilla, are altogether astonishing, and are further positive proof of my long-held conviction that ridleys are bewitched.

No sooner had the existence and destruction of the Mexican *arribadas* been made known than the discovery of two more breeding assemblages was reported in 1972. Both were in Costa Rica. One was at Nancite, up near the Nicaraguan frontier in Santa Rosa National Park; the other was at Playa Ostional about a hundred kilometers to the south. Both were found by Joseph Richard and David Hughes during the course of an aerial survey along the Pacific coast. There is a settlement at Playa Ostional, and the *arribada* there was being heavily exploited for eggs— some of which were being fed to hogs. At Nancite the turtles have undergone no exploitation at all. Later on, David Hughes took up residence there to observe the *arribada*, and was rewarded by a rare daytime emergence. The photographs that Hughes took rank with the great animal photographs of all time.

When the Nancite *arribada* came to light the government was immediately importuned by outside entrepreneurs seeking concessions to exploit it. One of these threatened to kill Billy Cruz, vice president and Costa Rican representative of the CCC, if he should try to block the effort. Billy tried anyway, and he lives on; and it is a good thing because we would be hard pressed to get along without him. The government has staunchly resisted all efforts of hide people to get concessions to exploit the colony.

Nobody lives near Nancite, and the 2-kilometer crescent of beach is washed by heavy surf and hovered by rocky headlands and rugged inland hills. The beach is located in Santa Rosa National Park, and the *arribada* is by all odds the best protected one in the world. Access to it is extremely difficult. During the last three seasons Dr. Steve Cornelius has attended the gatherings there, under contracts with World Wildlife Fund, Inc., and the U.S. Fish and Wildlife Service. In 1981 the CCC donated funds to the Costa Rican Park Service for construction of a small building to house surveillance and research personnel.

So the Nancite *arribada*, one of the great ecological treasures of our time, seems safe from the egg hunters and the avid leather people. I have never successfully connected with any *arribada* on shore. But one day I did see the whole Nancite fleet massed in the little bay, ready to go ashore, and the sight was stupendous. We came suddenly upon it after flying up the rocky coast for 20 miles. The pilot of the plane yelled *Santa Madre!* and jerked us into a diving turn. For ten minutes we circled 400 feet over the little bay, looking down, not on water, but on a 300-acre mosaic of ridley backs, little high-shelled females and long-tailed males, massed shoulder-to-shoulder in a tight tile deck of turtles on top of the sea. We circled too fast to see what they were doing down there, waiting for their signal to swarm up onto the shore in their wild, unaccountable, self-destructive nesting horde. It was high noon of a brilliant Guanacaste day. The olive ridley leans to windy nights as times for *arribadas*, and I could count only half a dozen overeager females moving up from the surf toward the trees and the thin ridley trails of a few others up the flat to the tree line.

After a lot of backing and filling, the poaching at Playa Ostional, where the ridleys arrive in an inhabited area, appears to be at least partly under control. A managed egg harvest is permitted there. The turtles are tagged each season by students of the University of Costa Rica supervised by Douglas Robinson. In 1982 the President of the Republic declared Playa Ostional a "protected area," and though there was no clear definition of that designation, it has an encouraging sound. So the Nancite colony is not only one of the biggest *arribadas* on earth, it is the only one in the world that is free of human abuse.

Even the discovery of the Costa Rican *arribadas* was not the end of the olive ridley saga. The next development was a report of massive slaughter of ridleys far down on the Pacific coast of Ecuador. This was doubly astonishing because no ridley nesting was known to occur south of Panama. In due course it came out that the Ecuadorian turtles were not a breeding aggregation, but were vast flotillas of subadults that evidently migrated down there to feed on the teeming macroplankton in coastal upwellings. As in Mexico, the turtles were being killed for their hides; and these were going to the same European markets that received Antonio Suarez's exports from Oaxaca. Antonio took a dim view of this enterprise, and he pointed out indignantly that the Ecuadorians were not even allowing the turtles to mature before they killed them. You hear this quite a lot from the harvesters of sea turtles. The reasoning on which it is based is very strange.

As of 1979, up to 148,000 ridleys per year were being killed in Ecuador; and this was disillusioning, because that country is known for its conservation conscience—as revealed in the Galapagos, for example. It later was revealed that the slaughter had been permitted because of a breakdown of communication between local government and the CITES (Convention on International Trade in Endangered Species) authority. In July 1981 the killing of turtles in Ecuador was made illegal by the Ministry of Natural Resources.

Shortly after that sensation had quieted down the next one came. There was sudden word that in India, Robert Bustard had located the biggest *arribada* ever seen anywhere, on the Orissa coast near Wheeler's Island, on the western shore of the Bay of Bengal. According to the report, Bustard had put tags on 158,161 Orissa ridleys during one fortnight. There was not time to ponder that development before word came that ruinous exploitation of both eggs and turtles was going on there. After that, still another

huge ridley aggregation came to light in West Bengal, and with
that news came word that this one too was being decimated, to
supply Calcutta markets.

At that point some people began to feel worn-out with emotion
over *olivacea*—irrationally exasperated with the poor creature for
the expenditures of adrenaline it evoked, and outraged with the
Mexicans and Bengalis for their treatment of it. In the *Marine
Turtle Newsletter* for December 1982, Nicholas Mrosovsky, Peter
C. H. Pritchard, and Harold Hirth pointed out quite correctly that
there was a fundamental difference in the exploitation that *olivacea*
was suffering in Mexico, where rich entrepreneurs and European
pimps were the chief benefactors, and in India, where hunger
was being assuaged. They wrote as follows:

> Meat from the turtles killed in West Bengal and eggs from the
> beaches also find their way into the markets in Calcutta. Here they
> go to feed . . . people who need better nutrition. The price of
> turtle meat and eggs is not especially high—they are not just luxury
> items. We have here a classic clash between the immediate needs of
> people and the conservation of resources. In the long run, of course,
> these are compatible. There will be less food available if these
> ridley *arribadas* go the way of those . . . in Mexico. So we urge
> you, whatever your conservation philosophies, to write Mrs. Gandhi,
> urging her to look into the matter, and devote more research funds
> to divining ways of improving the situation.

Where it all will end nobody can say. Whether the destruction
of the beleaguered *arribadas* can be stopped, and whether, if not,
the species can be sustained by the widespread separate nesting
that occurs—both are imponderable.

One point stands out, however: in its very redundance, an
arribada is one of the wonders of the natural world. The losses
that ridleys have suffered have degraded two related natural
assets—the wild species involved, *L. kempi* and *L. olivacea*, and
the *arribadas* in which both reproduce. Concern over the threat
to the existence of wild species is widespread, but the obligation
to preserve biological phenomena and organization is less widely

recognized. Like the Serengeti fauna, the hawks of Hawk Mountain, and the monarch butterflies of the Sierra Chinqua, the *arribadas* are phenomenal, mind-gripping examples of biologic order, scientific and esthetic treasures of the living world. There is no civilized way to escape the obligation to save them.

One of the changes in my outlook since this book first appeared in 1967 has been the realization that farming turtles for international trade, instead of being a conservation tool, is more likely to complicate the problem of protecting wild populations from abusive overexploitation. Back in the days when I saw promise in turtle mariculture, the strategy I visualized was to rear young turtles from hatcheries to an age at which they could graze and digest turtle grass, then place them on tracts of ungrazed pasture to grow to maturity or marketable subadulthood. I saw this as a way to accomplish the dual aim of feeding people and saving wild populations of the green turtle.

A basic weakness in that vision was the impracticability of penning turtles in the open sea—even the shallow open seas where *Thalassia* grows. So, when the present big turtle farm was set up on Grand Cayman, growing turtles on natural pastures was never even attempted. The little turtles were raised to market size in magnificent big aquaria set up on shore. At first an effort was made to feed them on fish and on turtle grass mown on local flats by an ingenious machine. But that too proved impractical, and an artificial, well-constituted, high-protein pellet was adopted. At that point any resemblance to my old notion of turtle farming was lost.

I am no longer a proponent of raising turtles for international commerce. My most serious objections are that it will keep alive and expand markets for turtle products, stimulate poaching, and provide a customs screen for smuggling operations.

A major potential for trouble in sea turtle conservation is the insatiability of international markets, once demand has been awakened. It is this factor that makes the poaching and smuggling of turtle products so hard to control. Not long after *So Excellent a Fishe* appeared, the green turtle was given endangered status in the *Red Data Book* of the Species Survival Commission of IUCN (International Union for the Conservation of Nature and Natural Resources). A few years later the advent of CITES offered the first mechanism for effective international controls. When the first meeting of the Marine Turtle Specialist Group of IUCN was held in Morges, Switzerland, in 1969, John Lusty, purveyor of turtle soup to His Majesty, The King, told us that international commerce in green turtles was largely confined to imports of green turtles for his soup kettles. He estimated that commerce in *Chelonia* beyond local subsistence trade involved no more than ten thousand turtles a year, most of which were used to make soup. A few years later, during the last months of the Somoza regime, three Nicaraguan packing plants were exporting ten thousand turtles from Miskito Bank alone, mostly to U.S. markets. The demand there was not by makers of soup. As Mr. Lusty pointed out, the U.S. soup market has always been weak. The U.S. demand was for meat.

With the return of personnel from abroad after World War II, more open-minded eating habits spread rapidly in the United States. More exotic dishes appeared on restaurant menus, and the demand for seafood of all kinds grew apace. Rising prices stimulated overfishing, and there was a serious decline in the fisheries of American waters. To fill the gap there has been a steady growth of demand for novelty items for the menus of restaurants in the United States and throughout the burgeoning tourist islands of the West Indies. This is a serious threat to Caribbean *Chelonia*. Given free access to Caribbean sea turtle populations, the restaurant demand could destroy them in a decade or less.

The main deterrent has been CITES. In 1978 importation of green turtle products from turtle farms was made illegal in the United States. This was a blow to Cayman Turtle Industries, the present name of the enterprise which, under my uneasy gaze, has grown from its beginnings as a few hundred Tortuguero hatchlings in live cars in the Florida Keys to a multimillion-dollar investment in tanks, plumbing, and personnel in the Cayman Islands. Various features of the Cayman operation were cited in imposing the ban. One was the difficulty the immunity of farmed products caused for the border agents who had to distinguish the farmed shipments from poached products. Very recently, CITES has reduced its effectiveness by getting involved in hair-splitting, making more or less irrelevant distinctions between "farming" and "ranching" that encourage maneuverings by signatories to apply for exemptions that will permit turtle mariculture for international trade. For those who believe that taking eggs from wild populations is the principal sin of farming, these exceptions are worthy of debate; but the loss of wild eggs is usually not the most important issue. It is the stimulus to poaching and smuggling that comes from the expansible international markets that farmed products keep alive.

The problem is very real. A fantastic example of what can occur came to light recently through the ingenuity and quiet dedication of Special Agent Charles Fuss of the Law Enforcement Group of the National Marine Fisheries Service. Long after the U.S. ban on turtle products went into effect, Mexican sea turtle meat—probably mainly or entirely that of the olive ridley—was still being imported into Texas under the fictitious label "Tabasco River Turtle." The irony of this was that the Tabasco turtle (*Dermatemys mawi*) is itself an excessively rare species that is increasingly exploited by Mexicans for food. Instead of getting the protection it badly needs, its name was being used as cover for smuggled ridley meat. This is a peculiar twist to the "look-alike" problems that customs people face; but over a quarter of a million pounds of "river turtle" meat was confiscated by the National Marine Fisheries Service.

And that was ridley meat, which is far less palatable than green turtle. The demand for green turtle meat, though not of the magnitude of the market for marijuana, is capable of generating the same kinds of intractable problems of control.

At the time I write, a strong lobbying campaign has been mounted by the turtle farms to bring about a retraction of the U.S. ban, and government agencies show signs of weakening. If the ban is lifted, the outlook for wild Caribbean turtle populations will decline and the stimulus to turtle farming will weaken the position of *Chelonia* in other parts of the world. This new threat comes at a time when the restaurant demand has eradicated soft-shell turtles from much of their former habitat in Florida; the huge alligator turtle, *Macroclemmys*, is disappearing from whole stream systems; and the common freshwater snapping turtle is declining nearly everywhere. There is today a lively trade in illegal alligator meat that by far exceeds the volume that could possibly have been derived from 'gators taken under license. And all the time, seafood prices and demand are rising, supplies are shrinking, and the poachers and smugglers are eagerly awaiting the customs screen that will allow a renewal of their operations in the Caribbean.

Of the gaps that persist in what is known about sea turtles, none is more irksome than not knowing how many kinds there are. Not only is that scientifically embarrassing, but to try to carry out realistic conservation programs without knowing what genetic entities are being dealt with is a simple-minded exercise. Our ignorance is partly a result of the loss of prestige that taxonomy suffered when the study of small bits of animals became so much more rewarding to graduate students than the old concern with entire, assembled creatures. But partly, also, it is because sea turtles are intractable subjects for taxonomic study. The five major groups of sea turtles—the genera—are quite distinct; but when anybody asks how many species and subspecies there are, turtle people look insecure, and justifiably so. There is not time to go very far into the reasons for this, but a rough inventory of the troubles is as follows.

Three of the genera of marine turtles, *Caretta*, *Eretmochelys*, and *Dermochelys*, are currently each considered a single world-wide species. We thus speak of *Caretta caretta*, the loggerhead; *Eretmochelys imbricata*, the hawksbill; and *Dermochelys coriacea*, the leatherback. In my *Handbook of Turtles* I followed old authors in recognizing separate Atlantic and Indo-Pacific subspecies of each of these three. In his *Encyclopedia of Turtles*, Peter Pritchard did not. The distinguishing characteristics on which the old separations were based were very weak, and today most turtle workers call each of the three genera a single kind of turtle. That makes no sense of course, but to delineate the different races that are actually involved will take a lot more attention than the problem is getting at present.

The other two genera, *Chelonia* and *Lepidochelys*—the green turtles and the ridleys—are a little more in line with classic zoogeographic expectations, though not much. Each, at least, is clearly represented on the American shores of the Atlantic and Pacific by different species—or, in the case of *Chelonia*, possibly subspecies. In *Lepidochelys*, Kemp's ridley (*L. kempi*) breeds only at one place in the Gulf of Mexico and ranges through the Gulf to Florida and northward along the Atlantic coast. It is totally absent from the Caribbean. The olive ridley (*L. olivacea*) was once called the "Pacific" ridley because it was known to breed only on Indo-Pacific shores. It differs from *kempi* in shell shape, jaw structure, scale number, feeding regimen, behavior, and temperament. In recent years it has been found to breed on the Atlantic coasts of Africa and South America; and it is this kind of ridley that turns up as a straggler along the outside of the Antillean island chain as far as Cuba. These Atlantic ridleys are no doubt genetically different from those of the Pacific, but nobody has ever made a serious effort to show this. All in all, ridley zoogeography, like everything else about the creatures, is curiously anomalous. But at least the genus comprises two clearly distinguishable forms, *kempi* and *olivacea*.

In *Chelonia* there is an extremely distinctive animal, *C. depressa*, restricted to northern Australia and adjacent New Guinea. For the rest, the genus is a taxonomic mess. If you confine your concern to its members on the Atlantic and eastern Pacific shores of the Americas, green turtles are easy to split apart. In common usage, the eastern Pacific kind, which is little, black, and high-shelled, and mostly an eater of algae, is called *Chelonia agassizi* or *C. mydas agassizi*, depending on how much you think you know about its interbreeding and merging with other populations out in the Indo-Pacific somewhere. But apart from that glimmer of light, the taxonomy of *Chelonia* is no better than that of the other genera. It is worse, actually. The name *agassizi* was first applied long ago to specimens of *Chelonia* from Guatemala. Therefore, any population that is demonstrably different from that one, by classic regulations and for practical reasons, needs another name. Another name was once bestowed on the population on the Mexican coast. David Caldwell described it as *Chelonia mydas carrinegra*, but nobody has since been able to show how *carrinegra* differs from the black turtles of Guatemala—though it quite likely does. In any case, most people apply the name *agassizi* to all the black turtles of eastern Pacific waters.

But when you leave the mainland coast and go west across the Pacific the real trouble begins. There is a sizable population of *Chelonia* in the Galapagos Islands. Superficially, it is a lot like Guatemalan *agassizi*, but the question of whether the two are the same or different has not been seriously investigated. Farther west, out in the Hawaiian Islands, there is another colony of *Chelonia*. In some ways it is like mainland *agassizi* but it is a much bigger turtle. George Balazs, who works extensively with the population and knows the mainland forms as well, believes the two are different. So do I. Why the Hawaiian turtles have not been given a name is partly because there is even greater confusion still farther on across the Pacific.

In the western Pacific and Indian Ocean there are several good-sized, more or less isolated populations of *Chelonia*. Every one of them that I know anything about seems somehow or to some extent different from Guatemalan *agassizi*, but they are all bewilderingly variable, both within the populations and from one of them to another. Color illustrations of Indian Ocean *Chelonia* published by Jack Frazier and slides made by Peter Pritchard in New Guinea show the hopelessness of trying to use color and pattern to separate races of *Chelonia* in the Indo-West Pacific. The depressing fact is that in all the vast territory from the Pacific coast of the Americas throughout the Pacific and Indian oceans, *Chelonia* is a taxonomic shambles. The current, defeatist

policy is to call everything out there *Chelonia mydas*; but some of
the people who do that then speak of the mainland black turtle
as *Chelonia mydas agassizi*. By implication that makes the name
of all the other green turtle races of the Indo-Pacific grab bag
Chelonia mydas mydas. And that of course is altogether intolerable.

I am not sure the alternative is much better. It is to look around
in the scattered Pacific turtle literature and select the name with
the greatest seniority that has ever been applied to a population
of Pacific *Chelonia* within the grab bag area. That is what, in my
own mind, I do—realizing the weakness of the recourse. What
you find is that the Japanese population was long ago given the
species name *japonica*. Inasmuch as nobody can say how the
Japanese turtles differ from the other grab bag races, as a desperate
measure *japonica* could be applied to all the green turtles of the
Indo-Pacific, except for mainland *agassizi*. That leaves a lot of
messes to be cleared up, but it is not nearly as bad as calling
every green turtle from Hawaii to Ceylon *Chelonia mydas mydas*.

Once you go around Cape Horn and the Cape of Good Hope
you get into solid *Chelonia mydas* territory. Carl Linnaeus first
described *Testudo mydas* from specimens from Ascension Island,
so that colony becomes the meter stick for any attempt to bring
order into the nomenclature of the green turtles of the world.

The other Atlantic populations of *Chelonia*—those in Surinam
and Costa Rica, and on Aves Island, and the small ones in Yucatán
and Florida—are all similar in general appearance to the Ascension
Island colony, although the latter are bigger—the biggest in the
world. But even in the Atlantic, *Chelonia mydas* cannot be thought
of as a homogeneous group. The four largest colonies have all been
tagged and studied for long periods of time. They are strongly
site-fixed in their nesting, and copulation takes place on the way to
the nesting beach. Everything that has been learned about them
indicates that they are genetically isolated from each other. It is
thus logical to expect that divergence has occurred, but this is by
no means easy to see. Although they differ noticeably in size and
in details of reproduction behavior, coloration, and conformation,
they are all quite similar.

The lack of useful information from the kind of taxonomic studies that modern electrophoretic procedures make possible is a grievous deprivation. It furthers the pronouncement of commercial exploiters that if you have saved one turtle population you have saved the species. Analyses of serum and tissue proteins of the various colonies have been undertaken, and some interesting insight into the relationships among the genera has come out of them. But the biochemists have been dismally slow in providing a reliable inventory of the kinds of sea turtles in the world.

As if the conditions of sea turtle taxonomy weren't already bad enough, there is the possibility that turtle farms will make things worse. When Cayman Turtle Industries found itself overstocked with young green turtles because of the U.S. ban on its products, Dr. Judith Mittag, one of the proprietors of the farm, wrote Robert Scott, Executive Officer of the Species Survival Commission of IUCN, asking what the IUCN attitude would be if a couple of thousand farm-bred turtles should be released in the Caribbean. Mr. Scott wrote me, as an old turtle specialist, to ask my opinion. I replied as follows:

This is in reference to Mrs. Mittag's letter of August 5 to you, asking whether the IUCN would advise her to release excess green turtle hatchlings at Grand Cayman. This exemplifies the kind of problem that farming wild species generates. The present one may appear trivial, but to those of us who are concerned over the elementary state of sea turtle taxonomy it does not seem so. If the Cayman release were successful it would add to the difficulty of determining affinities and differences among the green turtle populations of the western Atlantic. If the hatchlings to be released are from captive-reared females, they could be hybrids of the three Atlantic breeding colonies—those of Ascension Island, Surinam, and Costa Rica, all of which, at one time or another, have been present in the Cayman breeding crawl. The release might thus involve turtles that would either fail to breed, or would modify the natural West Atlantic strains, and thus exacerbate the troubles facing any effort to use modern, fine-scale taxonomic procedures in the systematic study of the group. Nevertheless, if the release were certain to be a single isolated exercise, I, personally, would say go ahead with it—believing that so few of the hatchlings would grow to maturity that even the most discriminating biochemical tests of affinity would not be biased by their presence in the population. But there is also the precedent to consider. There are aspirant turtle farmers all over the world, and the kind of zoogeographic disarray that they could produce by indiscriminately releasing farm-bred hatchlings could completely block any effort to sort out the green turtle stocks of the world.

If I were you I would answer Mrs. Mittag by asking whether the genetic background of the stock to be released is known, how many turtles are involved, and what their age is. A few hundred very young hatchlings might not be worth worrying about. A few hundred yearlings of mixed origin probably would be.

I am sorry if I seem evasive, but when there is no real answer, there's no virtue in inventing one. The most nearly Solomonesque solution I think of at the moment would be to require Mrs. Mittag to rear the hatchlings to flourishing maturity, then to package and freeze their flesh and send it about to hungry people.

The farm went ahead and released the turtles, and there is no knowing what headaches for taxonomists of future times they may bring.

Of remaining threats to the future of sea turtles, one of the most direct and widespread is incidental catch, especially by shrimp trawlers. When turtle populations were big, and shrimp fleets and boats were smaller, their inroads were not demographically significant. Now, however, bigger trawlers drag bigger nets, usually in sets of two or even four, and the drag times are much longer than they used to be. More turtles are caught, and more of them are dead or moribund when they come up in the net. Reacting to growing concern over this problem in the United States, the National Marine Fisheries Service undertook the job of designing an excluder or ejector device that would reduce the number of turtles caught, but not the catch of shrimp.

After four years' work at the National Marine Fisheries Service

gear research laboratory at Pascagoula, Mississippi, a successful
excluder has apparently been produced. They call it TED—Trawler
Efficiency Device. The reassuring name reflects both its exclusion
of big objects and what appears to be a small increase in the catch
of shrimp by trawls equipped with it.

TED is a vertical grid, mounted in a frame that is sewn into the
throat of the trawl—the place where the wings taper back into the
bag. The grid slants upward and backward, and as the trawl moves
forward through the water, shrimp are washed straight back
through the grid and into the bag, while turtles, sponges, and the
like are shunted upward to the top of the net and guided out
through a framed trapdoor in the webbing.

Although the device increases trawl-drag by around 100 pounds,
because it ejects jellyfish and other big objects before they reach
the bag, drag is actually reduced and fuel saved. TED costs
around $600, and it is not hard to install or operate.

There now comes the problem of mounting an effective acceptance campaign, first among shrimpers of the southeastern United
States, some of whom have already reacted favorably. Eventually
the device will have to be introduced throughout all the other
regions where the habitats or migration routes of shrimp and turtles
overlap. The most critical encounters between turtles and trawlers
today take place within the U.S. and Mexican range of the precariously surviving Kemp's ridley. But incidental trawler catch is
worldwide, and the acceptance of TED will have to be worked for
everywhere.

In looking through the chapters of this book for notions and
trends that need reassessment, I was struck by the lack of progress
that has been made in solving the most challenging scientific
problem discussed. That is the guidance mechanism used by long-
range migrants that travel in, on, or over the open sea and arrive
on time at precise destinations. To account for this is the inescapable obligation of students of animal behavior; and it has by no
means been accounted for. When I reread "The Way to *Isla Meta*"
and pondered the spectacular gains made in the study of animal

orientation during the past sixteen years, I was struck by the contrast between recent advances in sensory physiology in revealing cues of and redundancy in the sensory guide-signs of short-range overland travel, and the durability of the puzzle of island-finding navigation. Ingenious investigations of the kinds and acuity of sensory signals that guide pigeons in homing flights have been carried out at Cornell University and elsewhere. The fact that the same bird may use different cues under different conditions corroborates the view that migratory animals must have evolved an ability to take advantage of every detectable guide-sign that the travel environment affords. The sun compass sense was long ago substantiated, but lately it has been shown that when signs from the skies are hidden, successful orientation can be achieved using backup signals. Recent tests show that pigeons respond to magnetic fields, polarized light, ultraviolet light, and low frequency sound—as from wind over broken ground, or from surf on the seashore. Italian scientists at the University of Pisa are convinced that the sense of smell can play an important part in the homing of pigeons.

It has long been evident that the homing of salmon to natal streams after their stay in the ocean is mediated by olfaction—by the special smell or taste of the water along the way. The climax of decades of work with the salmon came in some elegant experiments by Arthur Hasler of the University of Wisconsin and his colleagues. Salmon were hatched and reared in tanks treated with a specific chemical, and then tagged and released. When the time for their breeding return arrived, the tagged fish came back with clear statistical significance to streams treated with the same chemical that had been used in the nursery tanks.

Only recently it has been discovered that certain bacteria contain magnetic particles with which they orient themselves along lines of force in the earth's magnetic field. Later work has turned up such particles in a number of vertebrate animals, including sea turtles. When these little magnets came to light a lot of people started talking as if we finally had solved the navigation problem and shortly would be showing how long-range migrations of animals are guided. These are exciting discoveries, but they in no way lessen the main burden of animal navigation theory, which has always been to visualize the natural selection process by which an animal can be equipped with the map and almanac sense that presumably is necessary if environmental information is used to correct for off-course displacement. This is the obstacle that is holding up research into what seems to many people one of the most dramatic instinctive achievements of animals.

In the case of magnetic field navigation, two of the three components of a navigation process—compass direction and latitude—might be provided by the newly found particles. Direction could be determined because the magnetic field orients north and south; latitude could be found because dip (the steepness of the vertical angle to the pole) increases as the pole is approached.

That leaves longitude, which could be reckoned by comparing magnetic and geographic north. To do that, however, celestial bodies and a biological clock are necessary, because there is no way in which a traveler using magnetic sense alone could detect geographic north. Thus, we have a dual magnetic-field and celestial-cue hypothesis, and this presupposes a genetic tour-de-force that seems no less staggering than the inherited earth-star almanac necessary for pure celestial bicoordinate position-finding. If the particle-bearing creatures do indeed use the particles as a compass and for detecting magnetic latitude from dip, this means that they have inherited an awareness of a grid of the whole earth in which dip-angle is plotted against polar differences; that they determine longitude from celestial sources; and then, after instinctively consulting an inherited grid of magnetic-field conditions, they locate their position on the grid and compare that place with respect to the location of the migratory destination as shown by an inherited geographic chart that is somewhere within reach of their senses.

I am not one to deprecate the power of natural selection. It has fashioned fantastic things in the biological world. I have to believe that a hybrid magnetic and celestial earth grid and map could be inherited—just as I once accepted navigation by celestial co-ordinates alone. But to accept either is a heavy responsibility.

The crux of the animal navigation problem is island-finding. The most promising procedure for clearing the experimental field for studying it is to track migratory animals—fish, whales, turtles, albatrosses—any creatures that make long ocean journeys and arrive on schedule at a pinpoint destination. Satellite tracking is nowadays a wholly feasible way to bridge the befuddling gap between the departures and arrivals of animals, either migrating, or homing after experimental displacement, across open sea. With the electronic facilities available today, to theorize about signals and senses used by ocean migrants without knowing the paths they take is a sack race, a self-imposed handicap, and one that is no longer technologically necessary.

In pondering the migrations of green turtles, we have cleaned up the theoretical premises a bit by subdividing their long-range reproductive homing travel into three stages. One is the open-ocean travel, across abyssal water separating feeding and breeding grounds, where topography and local hydrography supposedly offer no signals, and where guided travel must be by some sort of true navigation that involves the forbidding map and almanac senses. The next migratory stage is to locate the general region of the far-off home shore—in the case of the colony we work with, the 22-mile-long nesting beach at Tortuguero. After that is found, a final discrimination process brings a female ashore, not just anywhere on the ancestral beach, and not just on a part most favored by the nesting colony, but back to a place on the beach that is statistically close to where she has nested previously—and where, another theory goes, she most likely was born.

This way of subdividing the green turtle migration process relieves the inevitable confusion observers get into when they try to select a single mechanism that would both guide a migrant across open sea and take it ashore at a home site on the nesting beach. For example, the discrimination process by which the proper regional landfall is made could well be mediated by current shears, river plumes, or bottom topography, all of which could provide signals in coastal waters. This leaves the open-sea segment unexplained but more inviting as a field for theory and experiment because it is uncluttered by the shore-zone piloting behavior.

Ironically, the mechanism involved in the final fine-scale stage of homing—the return to some one short segment of the shore—has remained eerily elusive.

More progress has been made during the last dozen years in revealing the sensory versatility of path-finding animals than in all the previous time since von Frische discovered the sun-compass in honey bees. But, as nearly as I can see, we are no closer to explaining the island-finding capacity of open-sea migrants than we were in 1967.

The material in one chapter of this book needs no updating. It is timeless, and can stand no tampering with. I refer to the letters in "Señor Reward Premio." They are as valid today as they were when they were received. They have kept coming since the book appeared, and they still bring the same charm of the back-country Caribbean people. There is no room for the new letters, however, and this is a shame. But just to show that the correspondence has lost none of its verve and savor I offer the following from a lively lady on Roatan Island, Honduras, who had failed to send us the tag when she told us of finding one of our turtles:

> Dear Mr. Archie I just recive your letter and was glad to here from you I had give up hops on waiting on answer it was such a long time before I heard from you
>
> So I am so glad I got your letter well I had the little tag here but it got miss place here in the house So I cant fine it right now but I will still look it up and mail it to you but I had check of the nomber of it and the address and I am sending it to you I will still send it as soon as I fine it my son had found another one but that one is out of plastice But I not seen him yet to get the address of but as soon as I see him I will get the address of and send it for you so I am sending the nomber for you and if you still want to send the boy the check they will appreciate it Very much thanks for your kindness to them
>
> the nomber 4679
> fla gainesville
> fla usa

I want to ask you if it is either man up there that will like to have a wife I am looking a husband me and my husband sepered 15 years now and I really need one now but one the age about 49 to 50 or older Because I am trying to live for the Lord if it is either one that will be Instred in me he can send me his picture and I will send him mind right me right back quick and let me no from your friend. . . . Calabash Bight. Roatan, Honduras CA Write me by this address the one on the enelope is were the mail come but Calabash bight is my home town I will still get

The turtle was caught on a rock laying down they caught him with there hands the water was 4 feet deep in round the land

Please answer me right back quick is you receve this letter

That is a real woman talking. Although we were not able to locate an appropriate companion for her I am sure a man could do a lot worse, and I sincerely hope that she will have found one. Meantime, her name is withheld on the grounds that it might somehow complicate a happy new matrimonial arrangement.

INDEX

Roosevelt Roads, 22
Ross, Kip, 18
Russia, 220

Sahara, Spanish, 155
St. Augustine, Florida, 220
Salmon, 174–76, 203
San Andres Tuxtla, 135
San Blas, 139, 140
San Diego, California, 136
San Isídro, 141
San José, Costa Rica, 15
San José, Guatemala, 141
San Juan del Norte, 228
San Juan River, 2
San Lorenzo, Honduras, 139
San Luis, Brazil, 40
Santa Cruz, 216
Sarawak, 28, 229
Sargasso Sea, 99–100
Satellites, space, 197
Sauers, the, 173, 181, 184
Scales (laminae), 149–50, 151, 153 ff.
Schevill, William, 143–45, 193–94
Schnur, Rev. Fr. Ward, 53
Schools, turtle, 136–39, 142–46
Schroeder, Bob and Jean, 100–1, 235
Schulz, J. P., 154
Scotland, 213, 220
Scott, Peter, 212
Sea bass, 91
Sea-finding, 83–94
Sears, Elizabeth, 17
Senegal, 153
Sex ratios, 39
Sextant, use of, 178, 179, 185
Seychelles Islands, 30
Shells, 149–50 ff., 227–28, 229, 231. *See also* specific species
Side-neck turtles, 132–33
Sight (*see also* Celestial navigation): and sea-finding, 83 ff.
Sinaloa, 139, 141
Slaughter of turtles, 239
Sleeping habits, 94, 96
Smells, 167–68, 169, 177, 202
Smithsonian Institution, 239
Snakes, sea, 252
Snapping shrimp, 169

Sooty terns, 38, 39, 169, 177 ff.
Soto la Marina, 116
Sounds, navigation by, 168–69
Soup, turtle, 12, 13, 210, 229, 231
South Africa, 188
South America, 153, 162, 164, 226, 227. *See also* specific countries
Spain, 13, 125
Spanish Sahara, 155
Species, 215. *See also* specific species
Spectacles, use of, 88
Speed. *See* Coriolis Force
Stars, 173, 179, 181, 183–84, 185, 204. *See also* Celestial navigation
Stone, Doris, 6
Stubbs, Tom, 156
Suarez, Antonio, 251–53
Sun, 173, 175, 179, 181, 183
Surinam, 28, 153, 154, 156–57, 227, 263; leatherbacks in, 154, 156, 219; turtle from, found in Brazil, 39–40
Survival Service Commission, 212
Swim-frenzy, 233
Swimming, learning of, 85
Symposium on Continental Drift, A, 206
Symposium on World Sea Turtles, 240

Tags and tagging, 5 ff., 16–18, 25–40, 97, 98, 102–3 ff., 156–57, 160–62 ff., 240; baby turtles and, 38, 108–10; letters resulting from, 41–69; yellow turtles and, 218
Tamaulipas, 126, 129, 155, 226
Tamborito, 140
Tampico, 115 ff., 126, 129, 135, 156
Tanganyika, 150
Tarpon, 20
Tarpon Springs, Florida, 102
Tattooing turtles, 108–9
Teacapan, 140
Temperature (*see also* Cold, cold-tolerance): and hatching, 80–81; for turtle farming, 236
Tepiscuintle, 20
Terns, 38, 39, 169, 177 ff.
Terracais, 154
Texas, 115–16, 117, 259
Texas Park Service, 247